Care and Commitment

CARE
AND
COMMITMENT

Taking the Personal
Point of View

JEFFREY BLUSTEIN

New York Oxford
OXFORD UNIVERSITY PRESS
1991

Oxford University Press

Oxford   New York   Toronto
Delhi   Bombay   Calcutta   Madras   Karachi
Petaling Jaya   Singapore   Hong Kong   Tokyo
Nairobi   Dar es Salaam   Cape Town
Melbourne   Auckland

and associated companies in
Berlin   Ibadan

Copyright © 1991 by Jeffrey Blustein

Published by Oxford University Press, Inc.
200 Madison Avenue, New York, New York 10016

Oxford is a registered trademark of Oxford University Press

Library of Congress Cataloging-in-Publication Data
Blustein, Jeffrey.
Care and commitment : taking the personal point of view /
Jeffrey Blustein.
p. cm. Includes bibliographical references and index.
ISBN 0-19-506799-1
1. Caring. 2. Integrity. 3. Intimacy (Psychology)
I. Title. BJ1475.B57 1991
179'.9—dc20 91-8988

9 8 7 6 5 4 3 2 1

Printed in the United States of America
on acid-free paper

For Beverly, who wouldn't let me stop caring

Acknowledgments

Many philosophers took the time to comment on all or part of the manuscript of this book, and I wish to record my gratitude to all of them for their generous assistance and constructive criticism. I benefited greatly from the suggestions of Annette Baier, Owen Flanagan, Mark Halfon, Virginia Held, Ken Henley, John Kleinig, Joseph Kupfer, Michael Lockwood, and Diana Meyers. They read early versions of portions of the manuscript and many provided me with detailed written comments. I also received helpful written comments on penultimate drafts of large chunks of the manuscript from Neera Badhwar, Rosalind Ladd, and Margaret Walker. Special thanks go to Jonathan Adler, Chris Gowans, and Michael Stocker who read the penultimate draft of the entire manuscript and spent many hours discussing it with me. I am sure that my book has been much improved as a result of my attempts to respond to the points raised by these numerous readers.

I feel about this book much as parents feel when they send their children off to college. With doubts about the quality of the job I have done, I nervously send my offspring into the rough and tumble world, hoping that it is ready for the reception it will get there.

Contents

Part III: Intimacy

Care and Commitment

Introduction

Recent critiques of the traditional deontological and consequentialist theories that dominate moral philosophy have come from many quarters. Feminism, which is in many ways the inspiration for this book, is one. A substantial number of contemporary feminists have challenged the familiar approaches and have attempted to articulate an alternative ethical perspective that, in their view, is more faithful to the moral experiences of women. While there are significant differences between their various formulations, several common themes emerge: an emphasis on personal relations, nurturance and caring, maternal experience, emotional responsiveness, attunement to particular others in actual contexts, and the limited usefulness of principles in the resolution of moral problems. The ethic of care and responsibility that reflects these concerns and understandings is offered as an alternative to the deductive, calculative approach to moral decision making said to be characteristic of the dominant moral theories. In this sense, exponents of an ethic of care think of themselves as anti-theorists. In another sense, however, they are giving us a theory of their own, a conception of morality and ethical life for which theoretical precedents can be found in the moral philosophy of Aristotle and Hume, rather than Kant and Mill.

Explicitly feminist critiques of these moral theories dovetail with recent communitarian challenges to rights-based liberalism. Alasdair MacIntyre and Michael Sandel, two influential communitarians, fault the liberal view for ignoring the way in which we are "embedded" or "situated" in our social relationships and roles.[1] According to Sandel, communal aims and values are not just professed by the members of the community, but define their identity—the shared pursuit of a communal goal is "not a relation-ship they choose (as in a voluntary association) but an attachment they discover, not merely an attribute but a constituent of their identity" (p. 150). Whereas (communitarians argue) liberal indi-vidualists stress the autonomous choice of ends and begin with a moral agent who is separate from others, communitarians stress the discovery of already given ends and take as their moral starting point a self who is enmeshed in a network of relations to others. Similarly, feminists often say, an ethic of care sees the individual as making practical judgments not from an abstract and universal point of view, but from a point of view internal to particular rela-tionships with concrete others.

Communitarianism would be an implausible position if it denied the possibility of or need for critical moral reflection on the local practices, social roles, and particular relationships in which the self finds itself enmeshed. We can repudiate the roles and attachments in which we find ourselves because we come to view them as inher-ently trivial or degrading; room must be left for the kind of moral reasoning that can lead to this conclusion. Moreover, our different attachments sometimes make conflicting demands upon us, and moral reasoning that consists only in a process of self-discovery might still leave us without any way of resolving the conflict. Ques-tions about the value of the practices and relationships in which we are engaged and about the right way to resolve moral quandaries, it may be granted, are not to be answered by simple derivation from some comprehensive system of universal principles and val-ues. But this is not the only strategy of moral reflection that can be used to critically evaluate the worth and weight of our various constitutive attachments.

Communitarians argue, rightly I think, that the self is not com-pletely independent of its ends, free to choose its life plan totally unencumbered by socially given ends. But neither is the identity of the self entirely constituted by specific social relationships and roles, attachments whose meaning we can interpret but whose value we cannot question. We are not just what we discover our-selves, through some interpretive process, to be. We can, as autono-mous choosers of our ends, ask ourselves what kind of person we want to become. While we cannot perhaps directly freely choose our attachments, we can choose to engage in courses of action that we expect to create conditions under which certain attachments will develop. Moreover, from the fact that an attachment is, in some sense, freely chosen, it does not follow that it is dissolvable at will, or that it is something that we can just abandon or violate without any sense of personal loss or self-betrayal. For example, friendships are a manifestation of choice on the part of the individuals involved, but once someone has become my friend, the relationship is felt to demand loyalty and to impose serious constraints on choices and behavior affecting my friend's welfare. Contrary to what some communitarians seem to think, an autonomous chooser of ends is capable of deep and meaningful commitments.

Another leading critic of traditional moral theory, both Kantian and utilitarian, is Bernard Williams. Like the communitarians, he rejects modes of ethical thought that abstract from the particularities of social and historical context. Also, like feminist critics of an "ethic of justice," he holds that impartialist ethics fail to respect the personal point of view and do not take seriously the identity or integrity of agents. According to Williams, modern theory operates with a conception of morality in which all ethical considerations are subsumable under the category of obligation and declares that the fundamental obligations, from which all others are derivable, require a concern for humankind that transcends local loyalties and attachments. But such theory, Williams rejoins, oversimplifies our ethical lives and is peculiarly empty of content. The concepts it employs are too far removed from the realities of the social world, too abstract and thin, to capture real differences in things that make a moral difference.

In addition to offering a sweeping criticism of current patterns of ethical thought on the ground of their remoteness from actual social life, Williams considers what their adoption means for the agent. Aspiring to act in accordance with the requirements of theory thus understood, he contends, results in alienation from ourselves, that is, from those projects that are centrally definitive of ourselves. When we take the moral point of view, we view ourselves *sub specie aeternitatis,* in abstraction from our personal circumstances, and hence with a "detachment . . . from the level of all motivations and perceptions other than those of an impartial character."[2] Both utilitarianism and Kantian morality insist that the agent make decisions from this viewpoint. But this is incompatible with the subjective point of view from which we normally view ourselves. If we are to act as moral agents, we must be willing to sacrifice even those projects with which we most closely identify and that give us a reason for living. The demand that we do so, Williams objects, constitutes an attack on the agent's integrity.

I will look more closely at this integrity criticism, and at the different ways of interpreting it suggested by Williams' writings, later in the book. For now, I only want to note further that Williams' use of the notion of integrity to criticize the project of impartial ethics has a counterpart in feminist writing. Here the ethics of justice is faulted for excluding, among other things, the relevance of considering one's own integrity in making moral decisions. By contrast, among exponents of the care perspective moral deliberation is conceived of as a process in which decisions are made on the basis of the agent's sense of his or her own identity. The agent decides on a course of action by consulting personal standards and ideals, by using self-respect, and the integrity it protects, as a moral filter.

Traditional moral theory has also been criticized on the ground that it cannot accommodate the demands of special personal relations. It has been pointed out, by feminists and others, that we are not principally motivated to do things for our friends and loved ones out of a sense of duty or justice. I do things for my friend not as an instance of a type to whom I have certain general obligations (as Williams puts it, "this construction provides the agent with one thought too many"[3]), but in direct response to the particular, unique person he or she is. Moreover, some have suggested, because my relationship is with a unique individual, any demands this relationship imposes must apply to this person alone. The demands of justice or impartial principle are not so restricted in scope, and there is no place in an ethic of justice for respecting the particularity of intimate relations.

In this way, a dichotomy is set up between an ethic of care, which requires a regard for the individual other, and an ethic of justice, which requires us to adopt an impartial stance that abstracts from particular attachments. Carol Gilligan, whose work on moral development has played a major role in the call for a reformulation of moral theory, suggests at one place that the two perspectives are "fundamentally incompatible"[4]—that they involve seeing things in radically different and competing ways. The detached moral reflection of the justice perspective, with its considerations of fairness, right, and obligation, cannot be brought to bear on our cares without destroying the integrity of the caring perspective. Care and personal commitment preclude justice (and vice versa); therefore, we must settle either for an ethic founded on caring alone or for one founded on justice alone.

This is an implausible position. It is true that people have an innate predilection for emotional commitment and will commit themselves without needing to rely on some impersonal moral justification for this commitment. But I do not think that one somehow becomes an uncaring person, or that one ceases to be truly committed to something, merely because one is willing to consider the moral implications of one's actions and makes an effort to conform them to impartial principle. Nor do I find the notion of an ethic founded on caring alone, dissociated from justice, appealing. The qualities of devotion and loyalty associated with care are virtues only as long as the actions they encourage are not themselves morally wrong. The kind of loyalty that, for example, puts the welfare of those near and dear to us before all else, that blinds us to the legitimate needs and interests of other persons, is not a virtue. Nor is devotion to others a virtue—it is, rather, a defect—when it reflects an attitude of servility. Care must be subjected to moral constraints—constraints on how much energy and attention we may devote to the beneficiaries of our immediate concern as opposed to other persons, as well as constraints on the caring itself.

We better understand the relationship between care and justice if we do not regard them as competitors, but rather, as some commentators have suggested,[5] take the concerns definitive of each perspective to belong to different parts of morality. The care orientation focuses on ingredients and conditions of the good life: on commitment to the good of particular others, as in the several varieties of personal love, and on the formation and maintenance of a sense of self-identity through dedication to projects, principles, and so on, that give one's life meaning and direction. Loving concern for particular others enriches and energizes our lives. Concern for one's integrity is, at the deepest level, a way of taking oneself seriously, and lack of this concern indicates profound shallowness. The justice orientation, by contrast, relates to matters of right and focuses on duties, obligations, and rights. Since morality consists both of a theory of the good and a theory of the right, neither care nor justice can stand alone as a comprehensive theory of morality.

When we love another, we are responsive to that person in his or her wholeness and particularity. That person is more for us than a mere performer of functions, a bearer of certain abilities, or a holder of a certain status. He or she is valued for being a particular individual, not for being the bearer of a general property, nor even the property of being a unique and individual self. In respecting other people's rights, on the other hand, we do not take particular persons as our primary focus. From an impartial point of view, we could only speak about individuality in a nonperson-specific way. We might therefore say that a morality of care is particularistic whereas a morality of justice is universalistic (or something of the sort). While there is some truth in this claim, however, the contrast is also overstated because it is difficult to see how arguments for an attribution of moral good could be offered from the personal stand-point of the caring individuals themselves. The personal commitment that motivates a person to do good for a friend or loved one or to accord a certain priority to his or her community's interests could not be what motivates *us* to regard this individual's ties of personal and communal loyalty as having moral value. We need an argument for this that transcends the personal point of view, ego-centrically considered.

I have tried to indicate some of the ways in which a cluster of notions—care, personal integrity, personal and communal relation-ship—has figured in attacks on features of traditional moral theory. My own view is that while these objections have performed an extremely valuable service in focusing our attention on the agent who is to implement moral values, and on important aspects of human flourishing that any plausible moral view must take seri-ously, the criticisms do not succeed in discrediting impartialist eth-ics as such. At the same time, I want to leave open the possibility that a particular (sort of) moral theory may be objectionable be-cause it cannot accommodate certain claims made from the per-sonal point of view. For example, utilitarianism, I would argue, fares worse than Kantianism with respect to meeting the challenge of the personal point of view. Utilitarianism, and consequentialism generally, recommends the adoption of a viewpoint from which we regard our own personal concerns with indifference as means to the end of achieving some overall good.

In the first part of this book, I take up the subject of care, but not with the aim of pursuing the issues I have touched on in this introduction. I will not be mainly interested in care as it relates to metaethical issues or in presenting a conception of morally adequate care. Rather, I want to investigate the nature of caring as such and to explore a number of questions about care that do not only pertain to moral right and wrong. These questions include:

What are the differences between caring about, caring for, taking care of, and caring that?
What can be and what should be an object of care?
What motivates care and in what sense does the person who cares identify with what is cared about?
What is implied by the claim that caring supports a sense of the meaningfulness of our lives?
How does caring benefit the one who cares and what is the good of care?
How do we care about caring?

Discussions of care among feminist writers, focused as they are on the alleged absence of a concern with caring among contemporary moral theorists and on the political implications for women of being identified as caretakers, for the most part do not address these other matters.

The largest part of this book, however, is devoted to a study of integrity and what I call intimacy. Here I will return to critiques of moral theory from the personal point of view, but I will also be concerned about much else besides. In Part II, a preliminary discussion of Williams' integrity criticism of impartialist ethics sets the stage for a closer examination of integrity in its own right. A requirement that is fundamental to all types of integrity, moral and otherwise, is coherence, and I begin my analysis of the meaning of integrity by considering various sorts of incoherence that are connected with a person's identity and that preclude the possession of integrity. The person of integrity, as we say in everyday parlance, is true to his or her commitments, and since these sorts of incoherence indicate some kind of failure of genuine commitment, they also denote a lack of integrity. Commitment is not sufficient for integrity, however, if we think of integrity as a global phenomenon, that is, as something that only a person who leads or strives to lead an integrated life overall possesses. To make sense of this, I attempt to clarify the notion of the unity of a life.

In Part III, I take up once again the implications of including the evaluation of intimate relationships, by standards specifically appropriate to them, in the normal subject matter of ethics. Before doing this, however, a number of other important conceptual and normative issues are addressed. For example, a claim that is repeated at many places in the discussion is that (personal) love attaches to another individual in his or her particularity and that it is not transferable to another. This is a familiar characterization, but as I hope to show, it is hardly a perspicuous one. In clarifying it, we have to take seriously the charge, traceable back to Plato, that love so conceived must be groundless or irrational. Another topic concerns the value of the person. Neither utilitarianism nor Kantianism speaks of the distinctive value of the individual self, but the conviction that persons have value as the particular persons they are is a strong and deeply entrenched one. This conviction, I shall argue, animates personal love.

Though I focus on intimate relations of love and close friendship in Part III, I in no way want to suggest either that one cannot care deeply about people with whom one does not have close affectional ties or that one should not try to enlarge the scope of one's caring to encompass people for whom one has no personal regard. I do not confine or advocate confining caring to the private domain. Intimacy is of great interest to me, however, because it raises a number of intriguing philosophical problems about particularity in an especially vivid way.

Integrity and intimacy are linked. Deep personal attachments to particular people center our sense of self and contribute to our identity, and our integrity is bound up with making their welfare an overriding moral concern. Simply put, integrity has to do with commitment and our loves and close friendships are among our deepest commitments. Whatever it is that one is committed to, the person of integrity is obviously someone who cares deeply. Extreme apathy or indifference is incompatible with the possession of integrity because in such a case there is nothing that elicits enough interest from a person to motivate continuing and steadfast faithfulness. More than this, the materials out of which a person's integrity is constructed cannot just be transitory attachments or peripheral concerns, for the maintenance or attainment of integrity is, consciously or otherwise, a process of self-definition.

Though there cannot be commitment without care, there can be care without commitment. I might care about a person, for example, and not be committed to him or her, or about the condition of the environment and not be committed to doing something about it. We can thus both expand and sharpen our understanding of integrity and intimacy by examining the larger context of care within which they are located.

* * *

A major part of this book consists of conceptual analysis of key notions like caring (Chapter 2), commitment (Chapter 9), and personal relations (Chapter 15). I will occasionally make reference to how certain terms are used in everyday discourse, to what "we" say (see Chapter 11 and Chapter 14, for example), but I am not especially interested in reporting on ordinary usage. At the same time, I do not believe that my analyses depart so widely from ordinary language that the reader is unable to discern any affinity between them. My method is to begin with what I take to be some deeply held and widely shared beliefs about caring, integrity, and personal love, and to use these as starting points in a philosophical analysis of the concept in question. The expression "starting points" allows for the possibility that philosophical analysis will change our opinion about a particular feature of x: what was initially regarded as essential may come to be seen as only contingent, or even perhaps as hopelessly muddled.

My method can be illustrated as follows. I open my discussion of personal integrity with what I take to be a intuitively acceptable characterization: a person of integrity is true to his or her commitments. But a person normally has a number of commitments, and so we need to ask what being true to one's commitments means when they are conceived as a totality. The answer I develop works from the notion of coherence, extending this from coherence between principle and action (for the case of a single commitment) to coherence within one's set of commitments (for the case of multiple commitments). This in turn leads to an exploration of the practical bearing of the enlarged notion of integrity on the way we live our lives. By this point in the account, understandably, our intuitions about integrity may have run their course. For example, is there some lack of *integrity* in carelessly putting oneself in situations of conflict among one's most basic commitments, as I maintain there is (see Chapter 12)? I do not think there is any way to finally settle this matter. But what is important after all is that through plausible elaborations of the central organizing idea of fidelity to commitment—elaboration being a much looser relation than entailment—we are able to focus attention on a number of related considerations that bear on the appraisal of human lives.

While many of the claims I make in the text about caring, integrity, and intimacy are presented as conceptual truths, I frequently attend to empirical matters as well. For example, it is part of the concept of caring that the person who cares about something finds his or her own happiness in some ways contingent on whether the object of his or her care fares well or ill (see Chapter 2). There would be a contradiction involved in asserting that someone cares about *x* but is emotionally indifferent to whether *x* is enhanced or diminished. On the other hand, caring about *x* is only contingently connected to intolerance of ignorance about the current state of *x*. Here I make the following psychological observation: someone can care so much about *x* that he or she is terrified of inquiring into the current state of *x*. Elsewhere I briefly discuss the connection between intimacy and privacy (Chapter 14). Contrary to the view of some philosophers that, conceptually, there can be no intimacy without privacy, the view to which I am inclined (viz., that intimacy is jeopardized by lack of privacy for our experiences of intimacy) requires empirical support for its vindication. To give just one more example, my discussion of parental love (in Chapter 16) examines its causes, the particular distortions to which it is prone, and the obstacles standing in the way of a genuine love relationship between parents and their grown children. I include a discussion of parental love in the first place largely because of the critical role developmental psychologists have found it plays in the child's acquisition of an emotional foundation for the ability to love. At the same time, I regard parental love as a type of personal love and so intend my analysis of the concept of personal love to apply to parental love as well.

In addition to the conceptual analyses and the descriptive empirical findings, I put forward and defend normative or value claims of various sorts. For example, in Part I, I discuss what we ought to care about (Chapter 1) and the value of caring (Chapter 4); in Part II, I show why concern for one's own integrity is not objectionably self-centered (Chapter 7) and why integrity, important as it is, is not sufficient either for moral goodness (Chapter 11) or for the excellence of a human life (Chapter 12); and in Part III, I suggest a view of why persons matter that extends the Kantian critique of utilitarianism (Chapter 18) and indicate how impartialist moral theory can accommodate preferential treatment of friends and loved ones (Chapter 19).

The book I have chosen to write tries to do many different things, and I am well aware that its various pieces do not all fit together into a neat whole. The numerous chapters do not progress methodically from one step of an argument to the next, or from one facet of a problem to another, and to a large extent my detailed explorations of personal and moral integrity, and love and intimacy, proceed independently of each other. I hope, however, that this introduction will have situated my project within a larger context of contemporary philosophical debate and given the reader some sense of how I think this admittedly loosely constructed book hangs together.

I
CARING

1

The Importance of Caring and Caring about What Is Important

In 1826, at the age of nineteen, John Stuart Mill entered a mental depression, a "crisis," from which he thought he might never emerge. He describes this painful event in this well-known passage from his *Autobiography:*

> I was in a dull state of nerves, such as everybody is occasionally liable to; unsusceptible to enjoyment or pleasurable excitement; one of those moods when what is pleasure at other times, becomes insipid or indifferent; the state, I should think, in which converts to Methodism usually are, when smitten by their first "conviction of sin." In this frame of mind it occurred to me to put the question directly to myself: "Suppose that all your objects in life were realized; that all the changes in institutions and opinions which you are looking forward to, could be completely effected at this very instant; would this be a great joy and happiness to you?" And an irrepressible selfconsciousness directly answered, "No!" At this my heart sank within me; the whole foundation on which my life was constructed fell down. All my happiness was to have been found in the continual pursuit of this end. The end had ceased to charm, and how could there ever again be any interest in the means? I seemed to have nothing left to live for.[1]

The source of Mill's breakdown was not the realization that his moral ideals were not good ones to live by but rather that, worthy though they might be, they "had ceased to charm." The "changes in institutions and opinions" to which he had given his intellectual assent were not, he discovered, important to him, and this discovery undermined his will to live. With the same honesty with which he admitted his uncaringness with respect to his highest ideals concerning the improvement of mankind, he diagnosed the cause of his lack of conviction:

> [T]he pleasure of sympathy with human beings, and the feelings which made the good of others . . . the object of existence, [are] the greatest and surest sources of happiness. . . . My education, I thought, had failed to create these feelings in sufficient strength to resist the dissolving influence of analysis. (pp. 106–108)

Mill's education had nurtured in him the capacity to reason abstractly about rules, but not, as he came to see, to care about the people whose welfare was affected by his breach or observance of them. And because he did not care about them, he could get no joy or happiness from promoting their welfare. He could only go on with his usual occupations "mechanically, by the mere force of habit" (p. 108). His moral education had left him "without any real desire for the ends which [he] had been so carefully fitted out to work for: no delight in virtue, or the general good" (p. 108), and these consequences "required to be corrected, by joining other kinds of cultivation" (p. 111) with the cultivation of reason. Moral education must seek "a due balance among the faculties," "the cultivation of feelings" (p. 111) as well as of the powers of philosophic reasoning.

How do we help children develop a proper degree of sympathy or empathy for others, and thereby care about doing what is morally right and avoiding what is morally wrong? Several of Plato's early dialogues take up the issue of the teachability of virtue, but there are serious limitations in his treatment of the problem. In the *Meno,* for example, Socrates considers only those forms of moral instruction that would succeed in teaching virtue under the assumption that virtue is knowledge. If virtue is knowledge, Socrates suggests, then it ought to be teachable by giving lessons of some sort. Lessons take the form either of lecturing, where the aim is to get the pupil to memorize and eventually regurgitate information, or of training, where the goal is to get him or her to become proficient at a particular practical activity (as in the case of horseback riding or doctoring). But, Socrates goes on, we see that virtue is not taught in either of these ways; neither lectures ("the Sophists") nor practical exercises ("the Athenian gentlemen") succeed in making people moral. It would seem to follow, then, that virtue is not knowledge after all. Socrates then reconsiders his initial assumption and proposes instead that virtue is right opinion, concluding that "virtue is an instinct given by God to the virtuous."[2]

Gilbert Ryle, in his critical discussion of the Socratic question "Can virtue be taught?" agrees with some of this.[3] Moral development does not occur as a result of either of the preceding sorts of teaching. Memorization of standards is compatible with their not being the ones that the agent actually uses to appraise and guide his or her conduct, and skills can be exercised with or without moral sensitivity. But if knowledge is not sufficient for virtue, Ryle goes on to argue, virtue is still capable of being schooled. Moral education for Ryle does not culminate principally in children knowing the difference between right and wrong, but rather in children caring whether what they do is morally right or wrong. He proposes that we think of moral education not as a matter of "dictating and coaching," but of "civilizing" (p. 53), as a process in which, "under the influence of other people's examples, expressions, utterances, admonitions and disciplines, we too come to care deeply about the things that they care deeply about" (p. 51).

Some of these people (i.e., parents and schoolmasters) are aware of their influence on the child's development, of the child's desire to try to live up to them, and accept responsibility for the child's moral growth. These are moral teachers. The child also learns virtue from people who are not teachers of it; indeed, the child probably learns most of it this way. In any case, when a child learns virtue, he or she acquires certain qualities of character: qualities that are constituted in part by dispositions to feel, among other things, distaste for, revulsion against, and outrage at, immoral conduct of various kinds. These dispositions are necessary if the individual is not just to be knowledgeable about what is morally wrong, but to care about avoiding it. Such caring can be learned or taught, for caring is not "just a special feeling that we have been conditioned to register on certain occasions . . . of a piece with the seasickness felt by a bad traveller the moment he steps on to the still stationary ship" (pp. 51–52).

Of course, as Ryle points out, vices as well as virtues can be learned, and the young can come to care deeply about things that it is wrong for them to care about. [As an example, Ryle mentions "the young disciples of Fagin" (p. 56)]. Ryle's descriptive concept of moral education must therefore be supplemented with a normative conception specifying which character traits are desirable or worthwhile, and ought to be developed, and which should not be. This does not tell us, however, how much weight to place on normative analysis in the actual process of moral education. As Mill's case demonstrates, moral education will fail if it concentrates on winning the child's intellectual assent to certain moral requirements. One might decide to care on the basis of antecedent rational conviction, but it is a fatal mistake on the part of moral educators to suppose that the decision to care is tantamount to actually caring. Children will usually find themselves caring about morality if they care about the authority figures after whom they are expected to model themselves, and then sometime later, when their powers of abstract reflection have developed sufficiently, caring might become commitment. Still, the task for the moral educator is to get the child to care about the right things, and what is right is determined independently of the child's actually coming to care about it, or for that matter, independently of the educator's actually caring about it. As a practical matter, moral educators will be ineffective if they do not care about the moral requirements they are trying to get the child to care about. Children, as we know, have an uncanny ability to see through pretense. The justification of the requirements, however, does not consist in the fact that the educator cares about them.

This is not to suggest that the ability of people to care about the requirements of morality is not an important concern for a moral view. Something like Rawls' notion of "the strains of commitment" is useful here:

> In view of the serious nature of the possible consequences of the original agreement, the question of the burden of commitment is especially acute. A person is choosing once and for all the standards which are to

govern his life prospects . . . the parties must weigh with care whether they will be able to stick by their commitment in all circumstances.[4]

Conceptions of justice are to be assessed in part in terms of the degree of stress that would be experienced by members of a well-ordered society as they attempt to live up to the commitment they made in the original position. My interest here is not the Rawisian derivation of principles of justice, but what I regard as a plausible moral analogue of Rawls' condition: incorporating the requirements of morality into one's life should not have disasterous consequences for human personality. Morality may demand significant sacrifice and effort, but the cost of being moral should not be a distorted and undesirable personality.

A person may display, over an extended period of time, more or less stable dispositions to act in accordance with moral principles and still not care about doing the right thing. Moral conduct may, after all, just be habitual; however, our moral interest in ourselves and others does not stop at the question of what was or is to be done. It also encompasses questions about the spirit in which a person acts, including motives, desires, and the reasons for performing an action and upon which the person acted. A person can care about doing the right thing, and do it, for (what even that person takes to be) a poor or bad reason.

At this point, I want to move beyond the caring that pertains to morality and say something about the relation between practical reasons generally and caring. According to some philosophers (externalists), individuals can have reasons to act even if those reasons are not grounded in preexisting motivations. Others (internalists) find this an extraordinary claim, and argue that there are no reasons for acting that apply to everyone, regardless of their prior desires, commitments, and projects. Consider the following remark by James Rachels:

> In order for anything to count as an ultimate reason for or against a course of conduct, one must *care* about that thing in some way. In the absence of any emotional involvement, there are no reasons for action. The fact that the building is on fire is a reason for me to leave only if I care about not being burned; the fact that children are starving is a reason for me to do something only if I care about their plight. (On this

point the emotivists were right, whatever defects their overall theory might have had.)[5]

Both externalists and internalists can agree with this. But internalists would go on to contend that reasons for action must have their *genesis* in care. (Internalists may distinguish between reasons for believing and reasons for acting, with only the latter presupposing care and the like.) This intimate connection between caring and reasons for action holds whether the reasons are moral ones or not. I must somehow already care about the starving children's plight if I am to have a reason to help them, but why I care— because I want a reward, or because they are in need, or what?—is left open.

This internalist view, however, might not seem to agree with the ordinary use of "reasons." We say, for example, that the fact that children are starving is a reason for me to do something to help them, even if I do not already care about what happens to them, and that if I do not care, I ought to. I may not acknowledge that I have a reason to help them, but there is a reason for me to do so nonetheless. But what is the argument for the assertion that there is a reason for me to do it? If what is being suggested is that I am justified in believing that the children ought to be helped, and that this furnishes me with a reason to help them, then assuming that something is a reason for an individual to act only if it is capable of motivating him or her, it must be shown how reasoning which does not start with prior caring can by itself generate a new motivation. If *my* reason for helping the children is that, say, the world would be a better place if the needy children were helped, then this reason must be capable of motivating me. But in the absence of any antecedent caring on my part, the internalist contends, it cannot. The alleged external reason must become an internal one if my helping the starving children is to be explained by it. Simply thinking rightly about the children's plight does not create in me a motivation to do something about it: this transition can be explained only if we postulate some preexisting concern on my part to alleviate their condition.

The internalist position I have been sketching is not just that reason can work only if it appeals to preexisting caring. Rather, it offers a conception of practical reason according to which statements to the effect that someone has a reason to act in a certain way are falsified by the agent's lack of care. (Bernard Williams, another internalist, grounds reasons for acting in an individual's "subjective motivational set,"[6] which includes desires, intentions, patterns of emotional reaction, as well as cares properly so called.) On an externalist conception, by contrast, this is not so. Although internal reasons theorists may claim that persons can have reasons for doing something even when they think they do not, and that one's cares and commitments are not statically given but are alterable by rational deliberation, defenders of external reasons still fault these theorists for making practical rationality, as it impinges on the individual, too dependent on a person's actual emotional and psychological makeup. If the internal theorist is right, then external reason statements are at best misleading ways of expressing the conviction that things would be better if the agent so acted. More seriously, the use of such statements represents an attempt to "bluff" the agent into acting in ways the external theorist approves of.

The internalist characterization of an individual's reasons for acting has so far been that there is ultimately no reason for me to pursue anything if I do not already care about it in some way. An internalist might modify this characterization in the following way (here I adapt a suggestion made by Bernard Williams[7]): in order for something to count as a reason for me to do something, it must be the case either that I am motivated to act on the reason by prior caring or that I could come to be motivated to act on the reason as a result of serious reflection on my current motivations. On this view, it is possible for the "ought" in "S ought to care about x, whether or not he or she actually does care" to provide S with a reason for acting, but only if serious reflection on his or her current cares would lead to S's caring about x and thus to S's being motivated to act on the reason. If, on the other hand, S neither cares nor would come to care upon serious reflection, then the "ought" in "S ought to care about x" is being used to assess a situation, not to make a judgment about S. In this case, S has no reason to pursue x, even if it would be an especially good thing if he or she did so.

There is no need to discuss the internalism–externalism debate any further here.[8] I propose instead to consider whether there are some things that people ought to care about, whether or not the "ought" is translatable into a reason for action. Plausible candidates are things that can be identified as fundamental and important human goods: knowledge, life, play, aesthetic experience, practical reasonableness (including morality), and sociability (love and friendship). These things are indispensable elements in good human life and desirable for their own sakes in the sense that there is sometimes reason to acquire them even if nothing else desirable results from acquiring them. But what makes knowledge, for example, a basic human good is not that it is desirable for its own sake, apart from other things that form the content of a human life, but that it enables, supports, sustains, advances, and intensifies other important human goods.[9] The same can be said about sociability and the rest. *S* should care about these important human goods, whether or not he or she actually does care, because a human life consisting of them (or more accurately, consisting of them in a harmonious arrangement) and devoted to their enjoyment is intrinsically good.

(Again, for an internalist, *S* would have no reason to pursue knowledge, to cultivate sociability, to be moral, etc., if he or she did not actually care about these things in some way, or if he or she would not come to care as a result of serious reflection upon the things cared about. It is likely, however, that if *S* does not already care about these things, serious reflection on what is cared about would result in the discovery that the former give him or her reasons to act.)

Among the things that are important to a person are normally some things that are intrinsically important (because they are fundamental aspects of human flourishing). Indeed, it would be odd if the things that are intrinsically important were not usually important to people. For example, friendship or morality is important to most people and a basic element of human good as well, and the justification of caring about these things would appeal to their centrality in human life generally. But it is not just friendship generally, or aesthetic experience generally, and so on, that is important to people: also important are particular friends, particular aesthetic experiences, and the like. We ought to care about friendship, we ought to make it important to us, because friendship interlocks with, sustains, and advances a great variety of other things that make up the content of a human life, and we may come to care about it as a result of reflection on this. But we do not owe it to other people to become or to try to become their friend, and a concern for friendship is open-ended with respect to the particular persons we select to befriend. Moreover, no particular configuration or ranking of these basic human goods follows from the claim that living a life that combines these goods in a coherent, harmonious structure is intrinsically good. These things are worth caring about and ought to be cared about, but the explanation for this does not identify any particular instance of these goods, or any particular ordering of them, as something that ought to be cared about. I should devote part of my life, for example, to the cultivation of aesthetic experience, but this underdetermines the selection of such experiences and the importance they are to have in my life as a whole.

The basic human goods are instantiated in various ways in different lives. The particular things one cares about reflect one's individual history and circumstances, and it is absurd to claim that everyone should care about the particular things that are important to oneself. It would be unreasonable of S to hold that everyone should share the same love of fine wines, dedication to finding a cure for cancer, avidity for mountain climbing, or attachment to childrearing. It might also be unreasonable of S to claim that everyone should attach paramount importance to the same basic human goods. For example, morality might be of the greatest importance to some people but not to others; perhaps a convincing case can be made that it does not have to be if it is not.[10] In any event, it is difficult to object to the statement that there are some things that anyone ought to care about; that is, difficult so long as these things are described in quite general terms and the way in which these things as thus described are to be fitted together is not fixed.

I suggested earlier that moral development occurs through the cultivation of feelings and nurturance of the capacity to care about the well-being of others. It is necessary (but not sufficient) that a moral person be a caring person. We may add to this that morality, being a basic element of human good, is important enough that people ought to care about it. It is possible, I believe, for people to know what is morally right but not care about others who are affected by their actions, for those who are themselves indifferent to the moral rightness or wrongness of actions to be able to make sincere judgments about the moral propriety or impropriety of acting in certain ways. It is certainly possible for people who know what is right to care about doing what is right to different extents. To be sure, it can hardly be disputed that most of us do care about doing the right thing (as we see it) and avoiding the wrong thing (as we see it), and indeed this is one of the reasons why I began this discussion of caring by focusing on morality. But we care about much else besides, and sometimes even more than we care about morality. For example, we care about our personal projects, our friends and loved ones, and our nonmoral principles. The study of caring as such, according to Harry Frankfurt, is "concerned with a cluster of questions which pertain to [a] thematic and fundamental preoccupation of human existence" different from that investigated by either epistemology or ethics.[11] The task to which I now turn is clarification of the concept of caring.

2

What Caring Is

There are many different uses of "care." The following list is not intended to be exhaustive. (1) "To care for," as in "*S* does not care for lobster," or as in this interchange: (wife to husband) "You don't care for me anymore"; (husband to wife) "Of course I still care for you." Caring for in these contexts refers to liking, having affection for, being drawn or attracted to, or being pleased by.

In another sense, we say things like "The medical doctor cares for our bodily needs, the priest for our spiritual needs," where to care for means (2) "To have care of." To have care of someone or something is to be charged with the responsibility for supervising, managing, providing for, attending to needs, or performing services. *S* can have care of sick and elderly parents, for example, and not care for them in the sense of liking them or having affection for them.

(3) "To care about," as in "The dedicated researcher cares about finding a cure for AIDS," or "The typical worker on the assembly line does not care about the quality of the products he turns out." Following Frankfurt, we can say that "a person who cares about something is, as it were, invested in it."[1] A husband can care *for* his wife (i.e., like her or have affection for her), but if his own welfare is not somehow bound up with hers, he does not care *about* her. Conversely a person may care about something or someone that he or she does not care for in this sense. For example, a teacher may

take a special and personal interest in a student and yet not find the student particularly pleasant or appealing. In addition, a person can have care of something or someone that he or she does not care about.

(4) "To care that," as in "Certainly I care that millions of people are starving to death in Ethiopia," or "The exiled White Russian cares that the Bolsheviks be deposed." Caring-that is propositional and has a situation as its object. I can care that the Bolsheviks be deposed and (perhaps because I am under surveillance) not devote myself to deposing them, and I can care that millions of people are dying of starvation and (perhaps because I am poor and starving myself) not do anything to alleviate their suffering. However, if S cares that x, then S is invested in x's happening or not happening, as the case may be. It could hardly be said that I care that millions of people are starving if I do not experience satisfaction or joy, disappointment or distress, at learning that their misery has or has not been relieved. Also if S cares about x, then S cares that certain things involving x happen. For example, if an art collector cares about his or her Van Gogh then he or she cares that the painting be displayed so that it merits can be fully appreciated, or that it not be damaged (perhaps only so that it can be resold at a much higher price), and so forth.

Parents, typically though not always, care for their children, have care of them, care about them, and care that they flourish. Friends also care for and about each other. Love certainly involves caring-for, and as the word is sometimes but not always used, caring-about as well. As I have suggested, caring-for and caring-about are not always found together, and various combinations of these four uses of "care" are possible.

Let us look more closely at caring-about. I have said that the person who cares about x is invested in x. Now what is usually intended by the expression "S cares about x" is that S wants to do something that will benefit x, or be welcomed by x, or that will enhance it in some way, or keep it from being harmed or damaged, and so on. (The bulk of Part III is devoted to an examination of a number of issues pertaining to personal love, which I characterize as involving active concern for the good or happiness of particular others.[2]) Could caring-about be negative as well as positive? Consider, for example, the claim that Senator Joseph McCarthy cared deeply about communism, so deeply in fact that little else mattered, including the civil rights and reputations of the victims of his red-baiting. It may be said in this case, however, that this is a misleading description of what McCarthy actually cared about: what he cared about was not communism but his crusade against it, and he certainly wanted this crusade to flourish. Still, we can devote ourselves directly to the destruction or diminishment of something without devoting ourselves to the *cause* of destroying or diminishing it. Such caring-about is negative in tenor. The things and people we care about negatively we often do not care for either. But it is possible to devote oneself to the worsening of some thing's or person's condition even though one likes or is fond of it or him, as when we say, "It pains me to do this to you, because after all I do like you."

The notion of "interest" can perhaps help clarify the nature of caring-about and the difference between its positive and negative forms. When one cares about x one has an interest in x and takes an interest in x. One has an interest in something, Joel Feinberg tells us, when one has "a kind of *stake* in its well-being," that is, when one "stands to gain or lose depending on the nature or condition of X."[3] In positive caring-about, one stands to gain if x's condition is improved or at least maintained at some level favorable to x, and stands to lose if x's condition worsens or deteriorates or remains at some level unfavorable to x; in negative caring-about, one stands to gain if x's condition worsens or deteriorates or remains at some level unfavorable to x, and stands to lose if x's condition improves or remains at some level favorable to x. It is in my interest that my family and loved ones prosper (i.e., I stand to gain if they prosper and lose if they suffer); however, it is in my interest that my enemies at least do not prosper, because I stand to gain if they do not and to lose if they do. An "enemy," as I am using the term here, is not just someone we hate—though we usually do hate our enemies—but someone in whom we have a negative interest (i.e., we are negatively invested in his or her well-being).

Persons who care positively about x experience the diminishment of x as distressing or painful; persons who care negatively about x experience the enhancement of x as distressing or painful. When something bad (or good) happens to someone or something they care about, something bad happens to them, and they are distressed or pained because of these changes in the other's well-being. The distress or pain may itself be a kind of loss as well, but there is a distinction between the distress or pain that is attendant on this loss and the distress or pain that is attendant on the belief in some other loss. Persons who care risk loss, and distress or pain as a result of loss. It is not necessary that those who care about x also care about the distress or pain that caring about x exposes them to. They might or might not. If they care about their distress or pain, then they regard distress or pain itself as a personal loss (here "diminishment of x" is to be understood as the worsening of their condition with respect to distress or pain), and in caring about their states of mind they expose themselves to distress or pain if they should suffer this loss.

The caring-about that is characteristic of love relationships and friendships is only one sort of positive caring-about other people. Persons who love each other or who are close friends are strongly, durably, and deeply invested in each other's well-being, and one's well-being is directly a part of the other's. When a loved one is harmed, I too suffer a setback, and not because (or only because) I will then have to take time away from other things I enjoy doing in order to provide needed assistance, or because helping will be so emotionally draining that I will have little energy left for other projects, and the like, but because I am directly affected for the worse by knowing about the change in my loved one's well-being. And it is one's susceptibility to being directly affected for better or worse by changes in another's well-being, rather than having to suffer other incidental losses, that is paramount in a love relationship. In other cases of positive caring-about, identification with the good of the other, as an end in itself, is either missing or secondary. I may positively care about you because I am dependent upon you for the advancement of my own interests. An employer typically cares about employees in this way, because the employer's fortunes rise or fall depending on the well-being of the employees. We can mark the difference between these two forms of positive caring-about by saying that in the first case, I first and foremost care about *you* in *relation* to me, whereas in the second, I self-interestedly care about you as a *means* to the promotion of my own self-regarding interests, or unself-interestedly care about you only so long as on the whole I continue to get pleasure or benefits from you. There is also a parallel distinction between two types of negative caring-about other people. I may desire your ill-being as an end in itself or constituent of my own good, or I may desire it as a means to the promotion of some ulterior aim of mine.

Some positive caring-about, like the caring in love and close friendship, is basically disinterested care; that is, care that is given for the benefit of the recipient and that is not aimed at our own advantage or made conditional upon his or her being generally advantageous to us. The several varieties of love and friendship are also instances of affectionate disinterested care. Disinterested care can take other positive forms as well. We may simply show loyal, unselfish, and benevolent concern for the good of people with whom we are not acquainted, or solicitous concern for those who need our protection. On the other hand, there is basically self-interested caring-about; that is, care that is given primarily as a means to our own good or that extends only so far and lasts only so long as the other remains advantageous to us. Such caring-about can be affectionate, as in the case of Aristotle's pleasure- and advantage-friendships, or not, as in the typical case of the employer who cares about employee welfare.

One can *have* an interest in x and yet not *take* an interest in it, and one can take an interest in something one has no interest in, but caring-about requires both. In order to care about my children, for example, I must both have an interest or stake in their well-being and take an interest in their well-being. In general, I take an interest in the things and people I care about when I make their condition my active concern because I identify myself with them in some way. (As just noted, there are different ways of caring about other people, different foci of concern in identifying oneself with others. Even the employer in my example identifies him or herself in some way with the employees, or else the employer would not care about them at all.) On the other hand, there are many things and people that I take an interest in during the course of my life that I do not care about. I may take an interest in something simply out of idle curiosity or out of a desire to have something to take an interest in, and once my curiosity has been satisfied or my ennui dispelled I get on with my life. Taking an interest in someone or something might last for no more than a moment. But though there is nothing in the nature of "taking an interest in" that requires it to endure, with respect to the people and things I care about I take an interest for some more or less extended period of time. A person who cares about something must *direct* his or her life and conduct with reference to it,[4] and one who takes an interest in *x* for just a moment, even if he or she has a long-standing interest in *x*, does not take enough of or the right sort of an interest in *x* to care about it. (Of course, even among people who care some may take more of an interest in what they care about than do others.)

It is not possible for us to care *about* someone in whom or something in which we take no interest. On the other hand, it is possible to care *for* someone or something without taking much of an interest in the person or object. I might meet someone at a party and take an immediate liking to that person, but the interest I take in this person may be exhausted by this one occasion on which we met. Similarly, I can care for things that do not greatly catch my interest.

According to Annette Baier, one way of testing whether one really cares about something is given by this: "A reliable sign of real caring is the intolerance of ignorance about the current state of what we care about."[5] The person who really cares about *x*, whether positively or negatively, takes an interest in *x* in this way: he or she needs "constant contact with and news about the welfare of what is cared about" (p. 274). The difference between a person who needs this and one who does not is thus not that the latter cares less strongly about *x* than the former, but rather that the latter may not really care about *x* at all. *X* may still be important to this person, but tolerance of ignorance about *x* usually indicates that he or she has not made it important to him or herself by caring about it. For example, a mother identifies with her child, reacts with distress to the child's misfortune, feels pride in the child's accomplishments and takes delight in the child's well-being. Nevertheless, her attitude with respect to her child is "No news is good news": she is content to remain in the dark about how her child is faring. She will listen attentively when her child confides in her and will solicitously offer her advice and help if they are appropriate and asked for, and perhaps even if they are not asked for. But though she is distressed at bad news about her child, she is not distressed at not *knowing* whether there is bad or good news to relate about her child. She takes an interest in her child, but only so far and no further. For this reason, Baier would claim, such a parent's profession of caring is suspect. (Similar examples can be constructed for things. Distress at mere ignorance of their condition is also a test of really caring about them, according to Baier.)

I think it should be noted, however, that real caring may fail to pass Baier's test. One can care so much about x that one is terrified of receiving bad news about x and, as a result, be unable to bring oneself to make inquires about x that invites such devastating information. "Constant contact with and news about the welfare" of what we care about may be more than we can bear, and we may resort to denial in order to defend ourselves and survive intact. For example, a parent may see symptoms of a serious medical condition in a child and proceed to deny that there is any problem. (Does this mean that the parent really only cares about the child in a self-interested and not disinterested way? This may be true in some cases, but it is too glib to suppose that this must always be so.) Caring about someone or something does have its risks. People who care invest themselves in what they care about, and there is usually a risk associated with an investment. But as the use of denial shows, there may be limits to the risks that any given person who cares about someone or something is willing or able to take in caring.

My objection is only to a claim that "intolerance of ignorance about the current state of what we care about" is necessary for genuine caring. We can still think that some caring is better than others, in particular, that caring marked by this intolerance is better than caring that is not, either as a general rule or in specific situations. In analyzing the concept of care, it is hard to avoid building into it certain normative beliefs. But not all care is, all things considered, *good* care or equally good care. I shall have a bit more to say about this at the end of this chapter.

Caring about x involves being moved, either disinterestedly or self-interestedly, to do something that enhances x or to prevent something that diminishes x from happening (positive caring-about); or alternatively, to do something that diminishes x, or to omit to prevent x from being diminished, or to prevent something that enhances x from occuring (negative caring-about). Caring-about presupposes the ability to identify some states or conditions of the objects of care as good, and some as bad. (How it is to be decided what counts as good or bad is a question I shall not get into here.) Someone who makes no judgments at all about the goodness or badness of x being in certain ways cannot properly be said to care about x, whether disinterestedly or self-interestedly, affectionately or nonaffectionately.

There is clearly a significant difference between people and things that bears upon our interpretation of notions like enhancement and diminishment. Persons have interests of their own with which we can identify, but things do not. As Feinberg argues,

> mere things have no conative life; neither conscious wishes, desires, and hopes; nor urges and impulses, nor unconscious drives, aims, goals; nor latent tendencies, directions of growth, and natural fulfillments. Interests must be compounded somehow out of conations; hence mere things have no interests.[6]

Because "mere things" have no interests, they can have no good of their own, and so it is not possible to benefit or harm them. Thus, people who care about such things as historical landmarks, political or religious traditions, artistic creations, or ideas cannot be engaged in doing something that is literally good *for* these things. Feinberg does allow, however, for an extended or derivative sense of benefit and harm in the case of things. Harming or benefiting a thing can be regarded as "elliptical for the harm [or benefit] done to those who have interests" in the thing, "those who have in a manner of speaking 'invested' some of their own well-being in the maintenance or development of some condition"[7] of the thing. For example, if I care about a historical landmark, then I will typically do things like see to it that no one defaces it, contribute money to its restoration if it should fall into disrepair, pay it an occasional visit, point out its significance to others, and so forth. Clearly it is better for me if the landmark is in good repair rather than disrepair, intact rather than defaced. But it is not better for it to be in this condition. It is only better for those who have an interest in its being or remaining in this condition.

This is not to say that when I care about a thing, I "really" only care about the people who have an interest in it, or that the value of a thing is only its value to individuals who experience or use it.

A historical landmark, a way of life, a painting, or whatever, can possess a distinctive character that we can hold dear in itself, even though it cannot itself, independently of the interests of those who have a stake in its being a certain way, be benefited or harmed. We can value things in their own right, but we cannot be trustees of their well-being.

What I do for or to or with the objects of my care depends, among other things, on the character of what I care about, on my relation to it, and on the particular kind of concern that I feel for it. I care about an idea when I devote myself to discovering and exploring its essential traits, to widening and clarifying the scope of its application, to disclosing its relationships to other significant concepts, or perhaps only to assisting others in doing so. I care about other people when I act to benefit them simply because of the feelings of goodwill that I have for them, or because of this as well as feelings of special tenderness toward them; sometimes I care best when I do not try to help. I care about a cause when I commit myself to its promulgation and to winning converts to it. I care about a principle, moral or otherwise, when I devote myself to exemplifying it in my own life. When I care about an idea, person, cause, or principle in a positive and disinterested way, the worth that each is felt by me to have is inherent and not just a function of what it is able to do for me. Even what might be called "personal principles"—principles that I seek to exemplify in my own life but do not expect others to exemplify in theirs, that I do not criticize them for not exemplifying in theirs, and that I am not rationally required to extend to others—can be experienced as having worth in their own right. Of course, I cannot benefit or harm my personal principle itself; benefit or harm must here be understood in a derivative sense, as referring to the interests I have in the exemplification of the principle. But I am still attached to the principle itself and am prepared to judge myself according to how I measure up to it; my caring is not reducible in any simple way to caring about my own satisfaction or advantage, or more particularly, to caring about an image of myself as caring about these principles. As we shall see in Chapter 7, such an interpretation of caring about one's principles would leave us without an adequate appreciation of the force and import of claims about personal integrity.

There is an enormous variety of possible objects of care, and there are different kinds and activities of care appropriate to different sorts of recipients. But according to Milton Mayeroff,

> in any actual instance of caring it is always someone or something specific that is cared for [about]: the writer cares for [about] *this* idea, the parent cares for [about] *this* child, the citizen cares for [about] *this* community.[8]

What does he mean here, or more importantly, under what interpreation of these remarks would they be true? Perhaps the claim has to do with the intentionality of caring. Emotions, unlike feelings, are "about" something; they involve patterns of behavior of a consistent kind directed toward some object.[9] (The prevalent view is that the intentionality of emotion is to be understood in terms of the intentionality of its propositional or judgmental component, but this has been contested.[10]) Though I may not at a given time be able to identify the object of my emotion, or be able to identify it correctly, typically at least emotions are not freefloating. Moods, which are much like emotions, are different because they are not directed. If I am in an irascible mood, for example, I am unusually susceptible to the emotion of anger, not yet angry about anything in particular; if I am in a euphoric or depressed mood, this may be caused by some particular incident, but my euphoria and depression are diffuse and not *about* something specifiable. Now if Mayeroff is relying on some such distinction, his point about caring is well taken. I may be able to care about nothing in particular, if what is meant is that I do not care at all, but I cannot care about nothing in particular, if what is meant is that I do care but just not about any specific object.

On another interpretation of Mayeroff's remarks, what we care about must not only be some specifiable object, but a particular as opposed to a universal object. This view might be more fully expressed as follows. In any given case, when I care about *x* I care about it for itself alone, as a particular instance. I do not care about an idea or a child or a community merely as an exemplification of a type, but as a particular instance as distinct from other instances. Could I not care about a universal object as well? Not if in doing so I would be committed to caring about any instance of it only as an exemplification of a type. If caring about a universal object entails that I do not really care about its instances for themselves alone, and if I do care about things in this way, I cannot care about a universal object.

Now if Mayeroff intends to limit caring in this way, I believe he is mistaken. We can care about both particular and universal objects. I can care about *x* either for itself alone or only as an exemplification of a type. It is logically true that what we care about only as an instance of a type we cannot also care about as a particular or unique individual. But even if we assume that all caring-about must involve caring about a particular object, we cannot conclude from this logical truism that we can only care about particular objects and not also about some of the universals that the unique individual exemplifies. I can certainly care about my friend as a particular or unique person and about some of the qualities he or she exemplifies; I can care about the war in Vietnam for its own sake and as an instance of war in general; I can care about this particular philosophical idea and about the activity of philosophizing that my examination of it represents. In each of these cases, insofar as I care about *x* as an exemplification of a type, I am certainly committed to caring about the indefinitely large number of its instances simply because they are instances. But this does not prevent any given instance of caring-about from also being focused on a particular object: the object of my caring does not thereby become replaceable by something or someone else that instantiates the same universal. And again, I can care about a universal object without also caring about a particular one. My caring about a universal object will normally motivate me to try to exemplify it, but I might care about its exemplifications only as instances of a type.

In some sorts of caring-about, there cannot only be a universal object. As I shall explain more fully in Chapter 17, close friends or loving intimates do not care about each other merely as instances of a type, but such essentially particularistic care is only one species of (disinterested) caring-about. Not even all instances of love belong in this category. There is, for example, what Rawls calls "love of mankind," which "shows itself in advancing the common good in ways that go well beyond our natural duties and obligations,"[11] and such love is not concerned with others as particular and unique persons.

The variety of possible objects of care is only partly due to the diversity of particular things, people, and such, that we can care about as particulars, for we can care about universal as well as particular objects. In addition, there is another distinction to be drawn—between caring about x and being committed to x. In general, people care about the objects of their commitment, but not everything or everyone people care about is an object of their commitment. I might, for example, save a person's life because I care about that person for his or her own sake. However, if the person is only a distant stranger, there are quickly reached limits to how far I am willing to go on his or her behalf. Thus, I cannot properly be said to be committed to the person or his or her well-being. I might also feel some pride when the object of my care prospers, even if only a distant stranger, but this will of course be very different from the pride I feel when my friend or loved one, to whose well-being I have committed myself, prospers. Caring can be distinguished from commitment in terms of Bernard Williams' notion of "deliberative priority" (which he employs in arguing for the thesis that there is no uniquely moral form of obligation):

> A commitment has high deliberative priority for us if we give it heavy weighting against other considerations in our deliberations. (This includes two ideas, that when it occurs in our deliberations, it outweighs most other considerations, and also that it occurs in our deliberations.)[12]

Commitment, but not caring in general, is expressed in according deliberative priority to projects that embody it. If I care about something, it must be important to me, and the only valid test for whether something is important to me is whether I do or try to do something about it. But I need not give deliberative priority to projects that express this concern or to projects that do not interfere with them.

I want to conclude this chapter first with the reminder that I have only been interested in providing a (partial) descriptive account of care. I have tried to put normative issues aside. It remains to be decided, therefore, even in the case of caring-about that is directed at the good of its object, when caring is good caring and when it is not good or is defective in some way. I shall now make a few remarks about this.

One can care about something despite one's values, having as the object of one's caring something that one judges to be inferior and unworthy. For example, consider the case of an overweight woman who critically reflects on and is persuaded by feminist critiques of the ideology of slimness and who therefore does not value slimness. Nevertheless, she cannot help caring about her weight. Despite her better judgment, she has an interest in being slim and devotes herself to dieting. Since she cares about being slim, being slim is important to her, but she repudiates her caring about it and her treating it as important. (Similarly, one person might love another even though that person judges that it would be better not to do so. To be sure, we cannot love a person whom we take to be completely worthless, but we may think this person is unworthy in many respects.) Caring-about that is not in line with or consistent with one's values in this way, one's important or central values, is felt as self-betrayal and diminishes one's self-respect.

In addition to such caring-about that is against one's will, there are other cases in which caring is uncritical. There might be no absence of favorable evaluation of what is cared about, but rather undiscriminating overvaluation of it. The man who is infatuated with his beloved[13] typically exaggerates her charms and praises common qualities and ordinary performances as outstanding. He persists in this despite the facts that are there for all to see, and not merely because of misperception of or lack of information about the beloved. One can display a lack of sound judgment about all sorts of things one cares about, such as one's artistic or intellectual or other accomplishments, one's prized possessions, family traditions one upholds, the causes to which one devotes oneself, and so forth. In each of these cases, those who care are, unless exceptionally well-defended, courting disappointment and disillusionment, exposing themselves to more than the usual risks incurred whenever anyone cares about someone or something. In either event, whether one cares about and places importance on x even as one attaches considerable negative value to (caring about) x, or one cares about and places importance on something or someone that one undiscriminatingly overvalues, there seems to be something wrong with such caring. (Whether one should be *blamed* for this is another matter.) Caring should ultimately be integrated with one's important or central values (which is not to suggest that the values themselves are not subject to assessment in light of one's carings) and appraisal of the object of care should reflect sound judgment.

There are many ways that caring-about can fall to meet normative requirements. One might care about another person in such a way that one does not leave the other sufficient scope for the expression and development of an independent personality. One might also care too much about x in the sense that x occupies too much of one's attention. My appraisal of x itself might be sound enough and x might not be something or someone that I wish I did not care about, but I might be so preoccupied or obsessed with x that I am prevented from leading a happy and productive life. I give x or let x assume too much importance in my life as a whole. Or perhaps I pay so much attention to x that I neglect my moral duties and obligations to others. Even if it is morally permissible to give special preferential treatment to my loved ones and friends, caring about them can become excessive. It does so when I give my entire attention to them, despite the fact that further attention to them would produce minimal good for them compared to the much greater good that I could produce by giving my attention to others. Caring is also morally objectionable when a person is so preoccupied with a cause or with principles that the concrete interests of fellow human beings are ignored or undervalued. Finally, Annette Baier proposes as a normative requirement of caring that "it not depend on ignorance of its own nature and history."[14] For example, a lover who is drawn to someone by unconscious needs, desires, and wishes might find that love fade with growing awareness of the real reasons behind the attraction. This love may not be able to withstand exposure to all the relevant information available to the person about the love. According to Baier, one instance of caring-about is better than another to the extent that it can survive exposure to the facts about its origin and history. If the caring changes as a result of such exposure, as it very well may, it is better to the extent that the change is in the direction of deeper and more satisfying attachment.

Much more can be said about the ways in which some care is better than others. Care can be morally problematic or corrupt or irrational in ways that I have not yet discussed. Enough has been said, however, to show why any attempt to build an ethic on caring alone must fail. Nel Noddlings, for instance, writes:

> Moral statements cannot be justified in the way that statements of fact can be justified. They are not truths. They are derived not from facts or principles but from the caring attitude.[15]

It is difficult to understand how the claim that moral statements are derived from the caring attitude can be reconciled with the fact that we make moral demands of caring, and that caring may or may not meet these demands.

3

Caring and Personal and Impersonal Value

I can care about something even though I do not place value on it or disvalue it in some way. I can care about something despite my values and against my will. Placing importance on x is necessary to caring about x, but valuing x is not equivalent to placing importance on x. On the other hand, we often do value what we care about, and this chapter is concerned with such cases. Whatever other kind of value it has or is believed to have, it has value *for me,* or what we might call personal value. On occasion, I care about something under a description that contains a first-person indexical. For example, I may care about *my* getting a grant to pursue research, or about *my* finishing the novel I began last year. If in caring about these things I also value them, then the value is personal in a straightforward sense. These things have value for me in part because I attach some independent value (independent of the end achieved) to its being me who does or enjoys them. It is not necessary, however, for personal value that the description of what I care about essentially include a reference to me. For example, I can care about finding a cure for cancer, and finding a cure for cancer can have personal value for me, at the same time that the value of my finding a cure entirely derives for me from the fact that a cure will thereby be found. I view myself, as it were, as an instrument for the achievement of a valued end and yet still derive personal value from the impersonal pursuit. How is this to be explained?

Personal value in this sense is value that is posterior to the activity of caring-about. It is value that we give to the objects of our care by caring about them. Consider two persons, one of whom cares about bringing about some state of affairs x, and one of whom does not. Both may acknowledge that this project is worthy of being undertaken and merits achievement, whether or not they invest themselves in pursuing the goal. But x may have an additional sort of value in the former's case: personal value because care about x does in fact exist. Moreover, the fact that x has personal value for that person, if it does, may weigh heavily with him or her in practical deliberations. The importance of x in that person's life may be such that even if it is acknowledged that y scores higher than x on some standard of value that is not relativized to him or her as an individual, this may not be sufficient to induce a transfer of allegiance from x to y. If x is something that he or she cares deeply about, and if success or failure as a person is judged with reference to his or her efforts on behalf of x, then the assertion "x is my deep concern" will be regarded by him or her as a significant reason in itself for opting to be guided by it rather than by some alternative end y, quite apart from how an impersonal standard of value ranks x and y. This is in part what Samuel Scheffler has in mind when he speaks about "the independence of the personal point of view."[1]

Caring can generate value only for those who actually care, not for those who once cared but no longer do or who will care sometime in the future. The person who does not care about x can appreciate that x is the object of someone else's caring and so possibly a locus of personal value for *that person*, but not being personally invested in x, he or she does not create the same sort of special value of x for him or herself. (That person may then decide to care about x, but deciding to care is not tantamount to caring.) I care about my friends and loved ones, for example, and find personal value in my relationships with them, while others may profess that they cannot understand what "I see" in them. But having intimate relations of their own, I still expect others to respect the importance particular relationships have for me, to take seriously the fact that they are a source of personal value for me, even though others do not share my specific concerns and commitments. I say "find personal value" because caring about my friends and loved ones, indeed caring about much else besides, is not usually preceded by a decision to care, and the value that is generated by caring is not usually preceded by a decision to create personal value. Who our friends and loved ones are, and what it is we care about, is less chosen than discovered. Nevertheless, the value that we find in them is created by the very fact that we care and are invested in them.

Personal value is value for a particular person, conferred by that individual on something in and through caring. The concept of impersonal value, on the other hand, can be understood in different ways. Something might be said to have impersonal value if it would be a good thing for it to exist even in a world without conscious, desiring beings, even if it were never experienced by anyone, never the object of anyone's hopes or ambitions, never involved in anyone's life fulfillment. But the notion of value that is independent of the responses of *any* valuing subject might be thought too metaphysical and hard to make intelligible. Second, impersonal value might be value that is relative to some valuing subject or other. The value of x is here dependent on its being realized in the life of someone, somewhere, sometime, and not on its being realized in the life of someone in particular, at some particular time or place. Third, we might hold that impersonal value is interpersonal or intersubjective value. Impersonal value in this sense is relative to a valuing community: to ascribe this sort of value to something is to identify with a community whose values I share. The relevant group of valuing beings can be, but is not confined to, the members of one's particular culture or society.

I do not want to commit myself to any of these particular interpretations of impersonal value. Rather, I regard impersonal value only as objective value, that is, as value that inheres in something apart from my caring about or wanting it. Its relation to *me* drops out of the picture in this way. Further, the distinction between personal and impersonal value does not coincide with the distinction between agent-relative and agent-neutral value, as these terms are normally used.[2] Agent-relative value may be impersonal in my sense.

Caring-about does not always generate personal value. As I noted earlier, in cases of weak-willed caring, where the person's caring about something goes against his or her values, the object of this care does not provide a personal standard of value for guiding actions, even though the person has invested time and energy in it and directs his or her life with reference to it. But perhaps a more interesting case to think about is one in which the one who cares does not regard what he or she cares about as having some impersonal or nonpersonal value. It is possible, I believe, to care about something, even to care very strongly, without also thinking that the activities one engages in with respect to it have a value that transcends our individual preferences. In such a case, can what one cares about be personally valuable to oneself? Can one find value-for-oneself in something in the absence of any conviction of impersonal or nonbestowed value?

According to Loren Lomasky, these questions must (at least sometimes) be answered in the negative. "Personal value," he argues, "necessarily rests on a foundation of preexistent impersonal value."[3] Caring-about can itself generate personal value, but experience of it cannot (always) be conjured up out of thin air. What has personal value must also be perceived to have objective value. Suppose a woman cares about the welfare of her children and that her caring about them engenders a personal standard of value in terms of which possible outcomes of action are appraised. Her commitment to her children may, however, come into conflict with other things that she cares very much about, such as establishing a career for herself outside the home. Whatever she decides to do, she presumably does not take the matter lightly and wants to decide wisely. She experiences both the welfare of her children and her career aspirations as making serious demands upon her, and the predicament she finds herself in is an agonizing one for her. Now she could not experience her situation in this way, Lomasky would claim, unless she supposed that some value inheres in her childrearing and her career ambitions that is independent of the fact that she cares about her children and a career. It cannot be that attending to the needs of her children and establishing a career are regarded by her as valuable things to do simply because she cares about them. Such a characterization of her predicament trivializes it. She must also believe that they (that is, the activities, not necessarily *her* doing them) are impersonally valuable, that is, that they "hold out realizable value (for someone or other)" (p. 233). She must believe that childrearing and having a career have a sort of value that is expressible without self-reference, which means, for Lomasky, a value that derives from their standing in a certain sort of relation to *someone*.

In his elaboration of the claim that perception of personal value must be based on a conviction of impersonal value, Lomasky focuses his attention on instances of substantial commitment and on conflicts between objects of care "where the direction of a life is at stake" (p. 236). Indeed, it seems extravagant to require that the personal value generated by all caring, no matter how serious or trivial this caring might be, point beyond itself to impersonal value. Perhaps when one cares seriously about something that one values, one must suppose it to have a kind of value that does not simply derive from one's own individual caring about it. But not all caring has consequences that reverberate through the substance of one's life. It is purely arbitrary to declare that caring must be weighty, and capable of figuring in some agonizing personal predicament, if it is to be caring at all. Much of what we care about and that has personal value for us we could forego with relative ease, even if not without any personal disappointment or pain whatsoever. A particular hobby, for example, might be such a case (one person's hobby can of course be another's all-consuming passion). The person who cares about it and who gives it personal value through caring need not believe that it is also valuable from an impersonal or nonegocentric point of view. Though that person cannot believe, for example, that the objective truth about what he or she is doing is that it is a waste of time, it may be a relatively slight matter to him or her whether or not to remain occupied with this particular hobby or, for that matter, whether he or she has some hobby or other.[4]

It is only in connection with what we might call deep-seated caring that the one who cares must see the value of what he or she cares about as lying both within and without him or her. In cases of peripheral caring, this is not necessary. What is required here is, I think, something weaker than positive endorsement from a nonegocentric point of view. In any sort of caring, what one cares about doing cannot be viewed as having personal value for oneself if one judges that, regardless of the value one bestows on it, it is a bad thing to care as one does. The projects that have personal value for us must at least be seen to be innocent in themselves, apart from their relation to us, and in the case of deep-seated caring, personal value must also be sustained by the conviction of impersonal value.[5] This is not to say that something can have personal value for me and be an object of deep-seated caring only if I am not indifferent to whether the people with whom I come into contact approve of my values. I might not think about this and still be seriously committed to what I am doing. But if it is deeply important to me, I must believe that it matters, that my devotion is to something that is worthy of it.

Normative judgments of objective worth do not play a prominent role in connection with much that people care about and that has personal value for them in virtue of their caring. Indeed, many of the things we care about have personal value to us even though we do not judge them to be positively worthwhile, impersonally considered, even though we do not ascribe to them a value that we ourselves do not bestow on them. A life in which everything we care about is believed to have impersonal value would be a life weighted down by a pervasive sense of seriousness and of the momentousness of our decisions and actions. At the same time, personal value that is not augmented by the conviction of impersonal value cannot make a person's life *meaningful*. As Stephen Darwall observes, "that which endows our life with meaning must be something whose value we regard as self-transcendent."[6] The reason for this, he claims, is simple:

> Values that give our lives meaning both inspire and root our lives. They give our spirits the very air they need to breathe. They give us a rootedness: a place to stand, to defend, and to hold precious. But the value of what both enlivens and supports us cannot be based on our own individual responses as such. (p. 164)

This is not merely a psychological observation about us. Rather, it is a claim about the condition of the possibility of seeing one's life as meaningful. If a project is to be the ground of my life's worth, then it cannot just give me a personal reason for living. I must also affirm that the life I have a personal reason to live is worth living from some impersonal point of view. By itself, personal value cannot make the difference between a life that seems well spent and one that seems empty and pointless.

The values that govern our lives can endow our lives with meaning only if they are personal ones. Impersonal value alone cannot give my life meaning. I can grant that a course of action holds out realizable impersonal value, even though I have not made this course of action my own and in doing so given it a special value for myself. But then I would not find personal fulfillment in the pursuit of this course of action, and though it might contribute to the meaningfulness of some life or other, it could not yet contribute to the meaningfulness of mine. On the other hand, if something that has value for me does not point beyond itself to self-transcendent value, if something that I care about is not believed by me to *warrant* my care because it has genuine worth and importance, then it cannot give meaning to my life. If commitment to something is to give my life meaning, then I must believe that my commitment is impersonally recommended and that the value of what I commit myself to does not emanate simply from myself.[7] As Darwall construes this, I must believe that other people would concur in my evaluations were they to view the objects of my care with full understanding and without personal bias, putting aside their own particular situation, commitments, and preferences. In any case, believing that it is not impersonally disrecommended is not sufficient. Hence, the objects of deep-seated or serious caring are capable of endowing our lives with meaning, but the objects of peripheral care that are not positively endorsed are not, important though they are to us to some extent.

An example might help at this point. Consider the action of building model airplanes. We can imagine a person caring about this and attaching some value to spending some time building them. In most cases this will be an object of peripheral care only, something that is not taken by the one who cares as important enough to give meaning to his or her life. But now suppose a person suffers from a crippling physical disease and that devoting time to the building of model airplanes is seen as a test of ability to conquer the debility. Unlike the usual case, this person seriously cares about building models and is fighting a crippling disease through it; the challenge of conquering the disease provides this person with an opportunity to invest his or her life with meaning. It can only do so, however, if the person believes that conquering the disease is something worth doing, that is, impersonally valuable.

As this example illustrates, even normally trivial activities—that is, activities that most people would only care about in a peripheral way, if they cared at all—can conceivably be implicated in some close way in the meaningfulness of a person's life and can be perceived as having value independent of the fact of our caring about them. (Consider, as another example, the elderly widow who regards the most mundane of everyday chores as a significant test of her self-sufficiency. It is important to her that she be able to do her own grocery shopping, but she may also believe that, given her particular life situation, it is an important thing for her to do.) Whether or not something we care about has personal value only, or personal as well as impersonal value, refers to how the object of care is perceived by the one who cares and the role it plays in *that person's* structure of concerns. If it were only necessary that there be someone or other who cares about what I care about and who regards it as impersonally valuable, or that I could so regard it, and not that I so regard it, then the significance of the distinction I have been at pains to draw between personal value that is backed by impersonal value and personal value that is not would be eroded.

A notion of impersonal value is not only needed to explain what is involved in viewing one's *life* as meaningful, but is also implicated in ascriptions to *oneself* of integrity. Plans and projects that have value for me but not value from an impersonal standpoint not only cannot endow my life with meaning, but also cannot have a direct bearing on my (perception of my) possession or lack of integrity. Personal integrity, as Gabriele Taylor, and more recently Lynne McFall, have argued,[8] requires what might be called identity-conferring commitments. Such commitments involve, in Taylor's words, a person's "centrally important" values, the ones that "contribute to her identity," and any change in them would have "particularly far-reaching consequences on the nature and order of her other evaluations" (pp. 130–131). Of course different persons can and do have different identity-conferring commitments, and these need not be moral in nature, but whatever the content of these commitments, they make us what we are and they place constraints on our lives from which we may not be able to unbind ourselves without self-betrayal and personal disintegration. Identity-conferring commitments, which are at the deepest level what our lives are about, support a sense of the meaningfulness of our lives and give us a reason to continue to live. That is, these commitments confer meaning as well as identity, or meaning in conferring identity. Personal integrity and the sense that one's life has meaning are, thus, intimately linked. To repeat what I have said already, they both involve concerns that are believed to point to impersonal value, to value that precedes the act of caring. If the things to which I am committed were not believed by me to be worthy of my allegiance, irrespective of the fact that I personally care about them, then I would not see my commitment as having a bearing on my integrity. Peripheral caring is insufficient to generate a sense of the meaningfulness of one's life, and it concerns itself with matters that are not taken seriously enough to implicate one's integrity.[9]

Integrity is the identity of the person in terms of his or her commitments, and identity-conferring commitments are personal. One who has such a commitment is not thereby committed to believing that other persons he or she knows or is likely to meet will approve of it. Indeed, individuals may have no confidence or belief that others will do so, nor must they universalize their commitments. But if these commitments are to play the role in our attitudes toward our lives and ourselves that they do, if in particular they are to be capable of supporting a sense of self-respect, then we cannot take our commitments to be merely innocent psychological quirks: we must suppose that impersonal value attaches to them. Otherwise our concerns are too slight a foundation on which to build a sense of self-respect and personal integrity.

Since, as Taylor observes, "a person's commitments are normally varied and cover different areas of activity" (p. 131), it is possible to maintain integrity with regard to some areas and not others. It is also possible for one's identity-conferring commitments to be incompatible with one another, so that integrity with regard to some area of activity cannot be coherently combined with integrity with regard to another. In this case one cannot have a coherent identity overall, but, we might say, only a number of ill-sorted identities. Persons can have comprehensive integrity, integrity of the entire self, only if their lives consistently reflect a coherent conception of the good and they are committed to living in accordance with coherent commitments.[10] For such persons, too, there is personal value resident in the pursuit and achievement of coherence, that is, value that is consequent upon their commitment to the construction of a coherent life overall. But this is not all. There is also a belief that impersonal value attaches to the creation of such a life for themselves. They believe this higher-order project is worthy of their efforts and that being all of a piece in terms of their commitments is something of genuine value. The impersonal value here is not the value that conditions the various subsidiary identity-conferring commitments, but rather the value of being a certain sort of person, a person whose life is structured into an integral whole. This normative conviction dictates no specific commitments or structuring of them. Different individuals not only have different commitments, but can and will order them in different ways. The impersonal value of being a person of integrity is *personalized,* and how this is done depends on the individual's particular history, situation, subsidiary commitments, and so on.

In this chapter I have argued that caring-about typically (but not always) creates personal value for the one who cares, and that personal value can support our sense of the meaningfulness of our lives and can have a direct bearing on our integrity as persons only if there is as well belief in the impersonal value of what we care about. I now want to conclude by returning to a point I made in Chapter 1, namely, that there are some things that are plausibly regarded as sufficiently important that we ought to care about them. There may of course be things that people ought to care about that an individual does not in fact care about and that have no personal value for that individual. Actual caring should align to some extent with what ought to be cared about by anyone, supposing there are such things. Conversely, there is much that people care about of which it cannot plausibly be said that anyone ought to care about it (unless, that is, it is described in such generality as to trivialize the point), and there is nothing to condemn in this. But if this caring generates personal value that is sufficient to support a sense of meaning and that implicates one's integrity, the one who cares cannot see the value of what he or she cares about as emanating simply from within: this individual must judge that it is impersonally valuable. (For example, long-distance running, if constitutive of the meaning of my life and bound up with my integrity, must be taken by me to have self-transcendent value.) I can believe this without its also being the case that, or my believing that, its impersonal value is so compelling that I, or anyone, ought to care about it in the first place.

4

The Good of Care

Before we consider the good of care, it would be a good idea to review the different dimensions along which instances of caring can be differentiated from one another. Persons care about some things and people more strongly and more persistently than they do about others. Some caring is essentially self-interested, some disinterested. Disinterested care can take different forms, ranging (in the case of caring about persons) from benevolent concern for the good of people whom we have never met to the tender care of ardent love. As I noted in the last chapter, objects of care can be ranked in terms of how closely they are related to core elements of the caring self. The objects of identity-conferring commitments are accorded a special status so far as our self-conception and life plans are concerned: these core commitments are central to making one the kind of person one is, constitute one's basic orientation to the world, and shape the meaningfulness of one's life. Identity-conferring commitments can be to other people, both known and unknown, to ideals, both moral and nonmoral, to one's "brain child," to the community or traditions in which one was reared, or to projects of various sorts. They can also be either primarily self-regarding or primarily other-regarding.

Though disinterested care is not care that is directed toward the satisfaction and advantage of the one who cares, it can still benefit a person in many ways. Of particular importance is the fact that disinterested care functions as an antidote to self-preoccupation: in so caring, one shifts one's attention away from one's self, with which one tends to be excessively preoccupied, to appreciate aspects of the world in a detached way. The shift of attention induced by disinterested care can be described in Ernest Schactel's terms as a move away from "autocentric perception" to "allocentric perception":

> The main differences between the autocentric and the allocentric modes of perception are these: In the autocentric mode . . . objects are . . . perceived from the perspective of how they will serve a certain need of the perceiver, or how they can be used by him for some purpose, or how they have to be avoided in order to prevent pain, displeasure, injury, or discomfort . . . the predominating feature of the perception is not the object in its own right, but those of its aspects which relate to the perceiver's more or less conscious feelings of the need or purpose which the object is to serve. . . . In the allocentric mode . . . the emphasis is on what the object is like. . . . The perceiver usually approaches or turns to the object actively and either opens himself toward it receptively or, figuratively, or literally, takes hold of it, tries to "grasp" it.[1]

A persistent state of excessive self-preoccupation is of course pathological, but less extreme forms are not uncommon, and in them the precarious balance between inner-directed and outer-directed attention is temporarily upset and our sense of self for a time becomes distorted. Excessive self-preoccupation unrealistically magnifies the significance of the self and prevents us from seeing ourselves justly, both in ourselves and in our relations to others. Disinterested care, insofar as it gives us a more detached and diminished view of ourselves, promotes self-knowledge.

Self-regarding care can also free us from inordinate self-preoccupation and promote self-knowledge. We are perhaps inclined to focus on disinterested care in this regard, but I believe the former is possible as well and not uncommon. Consider a man who cares deeply about mountain climbing.[2] For him, the real point of climbing is not to reach the summit, but to achieve a kind of personal victory against himself by struggling against harsh and dangerous conditions. The benefits of this struggle are primarily for himself, and yet by testing his abilities against difficult tasks, he gains a better understanding of the extent of his abilities and his limitations. Self-knowledge can also be promoted through self-regarding care in less spectacularly risky ways. For example, people may commit themselves to the task of mastering some craft, or some body of knowledge, or some skill. In each case, let us suppose, they act only for their own pleasure or advantage. Yet they struggle to meet the demands placed on them by their self-directed projects, and in the course of meeting, or failing to meet, these demands, they can gain important insight into their intellectual and practical capacities and even into their character. Admittedly, disinterested and self-regarding care are not the only sources of self-knowledge, but they are significant sources nonetheless, and it is in the affording of opportunities for greater self-understanding that the good of care partly consists.

Two further points about the relationship between caring and self-knowledge should be mentioned. First, disinterested and self-regarding concerns can be either peripheral or deep-seated. As a rule, the self-knowledge that is gained through caring will make a greater difference in the life of the one who cares, and will matter more to that person, when the self is centrally identified with the object of its caring rather than just peripherally so. Mountain climbing, for example, can be an avocation or an identity-conferring commitment, and in the latter case it obviously matters a great deal to me what I learn about myself through this arduous experience. Peripheral caring can distract us from our self-preoccupations, but it may not do so with any regularity or with much persistence; even if it does consume a lot of our time and energy, it is not the case that the more intense the involvement the more significant the self-knowledge acquired through it. On the other hand, our self-conceptions are tested by engagement with the things and people that are ranked highest in our hierarchies of values and concerns. Because we take our deepest commitments to be features of ourselves that are central to the persons we are, our conceptions of ourselves may change as we strive to meet the demands that fidelity to these commitments imposes on us. (Revision of self-conception is not bound to occur as a result of the self-examination occasioned by caring. Affirmation of self-conception is also a possible outcome.)

Second, though as we have seen disinterested care can be directed toward all sorts of objects, and among people toward intimates as well as nonintimates, relationships of personal love and friendship are especially important in providing means to the achievement of an enlightened self-concept. Friends and loved ones (at least insofar as they are friends, too) see themselves in one another, and discover and measure their strengths and weaknesses through the continual and sensitive feedback each gives the other. This mutual monitoring, based on prolonged and deep familiarity, is perhaps the most potent source of objectivity about ourselves available to us. Caring about ideas, traditions, strangers, and the like, can also help us to attain objectivity about ourselves as we gauge our success in dealing with them, but it is often easier in these cases than with friends to succumb to the temptation to gloss over our faults or to delude ourselves into thinking we have virtues that we do not.[3]

Because, as experience shows, we are apt to get a truer picture of ourselves in intimate relationships of friendship, intimacy also plays an especially important role in maintaining and fostering personal integrity. Integrity presupposes self-knowledge: if we are to be true to the principles or commitments that make us who we are, we must first know what our principles are and what we are committed to. Moreover, it is not enough to know what we are prepared to give our intellectual assent to. The self-knowledge required for integrity cannot just be of this purely intellectual sort, but must be knowledge of the principles and commitments that actually motivate our actions and actually have a major influence in our lives. Friends, by interacting with us on several levels and by providing us, in an ongoing way, with a benchmark against which to test our self-image, help us to attain the practical self-knowledge upon which integrity depends.

There are other goods in addition to self-knowledge that are associated with caring. Caring can elicit and nurture certain qualities that, when combined with other valuable traits and ends, it is good for persons to possess. Deep caring, whether about things or people, often draws upon our reserves of patience and persistence, and in testing our patience and persistence strengthens them. Musicians who care deeply about their playing, for example, are not prone to complain about the necessity for continual practicing or likely to abandon their efforts because of occasional discouragement and failure, and they school themselves in patience and persistence as they actively dedicate themselves to the mastery of their instruments. "Persisting in what we are doing and in holding on to what we have" is important because, as Max Deutscher observes, it is

> a condition of maintaining knowledge and understanding—objectivity, if you like—of what we are dealing with and of ourselves. It is in our sustained commitments to philosophy, painting, each other, to the ideals of democracy, to the possibility of radical social change, to motor racing, to the value of life as exhibited in sense and in sensibility that we become familiar with the ins and outs of these things, that our illusions about them are dispelled or shattered.[4]

Caring can also display and teach a sort of humility that enables us to recognize and appreciate the world and others for what they are and prevents blind or distorted forms of response. Self-preoccupied as we often are, we often lose sight of the fact that we must make our way in a world in which we are not always in charge, but caring may bring a cessation of manipulative striving. Nel Noddings describes this phenomenon as follows:

> I let the object [of my caring] act upon me, seize me. . . . My decision to do this is mine, it requires an effort in preparation, but it also requires a letting go of my attempts to control. This sort of passivity, it should be noted, is not a mindless, vegetablelike passivity. It is a controlled state that abstains from controlling the situation; it involves ongoing processes but not explicitly goal-oriented activities.[5]

Letting go of attempts to control partly characterizes the relationship of friends, for example. They do not try to impose their expectations and requirements on one another and they come to appreciate one another's independence as intrinsically valuable. When patience, persistence, and humility are related to our identity-conferring commitments, these qualities are definitive of the sorts of people we are and even our more peripheral activities are likely to partake of these qualities as well.

Sometimes people care in such a way that they regard themselves as having a calling, perhaps but not necessarily accompanied by a conviction of divine influence. More generally, caring that is serious enough to be called commitment benefits those who care by giving meaning and worth to their lives and, to quote Bernard

Williams, by "compel[ling] allegiance to life itself."[6] Further, the
good of care is partly the good of trust. The foundation of our
capacity to trust is laid in childhood. The evident intention of our
parents to take care of us and their fulfillment of this intention give
rise to our trust in them and prepare us, as well as we can be
prepared, to form relationships of trust in adulthood. Of course,
trust is good only when it is placed in the trustworthy, and there are
usually various ways to assure ourselves of the trustworthiness of
others. I do not only trust, and I am not only justified in trusting,
those who care about me.

These claims about the good of care are modest ones. Not all
caring adds much to our self-knowledge; caring can create illusions
about what we care about as well as shatter them; caring sometimes arrogantly assimilates the world to our own preconceived
structures; care does not inevitably engender trust; and the projects that we care about do not always "inspire and root our lives."
Further, even if caring facilitates self-knowledge and gives us a
more accurate conception of ourselves and the world, questions of
value still need to be addressed. Patience and persistence, for example, are not unqualifiedly good, for they can be manifested by
those who care deeply about some wicked project. I also do not
want to claim that it is only in and through caring that all the goods
and qualities I have discussed are acquired or manifested. The
explanation I have given of why it is a good thing to care tells us
neither that these goods and qualities are invariably associated
with caring (i.e., necessary features of caring as such), nor that all
of them are confined to contexts of caring.

There is one more good of care that I want to consider. This is the
good of what Milton Mayeroff calls "basic certainty."[7] As he characterizes it, it pertains only to what he calls "inclusive caring," caring
that integrates a life, and can be possessed only by persons whose
commitments are in harmony with one another and whose more
peripheral and passing concerns are appropriately subordinated to
the aims and activities that are intimately connected with their self-
identities. The main features of basic certainty include these:

> There is . . . stability. . . . I am steadied and centered in my living, and
> the discordant experiences of day-to-day living, experienced against a
> settled background, are more easily assimilated. . . . This stability is

the antithesis of the deep-seated uncertainty as to who we are and what we are about that goes with ambivalence and drift. . . . We discover also the *clarity* that results from the elimination of much clutter. A simplification takes place in my life through recreating it around caring. Much that is incompatible and irrelevant to my caring is eliminated, and I achieve a fundamental clarity as to who I am and what I am about. (pp. 67–70)

The sort of stability, clarity, and simplication Mayeroff speaks of is not enjoyed by persons who are torn between conflicting identity-conferring commitments, or whose conduct and choices significantly depart from their established priorities. They are enjoyed, however, by those whose actions regularly cohere with coherent commitments (their fundamental commitments do not conflict and their less important commitments are ranked). Basic certainty, Mayeroff stresses, is not merely a matter of how we *feel* about our lives,[8] and the good of basic certainty is not just the good of a deep sense of contentment. One might actually be divided within oneself and yet, because one is self-deceived to a considerable extent, feel centered or certain about who one is and what one is about. But then in this case one has not achieved fundamental clarity. Further, basic certainty is not an unqualified good, for, it seems, it could be possessed by the fanatic as well as the person of integrity.

The life of a person who works to harmonize a number of different identity-conferring commitments is in a sense more complicated than the life of a person who is single-mindedly devoted to some goal or ideal. As a rule, the more one cares deeply about, the more difficult is the task of integrating one's commitments and maintaining their integration over time. And there are many obvious respects in which even the life of a person passionately devoted to some single goal or cause may be extremely complicated. ("Clutter" is not the only thing that complicates a life.) There are multiple criteria of the complexity of a life, and according to some of these it may not be the case that "a simplification takes place" in a life ordered by inclusive caring. In any case, if some sort of simplification does occur, it is, in the life of a person of integrity, "a continuing matter, not something static and acquired once and for all" (pp. 68–69).

One final remark about the good(s) of care: caring can be good for us in many ways even if it cannot plausibly be maintained that what we care about is, from an impersonal point of view, something we ought to care about. Much of what we care about makes claims upon us only once we care about it and not in advance of our caring, but its significance as a source of important goods and as an occasion for exercising admirable qualities is not dependent on its conformity to some antecedent "ought." We are not enjoined to have the particular friendships and love relationships that we do, and the personal projects to which we commit ourselves often reflect quite idiosyncratic preferences. In such cases, noncommittally looking upon what we care about from a point of view external to our caring will or may disclose no reason why we ought to care about it. Nevertheless, in making particular people or projects important to ourselves by caring about them, we may significantly enhance our self-knowledge and nurture our capacity for patience and perseverance in a profound way. Further, as argued at the end of the last chapter, while something we care about can give meaning to our lives only if we believe that it warrants our care, we need not also think that everyone should give it the same importance in their lives that we give it in our ours. And we can be steadied and centered in our living by inclusive caring, some of whose elements are carings that make claims upon us only because of the importance we give them in our lives. These and other goods, for the one who cares as well as others, are possible with carings of this sort.

5

Caring about Caring

There is, in addition to caring about people, projects, principles, ideals, and the like, a second-order caring: caring about caring. One can care about the former and yet not care about one's caring. But this is an ambiguous expression, covering both caring about our specific carings and caring about the capacity that underlies them, and I want to conclude this part of the book with some brief remarks about what constitutes caring about caring.

In one sense, to care about caring is to care about one's ability to care deeply about things and people in general, to invest oneself in and devote oneself to something (or someone) or other. People can lack this ability for different reasons, and for longer and shorter periods of time. Carings that have sustained us, and around which we have built our lives, can seem upon retrospective appraisal to have been inappropriate or excessive. We may come to believe that what we cared about was not worthy of our devotion or not worthy of the degree of devotion we displayed. Given the centrality of these carings, our lives will be seen as having been profoundly misspent and a pervasive sense of the pointlessness and emptiness of life may set in. Under these conditions, we may find ourselves unable to summon up enough conviction or interest to care deeply about anything at all. Not only might we then cease to care about the things we once cared about, but, overcome by a sense of the meaninglessness of our lives, caring as such might seem pointless and vain. How long this lasts depends on diverse factors, and it may be some time before we begin to care about caring and take steps to restore our ability to care about things and feel connected with life.

In addition, a person might stop caring about something by realizing that it cannot be gotten or attained, rather than by coming to believe that what one cares about is not worth caring about. If what one stops caring about is something to which one has devoted a substantial portion of one's life, the effect on one's ability to care deeply about anything at all may be devastating. Again, people can lose the ability to care even when they do not come to believe that they were wrong to care about what they cared about or, what is not the same, that they cannot have it. The mother who has devoted her life to the upbringing of her children and who now, because of their departure from the home, has no children to take care of, or the husband who, because of death or divorce, loses the wife with whom he has spent many close and deeply satisfying years, may be unable to take an interest in what she/he once cared about or to form any new attachments. (This includes relatively peripheral attachments as well. The realization that what we have cared most about is foolish or unattainable, or that we no longer have it to care about, may have effects that ramify through the whole range of our carings.) The loss they suffer need not, though it may, move them to question the wisdom of their former carings. If they still care about caring, if it is still important to them that they be able to care deeply (about whatever), they will seek ways of reviving their interest in life.

The person who cares about caring in the sense I have been discussing is emotionally invested in being a caring person, that is, a person who takes an interest in and devotes him or herself to things, activities, and people in his or her world. A person who cares about caring and who realizes that he or she has stopped being a caring person or is in danger of becoming uncaring may deliberately takes measures (perhaps with the assistance of others) to find something to care about or to keep alive a sense of purpose and attachment to life. But it is not necessary that this person normally is consciously aware of the investment in being a caring person or that he or she normally retains some picture of self as a caring person that serves as an ideal toward which to aspire.

Further, though I have spoken only about positive caring about caring, that is, caring that is directed toward *having* cares, there is a negative counterpart as well. In this sese, caring about caring would be directed toward the *elimination* of cares, toward disengagement from life. Eventually, when we have severed our attachments to the world and freed ourselves from all first-order cares, caring about caring will also fall away. This seems to be the Buddhist ideal, and the classic Stoic ideal is in one important respect very similar. To be sure, achievement of personal happiness or well-being did not require the Stoics to renounce the world and its goods, but it did require the cultivation of indifference so that one could protect oneself from injury by the vicissitudes of life. The unhappy state of mind in which we are oppressed, burdened, or disquieted, or undergo tension and suffering on account of fear, worry, anxiety, or grief or sorrow concerning what we care about results, they argued, from the delusory belief that we can actually control external events. In fact, all that happens is in accordance with a preordained arrangement that we are powerless to change, and we must learn to give up our cares (that is, anxieties, worries, etc.) by accepting this. In this condition, in which we would not be bothered or pained even if we were aware that what we care about is defeated, or dead, or permanently absent from our lives, we cannot properly be said to care about it.[1]

Caring about caring also looks to our specific carings for the purpose of ascertaining whether we do indeed care about what we think we care about, or care in the way we think we care, or care to the extent we think we care. There are several ways we can be mistaken in our beliefs about what we care about. A mother who claims to care about her daughter takes no interest in her at all and does not react with distress or joy to bad or good news about her. (She erroneously thinks she cares.) A professional declares that a caring relationship to a client is merely one of benevolence motivated by a sense of duty, whereas in fact this professional feels a special tenderness toward the other and gives the other a special favorable place in personal estimation (thereby misidentifying the type of caring). A workaholic man professes to care about his family more than anything else in his life, whereas in fact his family, which he does care about, always comes second after his job. (He misperceives the relative weights of his carings.)

We sometimes fail to realize that our actions do not cohere with our avowals of caring, perhaps because we have deceived ourselves into thinking that they do. Caring about caring, in the sense I am now exploring, requires that we step back from these avowals and check for such discrepancies with the aim of eliminating any significant ones that may be found. The impetus for such introspective reflection on our carings often comes from a perceived discrepancy between the way we see ourselves and the way others see us: others identify us as caring about something, or caring about it in a certain way, or to a certain extent, but we do not, and we seek to determine whether we really care as they claim we do. For example, I may never have professed to love you and never have thought of myself as loving you (I never "led you on," as we say), but your insistence that I have given every indication that I do leads me to reflect on my true feelings. Perhaps I have been insufficiently attentive to them and careless about my carings.

Suppose we satisfy ourselves that we do indeed care about something or someone (in a certain way, to a certain extent). Will we, if we care about caring, guide ourselves away from anything that might alter or endanger this caring? Clinging to our carings in this way is one form that caring about caring can take. In this case, the person who cares takes only limited risks: one risks loss or defeat if the things or persons cared about are somehow diminished, but does not risk the alteration, devaluation, or loss of one's caring about them. This person loves someone, say, and in doing so ties his or her own fortunes to the fortunes of the loved one, but does not place love itself in jeopardy. The person does not seriously question whether or not to care this much about someone, perhaps because of fear of what might be learned and of what might then be decided about the continuation of the relationship. Critical scrutiny of our fundamental carings and core commitments is especially risky, and resistance to it is therefore especially strong, because such inquiry might (though it certainly does not have to) reveal the desirability of making profound and far-reaching changes in our lives. But even the loss of a less-than-profound caring can be the loss of a source of great satisfaction and some personal enrichment.

A second, riskier sort of caring about caring considers—and not just in a detached theoretical way—whether our carings should continue, or continue in their present form, or with their present degree of importance. We care about our carings enough to do this, we might say. If, in caring about caring, scrutiny of our carings supports them and we are reasonably confident that further inquiry will not lead us to change our minds, then it is reasonable for us to act so as to conserve our carings. If, however, in caring about caring we judge that it is better not to care as we do, or if we suspect that our judgment may be incorrect, then it may be sensible for us to take steps to change or eliminate our cares or to inquire further. Of course, we can no more stop caring at will than we can care at will, for caring, which is emotional, is not under a person's direct voluntary control. Still, we can form an intention concerning what to care about and how to care about it, and we can, by choice, work to extinguish or transform or reposition specific carings.

I do not say anything here about the tests that people do and should use to evaluate their carings, if they care about caring and therefore are willing to put their carings themselves at risk.[2] An interesting question here concerns the relationship between the structures of personal and impersonal value. Suppose I discover that the way my carings are arranged in my life does not mirror their ranking in some impersonal scale of values I accept. X has greater personal value to me than y even though I believe that, from an impersonal point of view, x does not have greater value than y. Should I work to reorder my carings so as to bring them into closer alignment with the structure of impersonal value as I see it, so as to only give prominence in my caring to what I judge to be of greater impersonal value? Such a requirement, it seems to me, would constitute an attack on the integrity of the personal point of view. In any case, there are certainly other normative requirements for caring that are less problematic than that the value to us of some impersonal value should reflect its impersonal importance.

Caring about caring may not change our carings, but it changes how they are related to us and how we express ourselves in our caring. Through critical reflection on our carings, the point of which is to reach a decision about whether or not to go on caring or caring as we do, and with the resolution to carry out this decision, we take control of our carings and make the decisions and actions expressive of them our own. Autonomy in our core commitments and fundamental carings is autonomy at the deepest level of who we are and what we are about.

II

INTEGRITY

6

Williams and Integrity

Integrity has not been much discussed in the philosophical literature as a topic in its own right. It has been much stressed, however,
in recent debates on whether modern ethical theories, utilitarianism and consequentialism in particular, paint a coherent picture of
the moral life. In a number of influential papers, Bernard Williams
has attempted to show that they do not because they force a rift
between the agent and his or her most heartfelt commitments.
Against utilitarianism's version of impartiality, Williams argues:

> The point is that he [the agent] is identified with his actions as flowing
> from projects and attitudes which in some cases he takes seriously at
> the deepest level, as what his life is about. . . . It is absurd to demand
> of such a man, when the sums come in from the utility network which
> the projects of others have in part determined, that he should just step
> aside from his own project and decision and acknowledge the decision
> which the utilitarian calculation requires. It is to alienate him in a real
> sense from his actions and the source of his action in his own convic-
> tions . . . this is to neglect the extent to which *his* actions and *his*
> decisions have to be seen as the actions and decisions which flow from
> the projects and attitudes with which he is most closely identified. It is
> thus, in the most literal sense, an attack on his integrity.[1]

Now if Williams is right about this, this is indeed a serious indict-
ment of utilitarianism, for his claim is that it makes unreasonable,

and not just disagreeable, demands of us. But the success of the integrity criticism clearly cannot be determined until we know what integrity means here, and it is mainly in order to get started thinking about the nature of integrity that I propose to begin with Williams. As for the difficulties that integrity supposedly raises for utilitarianism, I will suggest a number of possibilities and will argue that utilitarianism survives them. (In what follows, I mean by utilitarianism, act-utilitarianism. The rule and motive variants of utilitarianism and consequentialism are not considered.)

Who is it whose integrity is supposed to come under attack? Suppose a person has a number of individuating "ground projects" that he or she "takes seriously at the deepest level as what his life is about,"[2] but does not acknowledge any commitment to maximize utility. A utilitarian tells him or her to abandon some ground project(s) because it is nonoptimific, and without coming to embrace the utilitarian principle as a commitment (or having as a principle deferring to the wishes of others), he or she does what is demanded. I think we would agree in this case that the individual has lost personal integrity. But this has nothing particularly to do with the content of the demand that the utilitarian is making of this person. A similar loss of integrity would take place if, for example, I had it as one of my ground projects to become a poet and I capitulated to the insensitive demand of my parents to give this up and become an accountant instead because there is more money to be made from accounting, even though I did not share my parents' commitment to financial prosperity. Since this loss of integrity is not a special problem for utilitarians, it is not what I shall suppose Williams has in mind when he argues that utilitarianism strips us of our integrity. So let us consider the possibility that the agent endorses the utilitarian principle and has as a ground project the maximization of utility. Perhaps Williams wishes to maintain that people do not or cannot have this as a ground project, or that even if there are committed utilitarians, their integrity is placed in jeopardy by being so.

If we think of integrity in a formal way as what is manifested in a person maintaining his or her principles or deep commitments in the face of temptations or trials, then it is not clear why the utilitarian must lack integrity. For in the case of some people, maximizing utility may be a deep concern of theirs and they may hold fast to this principle. But this might be challenged. One might concede that if an agent makes a commitment to the utilitarian principle, then acting on this principle would not conflict with one's integrity, and then go on to deny that an agent can, "at the deepest level, as what his life is about," have the maximization of utility as a project. In other words, acting on the principle of utilitarianism could not count as acting with integrity because such actions are not motivated by the agent's commitments. Utilitarianism, then, requires one to set aside other projects to which he or she is committed for the sake of something to which he or she is not.

We might try to demonstrate a difficulty with the notion of a committed utilitarian in at least two ways. First, it might be argued, as Loren Lomasky has done, that if I am to be committed to some project of mine, then I must believe that I have more reason to carry it out than I have to fulfill the corresponding interests of others.[3] In other words, to be committed to my project requires that I have a certain attitude about its primacy. But I cannot deliberate and act as utilitarianism requires and yet accord my projects this primacy: I must weigh the relevant concerns of others equally with my own in deliberation and act impartially. Hence, "commitment" to the maximization of utility violates a necessary condition of commitment and so is incoherent. It is not hard to show, however, that this argument is confused, for utilitarians can coherently claim that their project of maximizing utility does have a certain primacy in the sense that they would have no reason at all to promote it if it were only someone else's end. What gives the utilitarian reason to treat everyone's interests alike is not the concerns of others, but his or her own concern for the maximization of utility. The utilitarian's pursuit of an impartialist end is compatible, therefore, with having the required attitude.

But even if there is no problem of incoherence in the commitment to utilitarianism, it may be alleged, further, that "maximization of utility" is an extremely abstract and remote end, too abstract and remote to be integrated with one's character or identity. Those commitments that the agent makes on the basis of what he or she, quite personally and partially, wants to see happen are vivid and immediate enough to compel one's allegiance, to be the object of one's deepest subjective concerns, but people just cannot generate much enthusiasm for the maximization of utility (or any impartial ethical principle). This argument is also unpersuasive. It is not only the welfare of some particular persons, friends or loved ones, to which people can and do dedicate themselves. As Sarah Conly observes, "while some may find it hard to imagine a person dedicated to "utility" *per se,* it is not so hard to imagine a person who is sympathetic and benevolent, who yearns for the happiness of others."[4] For such a person, utility is not a remote abstraction and the promotion of it is grounded in a heartfelt concern for the interests of other human beings.

The integrity criticism of utilitarianism might proceed along the following lines. It might be conceded, after the preceding discussion, that one can have as one's ground project the maximization of utility. But a utilitarian is not just someone who has a commitment to the maximization of utility on a par with his commitments to other partial, nonoptimific projects. Rather, the utilitarian recognizes that despite these partial commitments, there is a *duty* to act from the utility principle. In other words, there is an acknowledged commitment to utility that overrides any nonutilitarian commitments. But a person of integrity must have nonoptimific projects that he or she is not prepared to set aside for the sake of social utility, that he or she will not allow to be thwarted just because this principle prescribes that it is the impartially right thing to do so. So, though one can be a committed utilitarian, one cannot at the same time have the sort of strong commitment to nonutilitarian projects that the person of integrity must have. It is "quite absurd," Williams argues,[5] to require that when the demands of utilitarian morality conflict with an agent's personal and partial commitments, the former must win. And we might add that this requirement is quite absurd because it sometimes amounts to an assault on an agent's integrity.

There is no need to appeal to integrity here, however. A utilitarian agent does not have any personal and partial commitments that are strong enough to override utilitarian morality. As this person sees it, there is good and sufficient reason to do as utilitarianism requires when there is a conflict between these demands and other, partial commitments. To be sure, as Williams maintains, "there can come a point at which it is quite unreasonable for a man to give up, in the name of the impartial good ordering of the world of moral agents, something which is a condition of his having any interest in being around in that world at all,"[6] but for the person I am describing, setting aside personal and partial commitments is not tantamount to losing interest in life. The individual's "interest in being around" is just not dependent on having personal and partial commitments that can trump utilitarian demands. Perhaps it will then be claimed that one *ought* to have such commitments, that there is something impoverished about the life of a person who has an overriding commitment to the maximization of utility. For example, this person may lose out on friendship. According to William Wilcox, "an overriding commitment to the maximization of impersonal value . . . has practical effects that are too pervasive to leave room for the *commitment* to particular persons necessary for friendship."[7] Someone with such an overriding commitment may be able to care about some particular person for the person's own sake, but cannot be, as a friend is, committed to someone for that person's own sake, in the particularly strong sense of "commitment" Wilcox employs. Now we might agree with this, but this and other attempts to show that one ought to have nonutilitarian strong projects seem very different from a criticism in terms of integrity. It might be suggested that the value of close personal relations yields a positive reason for allowing agents to pursue nonoptimific projects and commitments, but those who have integrity do not necessarily lead rich or well-rounded lives.

In *A Critique of Utilitarianism,* Williams argues as follows:

> What projects does a Utilitarian agent have? As a utilitarian, he has the general project of bringing about maximally desirable outcomes. . . . The desirable outcomes, however, do not just consist of agents carrying out *that* project; there must be other more basic or lower-order projects which he and other agents have, and the desirable outcomes are going to consist, in part, of the maximally harmonious realization of those projects. . . . Unless there were first-order projects, the general utilitarian project would have nothing to work on, and would be vacuous.[8]

These projects are not "themselves projects of pursuing happiness," for "one has to believe in, or at least want, or quite minimally, be content with, other things, for there to be anywhere that happiness can come from" (p. 113). I think a utilitarian agent could accept this much. But Williams adds that among these first-order projects that the utilitarian agent must have are "commitments," or in a phrase that I have already quoted, projects that "he takes seriously at the deepest level, as what his life is about," and such projects cannot be regarded from a purely utilitarian point of view. The utilitarian is able to set aside some lower-order projects without a sense of personal disintegration when the general utilitarian project seems to warrant it, though there may still be a feeling of frustration when they are set aside and a wish that the utilitarian project allowed for pursuit of them. But abandoning one's *commitments* involves more than frustration: it involves a loss of one's integrity. In short, the utilitarian project is vacuous unless it is parasitic on other projects whose abandonment by the agent, even for the greater good, constitutes a grievous loss.

I believe that Williams has not demonstrated this. That the utilitarian agent has no first-order projects that in principle cannot be overriden by a utilitarian project hardly shows that this project is vacuous. It should be remembered that though one is able to set aside lower-order projects without self-betrayal, they might still engage the individual's emotions, hopes, and wishes; that is, the person might still care about them even though they are not commitments in Williams' sense of the word. I fail to see why, if the utilitarian agent must have first-order projects, they must be of this particularly strong sort.

Utilitarians who believe that acting on their lower-order projects is incompatible with their utilitarian project will, if they are rational, sacrifice the former to the latter. Moreover, they will arguably not be able to unreservedly commit themselves to their lower-order projects, because their overriding commitment to utilitarianism will pervasively intrude on their pursuit of those projects. (They may try to answer this objection by introducing a distinction between criterion and motivation, about which more shortly.) Perhaps we will fault the utilitarian project for not allowing strong nonutilitarian commitments that are central to what makes our lives worthwhile (commitments to friends and local communities, for example). Again, however, I think this is misleadingly characterized as an *integrity* criticism. Utilitarians may have a shallow appreciation of aspects of life that we regard as constitutive of human good, but one can achieve integrity by integrating all of one's subjective concerns into a life that serves a dominant utilitarian purpose.

According to Samuel Scheffler, Williams' integrity criticism should be seen as arising

> in response to the discrepancy between the way in which concerns and commitments are *naturally* generated from a person's point of view quite independently of the weight of those concerns in an impersonal ranking of overall states of affairs, and the way in which utilitarianism requires the agent to treat the concerns generated from his point of view as altogether dependent for their *moral* significance on their weight in such a ranking.[9]

The problem of utilitarianism and integrity might then be formulated as follows. People have a broad and diverse range of concerns and commitments, many of which are largely personal rather than impartial. This pluralistic psychology is the natural one, and being natural it has a privileged status that any valid moral theory must respect. A life lived according to utilitarianism, however, is fundamentally at odds with a life of pluralistic commitments, and so the former is unnatural and utilitarianism, which is all-consuming in its demands, fails to meet a condition of adequacy.

There are two difficulties with this version of the integrity criticism. First, what justifies us in claiming that the concerns and commitments alleged to be in conflict with a utilitarian life are *the* natural ones for people to have? The psychological makeup of the utilitarian agent may be atypical within our way of life. Such an individual will have interests and projects other than that of maximizing utility, but unlike most of us, this person's attachment to these interests and projects is conditioned by a willingness to give them up whenever it is recognized that they detract from the general good. (Since an agent can become exhausted in the furtherance of social utility, he or she may need to devote some time to the pursuit of nonmoral interests in order to be a better contributor to the general welfare.) But perhaps, as Gregory Trianosky suggests, the argument shows "too little regard for the plasticity of human nature, and hence for the vast range of psychologies which humans may with equal 'naturalness' instantiate."[10] Second, even if persons do not naturally act in accordance with the impersonal standpoint of utilitarianism, what is "natural" may not be appropriate, rational, or something we should cultivate or encourage. For these reasons, this attack on utilitarianism is inadequately supported.

Persons can be personally interested in, committed to, projects that treat their interests impartially: the logic of "commitment" does not rule such projects out. The project of maximizing utility can also be, though perhaps for most people it is not, the identifying focus of one's life. If Wilcox is right, then committed utilitarians cannot have friends, and if they have friends, then they must be self-deceived about their utilitarianism. For this reason they would lack integrity. But so far as we have seen, the commitment to utilitarianism is not itself inconsistent with personal integrity.[11] Integrity, as the Oxford English Dictionary tells us, is the state of being "undivided; an integral whole." In line with this definition, personal integrity is commonly seen to require internal coherence of different sorts: consistency among one's principles or commitments and coherence between principle and action. These conditions of internal coherence impose few constraints on the content of the principles or commitments a person of integrity may hold; in particular, they do not seem to rule out adherence to the principle of utility as a basis for ascriptions of integrity. There must be internal incoherence if there is to be a lack or loss of integrity, and utilitarianism does not necessarily violate a person's integrity by generating such incoherence. Utilitarianism need not alienate us from our own deepest convictions; it does not have to be conceived of as somehow coming between us and all those concerns whose fulfillment we cherish.

It might also be thought that internal coherence is sufficient for integrity, but here I think it is important to draw some further distinctions. As I shall argue in Chapter 11, types of integrity that presuppose personal integrity are not only a matter of formal coherence. Intuitively, at least, certain people who, admittedly, do not lack internal coherence are not even candidates for the possession of, say, moral integrity. But any constraints on content that would rule out the principle of utility are, I would maintain, arbitrary and unwarranted. Of course, this does not dispose of all the complaints against utilitarianism. Even if a utilitarian can have integrity, other criticisms, different from the integrity criticism as I have construed it but suggested by Williams' discussion, might be levelled against utilitarianism and consequentialism more generally.

It may be pointed out that while it is possible for a utilitarian to have integrity, *other people* might not be utilitarians. They might have nonutilitarian ground projects. The utilitarian agent will not interfere with their following through on these projects only if allowing them to do so maximizes utility. Thus, utilitarians are not respecters of other people's integrity for its own sake. They cannot regard the loss of integrity as particularly grievous in itself, but can disapprove of it only to the extent that it lowers utility. This, it may be maintained, is a serious flaw in utilitarianism because integrity is an important value and it is demeaned when it is treated as having only instrumental importance. Perhaps we can read Williams as making this kind of normative criticism of utilitarianism. In any case, I think he wants to make a deeper criticism as well (viz., that agents will lose their integrity if they attempt to act the way utilitarianism requires), and this is what I have focused on in this chapter.

Another objection is this. There are various sorts of personal projects or pursuits that have a high value on any plausible theory of the good, such as actions performed in the context of friendships or loving relationships. These are highly valuable pursuits that a consequentialist theory would certainly require to be enhanced. But the intrusion of an overriding consequentialist motivation into the pursuit of such relationships, the argument continues, would tend to destroy their friendly or loving character and, thus, block the realization of their distinctive value. If agents generally were directly motivated to attempt to act in accordance with the consequentialist criterion of right action, there would be a significant loss of human good. Hence, the general inculcation of direct consequentialist motivation would be self-defeating from the consequentialist point of view.

Now consequentialists have not been deeply troubled by this result. They respond that consequentialism itself shows why a certain type of motivation should not be generally inculcated. In their view, consequentialism is a theory about the ultimate basis of moral rightness, and it needs to be separated from the attempt to inculcate a directly corresponding moral motivation. For many philosophers, however, this defense of consequentialism comes at too high a cost. A moral theory that deems its own principles generally unacceptable as a source of motives, they contend, disqualifies itself from serious consideration as a moral theory.[12] In any case, there is no inconsistency in believing both that consequentialism disqualifies itself from serious consideration as a moral theory and that an individual may have integrity as an adherent of it.

Michael Slote has also expressed misgivings about Williams' integrity criticism of utilitarianism. Utilitarianism's denial of permission to pursue nonoptimific projects and commitments, he argues, is not best thought of as an attack on an agent's integrity. The integrity criticism in fact rests on a more fundamental justification for pursuing such projects. "Our moral permission to choose any innocent project or commitment whatever is naturally thought of as deriving from and expressing a reasonable and appealing ideal of individual autonomy."[13] According to Slote, the complaint against utilitarianism should be expressed in the charge that it "unreasonably infringes (or fails to respect) the autonomy of individuals' (p. 32). One can be a committed utilitarian, and have integrity as such ["even optimizing act-consequentialism allows for certain sorts of personal integrity," Slote notes, "namely integrity constituted by the desire precisely to produce the most good possible" (p. 54)], but the principle to which one is committed can still be faulted on the ground that it fails to respect moral autonomy. Of particular interest in Slote's discussion is his claim that the integrity criticism could only work in connection with projects and commitments one has in fact chosen, not in relation to those one might choose. One's integrity might be demeaned if one is denied permission to pursue projects one actually chooses to follow, but not if one is denied permission to undertake and pursue some other project than the one one is in fact interested in:

> [C]onsiderations of integrity . . . are only relevant to our freedom to pursue the particular projects we are committed to; and thus fail to account for our full moral freedom with regard to projects, life plans, careers and commitments. (p. 28)

The idea here seems to be that since integrity involves something like loyalty to one's principles or commitments, and one cannot be loyal (now) to a principle or commitment one may some day come to embrace, denial of the freedom to pursue projects to which we are not already committed could not raise any objection relating to integrity.

I take issue with Slote's position that it is inappropriate to claim a person's integrity is not taken seriously when one is denied permission to form an entirely new attachment to some object, to redirect one's concerns and devote oneself to something that this individual is not already invested in. A person might be engaged in various projects that to some extent are found to be fulfilling, but perhaps this person has not yet, as we say, "found him- or herself," found that career or project to which he or she can be wholeheartedly dedicated and which can unequivocally be embraced as the identifying focus of his or her life. This individual might not be aware of this. Even if this person were aware, he or she might for various reasons settle for projects already chosen and not attempt something new, or might attempt this and still discover that he or she is no or little better off. In any case, if one is denied the freedom to form new attachments that might be more self-fulfilling, more expressive of native talents and in accord with natural dispositions, I do not think it odd to say that this person's having integrity is not being treated as a matter of importance. For example, perhaps a woman has thought for a long time that she wanted to be a social worker, and has worked toward that end with some diligence. She begins, however, to have doubts about whether social work can truly fulfill her and at the same time she starts to think more seriously about law as a career. If she is denied permission to drop social work and pursue law (which she is as yet not sure she wants to commit herself to), she may, with good reason, regard this as a failure to show adequate concern for her integrity. This is so even if, as it turns out, she does not commit herself to law, even if she discovers that, contrary to what she thought at first, law is not right for her after all. In short, one way to take integrity seriously is to allow people the freedom to experiment with and refashion their ground projects, to develop new identities as their life circumstances and understanding of themselves change.

Now we might try to salvage Slote's claim about integrity by arguing that the woman in my last example has all along had a higher-order commitment to pursue the career that is best for her. Denying her permission to form new attachments prevents her from acting on this commitment and constitutes an assault on her integrity. Here integrity is still related to an existing commitment, even if not to a particular project that one is already committed to.

This is certainly an improvement over Slote's original formulation, but I doubt that, as a matter of fact, such a higher-order commitment is present in all such cases. Moreover, questions about whether integrity has been taken seriously can still be legitimately raised even in the absence of such a higher-order commitment.

The individual's moral autonomy with respect to the fulfillment of projects and commitments encompasses "any (innocent) project whatever" (p. 28), and some of these projects and commitments, since they do not contribute to an agent's identity, have nothing directly to do with the possession or lack of integrity. So in this way Slote's autonomy criticism of utilitarianism is more general than is Williams' integrity criticism. However, Slote's contention that it is only the permission to pursue the particular projects we are committed to that can be defended on grounds of integrity is too confining. As for the utilitarian, pursuit of nonmoral interests can be allowed on the ground that it makes one a better contributor to the general welfare than one would otherwise have been. The utilitarian can also recognize that an individual may lose interest in some personal project and that, if given the opportunity, may be able to develop new attachments that would make for a better contributor to the general welfare. If carefully monitored, both the having of personal projects and the pursuit of projects that one is not actually interested in (but might become interested in) are compatible with an overriding commitment to the utilitarian principle.

There is of course much more to be said about integrity than can be gleaned from the literature on utilitarianism. The sense of integrity that we find in Williams (i.e., a person's identification with his or her "ground projects") is only a starting point. Intuitively, integrity is a matter of being true to one's most important commitments, or of being committed to one's ground projects, but a complete account of integrity would give us the necessary conditions of commitment. When does a person lose or lack integrity? In addition, persons typically have a number of commitments, not all of which are moral in nature, and they may or may not have integrated the requirements of morality into their lives. The person of integrity must find some way of ordering or integrating commitments, and if this person has more than one fundamental commitment, the problem is finding how to be true to all of them. The utilitarian, who takes commitment to the principle of utility to be superior to other personal and partial concerns, orders commitments in one way, but there are other ways for the committed moral agent to unify his or her life. (And if someone does not accept the utilitarian ordering, then this individual's integrity would be assaulted if he or she were forced to act in accordance with it.) There is also a problem of explaining the familiar view that integrity requires such specific virtues as truth telling, honesty, and fairness; Williams' characterization of integrity does not help us with this. I will discuss these matters in later chapters, but I first want to say something about the importance of integrity. More specifically, I will next discuss the notion that one's own integrity is something each of us should be especially concerned about.

7

Integrity and Self-Indulgence

The integrity criticism of utilitarianism, as construed in the preceding chapter, fails. Though it is true that people lose their integrity when they ignore their own principles and follow the advice of an adherent of a moral code that they themselves reject, those who make up their own minds and embrace the utilitarian principle, and who act in a consistently utilitarian way out of their overriding dedication to social utility, seem not to have thereby lost integrity. Nothing has been said so far that convincingly shows utilitarianism per se is ineligible as a basis for a person's integrity. But while a utilitarian may be able to have integrity in the formal sense that has been discussed, there is a further question as to whether utilitarianism, or consequentialism in general, can give a satisfactory account of the relationship between an agent and his or her (moral) integrity.

According to Stephen Darwall, consequentialism "denies that a person has a special responsibility for her character or integrity in the sense that it denies that considerations regarding *her* character and integrity are in any way directly relevant to what she should do."[1] What can matter for a consequentialist is not whether, in performing some action, a person loses *her* integrity, but only whether integrity is lost. The wrongness of violating one's integrity is reduced to the disvalue of its being violated, and other things being equal, one loss of integrity is as bad as another. There is, therefore, no moral reason for a person not to violate her own principles and values that is not also a reason for her to prevent another person's loss of integrity. The common sense conviction that there is a special moral bond between a person and her own integrity, that a person is specially responsible for the maintenance and restoration of her own integrity, just because it is hers, is, for a consequentialist, misguided. In one way, then, integrity seems to present no challenge for utilitarianism: there is no problem here regarding the possibility of having integrity. If we grant that agents can act from a commitment to the principle of utility, then acting upon this principle would be consistent with an agent's integrity.[2] But in another way, integrity does pose a difficulty, if common sense is right: there is a problem for utilitarianism as an agent-neutral theory of the right. Utilitarianism might not threaten an agent's integrity, but its theory of the right cannot allow that agents bear a responsibility for their own integrity that they do not bear for the integrity of others. In other words, belief that one has a special duty to take care of one's own integrity is not compatible with commitment to the impartial principle of utilitarianism, properly understood, though an agent might consistently act on this principle and have integrity in so doing.

This view about an individual's responsibility for his or her own integrity with which the consequentialist theory of right conflicts would make sense of these famous remarks by Solzhenitsyn on the occasion of his receiving the Nobel Prize for Literature:

> And the simple step of a simple courageous man is not to take part in the lie, not to support deceit. Let the lie come into the world, even dominate the world, but not through me.[3]

As Jonathan Glover interprets this declaration, it expresses "resistance to consequentialist morality."[3] Solzhenitsyn acknowledges a restriction on what he may do to promote the best state of affairs that concerns an act's relation to *himself* (viz., that it would be a supporting by *him* of deceit). Taking part in the lie, even when this has the best consequences, is not something that he can in good conscience do, for it would constitute a diminishing of his own moral integrity, and he regards it as a special responsibility of his to preserve his own integrity. "Do not participate in a lie" is not a rule of thumb for him that he can set aside without a sense of crisis

when conditions seem to warrant it. If, on the other hand, Solzhenitsyn were a utilitarian, he could set aside this principle without loss
of integrity if this would produce the best consequences. But then
the preservation of *his own* integrity could not, on the conception
of right to which he then subscribes, be directly relevant to what he
ought to do. That is, to repeat, he could have integrity as a utilitarian, but as a utilitarian *his* having integrity could not have special
moral importance for him in this sense.

The utilitarian will dispute this view about an individual's responsibility for one's own integrity. Special concern for one's own integrity is incompatible with utilitarianism and it might be left at that.
But the utilitarian might argue instead that there is something
objectionable about the notion of having a special responsibility
for one's own integrity, and that what is objectionable can be recognized as such by those who are not already convinced of the correct-
ness of the utilitarian outlook. The objection would then constitute
some independent ground for accepting the utilitarian system and
would not merely be a reassertion of the utilitarian position.

The objection might be that those who regard their own integrity
as their special or fundamental responsibility and act accordingly
are guilty of self-indulgence. Williams explains the charge of self-
indulgence in this way:

> One thing the thought can express is the suspicion that what the agent
> cares about is not so much other people, as himself caring about other
> people. He has an image of himself as a virtuous [person], and this image
> is more important in his motivation than any concern for other persons.[5]

The person who is specially committed to the preservation of his
or her own integrity acts out of concern for a self-image as a
person of character. The individual is primarily concerned about
keeping this image untarnished, and so will carefully remain insu-
lated from the outside world and be guided away from anything
there that might cause him or her to question the self-image. This
person is in some ways like the extreme sentimentalist as described by Joel Feinberg:

> Sentimentalists, notoriously, are persons who deliberately cultivate
> their sentiments. . . . When the practice becomes excessive, and habit-

ual dependence is created, then the techniques of autogeneration become more demanding and the detachment from real life stimuli more marked. At that point the sentiments, being patently strained and artificial, are properly condemned as mere sentimentality, and the energetic efforts to remain absorbed in them, disconnected as they are from real life purposes, are described as "wallowing."[6]

Just as "sentimental absorption in symbols distracts one from the interests that are symbolized" (p. 30), so, too, does concern for one's own integrity distract one from the human interests in which one's ideals and principles are grounded.

Those who take their own integrity to be their fundamental responsibility, it might be said, put their own integrity above the well-being of others. Their thoughts dwell on themselves and their own character more often than is reasonable, and others are left to pay the price of their unwillingness to offend against their self-image. Moreover, such a person is highly susceptible to taking on superior airs. He or she is inclined to see him- or herself as being better than other people, for regardless of what others do (which, much of the time, violates their own principles and values), this person at least maintains *self*-integrity. Against the background of widespread corruption, Solzhenitsyn's resolution, "Others may support deceit but I will not," quite naturally generates an arrogant holier-than-thou attitude.

It might be argued that those who are specially concerned about their own integrity are not only self-indulgent: they also do not have the integrity they believe they have. The desire to be a person of integrity, which is assumed to be the motive of those who regard themselves as having a special responsibility for their own integrity, makes it impossible for one to have precisely that character. We can call this the *self-subverting* property of integrity. Not all of our concepts of moral evaluation have this property or are, to use Williams' expression, susceptible to this sort of "reflexive deformation."[7] The conscious aim to develop certain traits may not actually subvert their attainment. Acting from the desire to be honorable, for example, does not rule out acting from honor. But some moral qualities are subverted by the preoccupation with having them. To be humble is not the same as to be motivated by the desire to be a humble person; to be motivated by altruism is not the same as to be motivated by the desire to be an altruistic person. And in each case, there is a self-centeredness and a self-consciousness that fit badly with the having of the moral quality in question. (Another example of self-subversion in the case of a nonmoral quality involves spontaneity: actions that spring from a calculated desire to be spontaneous are thereby rendered unspontaneous.) Integrity, the argument goes, is in this respect more like humility and altruism than honor. What integrity involves is a kind of self-forgetfulness or outward focus of the personality, and this is just what persons who take themselves to have a special responsibility for their own integrity lack.

For someone who believes that an act's being a violation of one's own principles or values *is* directly relevant to what should be done, that an agent's fundamental responsibility is to maintain and repair self-integrity, it is necessary to explain why the reflexive thought "not through me" does not express mere self-indulgent refusal and why the person who has this thought is not focusing excessively on his or her own character. One response to this charge of "moral egoism," as Jonathan Bennett calls certain appeals to conscience,[8] is as follows. Agents violate their integrity by doing things that they would authentically judge wrong. What makes it wrong for them is not that they would lose their integrity if they did these things: their wrongness is explainable for them independently of the loss of integrity that would occur if they were done.[9] In other words, the person of integrity is not guided by the thought, "I am committed to *me* not doing x," where the reason for not doing x is that it would undermine one's own integrity, but by something more like "I am committed to *its* not being done through me," where the reason for not doing x is independent of the fact that this individual would sacrifice *his* or *her* integrity if it were done. (Since it is so independent, this person would not want anyone to do it.) This person's primary allegiance is to the objects of core commitments, not to some ideal of self that stands over and above them, and since the focus is not on the self but on the commitments, there is a kind of self-forgetfulness.[10]

Now in the sort of case I am considering, the actions that flow from these commitments have a unique kind of significance for the agent that they do not have for anyone else and which the actions that flow from the commitments of others do not have for that agent. This unique significance is captured in the idea that one takes oneself to have a special duty to maintain one's own integrity. But this duty is, among agents who have integrity, a second-order one: it is not on the same level as their core commitments, capable of competing with and overriding them. It is possible to take this duty seriously without at the same time elevating "one's integrity" to the status of an autonomous ideal in itself. Persons of integrity can sometimes have the thought, "If I do x, I will compromise my integrity, and I am specially responsible for my own integrity." But this is simply an expression of the kind of importance one's principles and values have for that person and the kind of steadfastness with which he or she adheres to them.

Persons who takes this duty seriously do not thereby care more about themselves caring about others than about others. Their refusal to compromise their principles in order to bring about the best states of affairs need not be an act of self-indulgence, but could be described instead as the particular way in which they express concern for others.[11] Further, it might be maintained that the refusal to do what will bring about the best state of affairs, as expressed in the resolution "not through me," is tantamount to the adoption of a personal morality of absolute prohibition, and that such absolutist refusals actually demonstrate a lack of integrity. For while the person of integrity is flexible and undogmatic, prepared to admit exceptions to principles, the absolutist is indifferent to possible additional features of situations that would alter moral judgments if considered seriously. But even supposing that the absolutist lacks integrity, this objection does not succeed. I have argued that a theory of morality that attends only to the value or disvalue of states of affairs cannot render intelligible those refusals to act, like Solzhenitsyn's, that reflect deep and direct concern about one's own agency. The wrongness of acting is here judged not just to be a function of outcome, independent of its being the agent who does it. But it is quite consistent with the acceptance of a special duty to tend to one's own integrity to be willing to retract one's refusal in certain circumstances. The former has to do with a particular way of seeing moral demands, with the relation between a person and *his* or *her* actions, not with the content of the demands themselves. (Specifically, to take the stand, "not through me," is not necessarily to commit oneself to absolutism in all circumstances.) Thus, even someone like Solzhenitsyn can consider what would be the respective consequences of refusing or not refusing "to take part in the lie": he does not embrace consequentialism merely because the consequences of not refusing are such as to lead him to change his mind about what he ought to do.[12] His fundamental responsibility is still his own integrity, though possibly what he considers responsible conduct will change with changes in the consequences of his refusal. What he cannot consistently do, however, is embrace a morality where total outcome is decisive and give his own agency any special, nonderivative, moral importance.

Consider the following case discussed by Williams.[13] Jim, an explorer in South America, happens upon a village where an overbearing and sadistic army officer, Pedro, is about to execute twenty Indians. The officer declares that because of Jim's arrival, the terms of the execution will be altered: if Jim will shoot one of the Indians, Pedro will let the other nineteen go unharmed; if Jim refuses, Pedro will execute all twenty. Moreover, Jim has profound moral objections to killing. Now a utilitarian, let us suppose, would argue that the right thing for Jim to do under the circumstances is kill the one in order that the greater number be spared. (One complication is this: Jim seems to have no reason to trust that Pedro will not kill the nineteen if he [Jim] shoots the one. If so, then maybe Jim should refuse to shoot the one after all. But we can alter the case somewhat to take care of this.) Refusal to do so, on the ground of his deep commitment to nonviolence, would show that he self-indulgently cares more about his own integrity than about saving nineteen lives. Or, as Jonathan Glover puts it, it would display "a possessive attitude to one's own virtue."[14] But this description represents someone who differs from the consequentialist, in that he finds it absolutely impossible to kill the Indian, as just some other kind of consequentialist:[15] if he were to shoot the Indian his personal integrity would be shattered, and since he values his own property highly, he will not do it. Now some people might have this thought, but not everyone who refuses the officer's offer must. Moreover, Jim has not started to think as a consequentialist just because he decides to shoot the one so that nineteen may go free, if he so decides. It is not inconsistent with integrity to set aside one's deeply held commitments under extreme circumstances, and in so doing Jim could still believe that what is fundamentally important is how *he* conducts himself.

It is not only morally objectionable actions like promise-breaking or lying or killing that one can regard *oneself* as being forbidden to perform. Concern for one's own integrity can also be shown in connection with one's nonmoral principles and values. An artist who takes pride in his or her originality, for example, might refuse to turn out paintings in machinelike fashion just to please the public and garner wealth and fame. His or her artistic integrity, the artist believes, would be compromised by such pandering to the tastes of the undiscerning masses, and we can imagine a statement something like Solzhenitsyn's: "Let others contribute to the commercialization and trivialization of art in our time, but I will not be a part of it." The artist's first responsibility is to self, not to sell out: compromising one's artistic integrity has a unique kind of significance for him or her because it would be *his* or *her* integrity that is being compromised. We should not suppose, however, that such a person must really care about personally caring about art more than about art, or that what is prized above all is self-image as a person who will not violate artistic values. (This is the analogue of the self-indulgence charge considered earlier.) It may rather be that certain artistic standards are so personally important to artistic individuals that they judge themselves by them and would condemn themselves for lacking integrity if they failed to live by them.

8

Wholes and Unities

The integrity I am concerned with is the integrity of persons as opposed to the integrity of physical objects, institutions, ways of life, and so on. More specifically, it has to do with a person's commitments. But there are common features shared by these various applications of "integrity."[1] Integrity is a state of being whole ("integrity" comes from the Latin *integritas,* one of whose meanings is wholeness) and it is a necessary condition of something being a whole that it is not identical to the sum of its parts. Formulated modally, something is a whole if it could survive a change in its constituent parts.[2] For example, the living human body is a whole relative to its cells because the same body endures through time despite the normal processes of cellular growth and decay.

One way of understanding personal integrity is this: the identity of the person in terms of his or her commitments can be maintained over time even though the commitments at time $t2$ are not identical to the commitments at time $t1$. While it often happens that over some stretch of time a person of integrity keeps all personal commitments and gains no new ones, it must be possible to remain the same whole person even if this does not happen. If this person must continue to have precisely these commitments, if to abandon any single commitment or commit oneself to something new is to make a different person, then with respect to personal commitments this individual is not a whole. Similarly, if to change a single note in the score of a musical work is to make a different work, then it is not a whole relative to the notes. The integrity of the composition is not maintained through a change of these parts.

By comparing personal integrity to bodily integrity I do not mean to suggest that questions about personal integrity are to be settled with reference to some metaphysical account of the sameness of persons over time. In fact, I am not interested in personal identity as philosophers usually discuss it (i.e., as a metaphysical problem), but more nearly in the sort of thing we have in mind when we say that someone is having an "identity crisis." What is important for me is whether a person's self-conception could survive intact despite some changes in commitments. Personal integrity, as I am here using the expression, presupposes that one is, by some objective criterion, the same person, but of course, the loss of integrity does not literally make one a different person.

The parts of a whole also make up a unity: they are as one in the whole. The mere continued existence of all the parts of a whole is not enough to maintain the existence of a whole because it is also required that the parts remain in certain (unifying) relations to each other. For example, an orchestra is a unified whole, for it is not just composed of parts, some of which are the player and conductor and another of which is the relation they have to one another, but rather of parts in that relation. Further, the parts of a whole can be more or less tightly unified and more or less diverse.[3] The parts of a living human body, homeostatically regulated in complicated and intricate ways, are bound together more closely than the components of whole ecological systems; the themes and characters that are unified to a certain degree in one novel may be more diverse than those unified to the same degree in another. In general, the more diverse and apparently disparate the parts that are to be unified, the more difficult it is for us to unify them to a high degree. With respect to personal integrity, the person is a unified whole in terms of commitments. The degree of unifiedness of a person's commitments may vary from one period of life to another, or it may be more or less than that of another's: the tighter the relations among a person's commitments, the more unified that person is. The diversity of these commitments might also vary, with or without a difference in the degree of unifiedness of the commitments.

These remarks about integrity are very abstract and preliminary. Integrity, in its various incarnations, is a condition of unified wholeness, but what this means in particular cases must be spelled out in terms of the identity conditions and unifying relations appropriate to them. In the case of personal integrity, we need to know what kind of life would exhibit the required unity. How much structuring, and what kind of structuring, are needed? Is the demand for unity the demand for a life lived according to some preestablished plan to which one more or less rigidly adheres? Is it compatible with a more organic, less deliberate, life-style? If the former, then maybe integrity is not actually as valuable as or has a much more limited kind of value than many of us have thought. I will come back to these problems later (see Chapter 12), after we have a better grasp of the nature of commitment and of various sorts of failures of commitment.

9

Lack of Integrity

"Integrity," according to John Kekes, "is a complex notion. In one of its senses, it is principled action; in another, it is wholeness."[1] (My concern in this chapter is only with the first sense.) Kekes construes "principled action" broadly to mean action in accordance with commitments one has made.[2] "Principled action" can also be given a narrower reading: action in accordance with one's principles, where "principles" is not used as a synonym for commitments but refers instead to a specific sort of commitment, namely, commitment to principles. Integrity standardly has to do with principled action in this second sense. In what follows, however, I shall not suppose that one must subscribe to some principle in order to have integrity. Williams, as noted earlier, takes integrity to involve a person's identification with a "ground project or set of projects which are closely related to his existence and which to a significant degree give meaning to his life,"[3] and ground projects are not always describable in terms of principles.

Sometimes persons of integrity do things (or refrain from doing things) *on principle,* moral or otherwise: as we say, they make it their principle to do something, or it is a matter of principle with them to do something, and they act accordingly. Acting on principle, as I am using the expression, is plainly not just acting with conscious intent, for the former has implications for the agent's future conduct whereas the latter does not. That is, someone who is on principle opposed to (or in favor of) doing x is opposed to (or in favor of) doing x-type acts. For example, a conservative U.S. senator might on principle refuse to vote for a particular arms control treaty with the Russians because of a conviction that the Russians always exploit treaties to their own advantage. Further, a person does not act on principle if some settled policy of action is only inferrable from that person's conduct over an extended period of time. It must be consciously entertained (but not necessarily deliberately adopted) and it must play a motivational role for that individual: what this person does must be the result of explicit reflection on some policy as to how he or she will act in a certain kind of situation. Action on principle is self-conscious rule-governed behavior where the agent is moved to do what is taken to be prescribed by his or her principles for the simple reason that it is so prescribed. A person who acts on principle is also naturally described as standing *for* something, and not just as being willing to stand *by* what has been done.

Many actions in accordance with one's commitments are not principled actions in this sense because they are not the result of explicit reflection on some rule or other. There is a difference, for example, between a person who is committed to a Bohemian way of life on principle, perhaps as an act of rebellion against conventional society, and another who simply lives this life as an expression of deepest impulses. The latter might also have and act on a higher-order commitment to the principle not to abandon a chosen life-style, however unorthodox it may be, but the first-order commitment is not to a principle. (It can be a matter of principle for a person to stick to commitments that are not themselves commitments to principle.) Or if principles are involved, they might play a secondary role. A grown child might take care of an aged and needy mother because of a commitment to *her,* not just because that child is committed to some principle of filial responsibility; or a husband might be faithful to his wife mainly because he loves her, not because he is committed to a principle of marital fidelity. He may be committed both to the person and to the principle, but he is not primarily motivated by the thought that care or faithfulness is dictated by his principles. Commitment does not have to be principled to be genuine or important or worthy. Indeed, some of our strongest commitments, those to friends and loved ones, are not grounded, or only grounded, on principle, even of a quite personal kind. In such cases, commitment is primarily nonprincipled, not unprincipled.

In the larger sense of principled action that Kekes employs, a person displays integrity only "if he has made a commitment and acts according to it."[4] Commitment, as the term is mainly used in a characterization of integrity, must be active, something that one makes, not passive, as when we say that a person is committed to believing *p* by virtue of a belief in *q*, on account of the logical relations between *p* and *q*.[5] A person's belief may commit that person to act in a certain way without there being any active commitment to it. Further, to prevent misunderstanding, I would add that we do not have two conditions here that can be satisfied independently of one another: namely, making a commitment and acting according to it. For one must, to some extent, act according to one's commitments if one is to be committed (in the active sense) at all. Thus, a person cannot properly be said to commit him or herself to God if, while believing that there is a God, this belief is not allowed to influence his or her way of life at all. This person may accept that there is a God who will call him or her to account and be genuinely afraid of the consequences of disobeying Him, and yet be determined to go on pursuing selfish pleasures. Though this person is not an atheist, there is in this case only acknowledgement of God without any commitment. (We might say here that while the individual believes *that* there is a God, there is no real belief *in* Him.) Commitment is not to be identified with mere belief. If it were, then a person could not question beliefs without thereby weakening commitments. But one can entertain intellectual doubts about God, say, while remaining as committed to Him as before.[6]

People who accept that there is a God but remain totally indifferent are not religiously committed because they fail to make any effort to act on their religious beliefs. And if to have religious integrity one must be true to one's religious commitments, then those persons obviously cannot possess religious integrity. Apathy or detachment is one explanation of lack of commitment, but there are others as well. For example, one is not a committed Marxist if one only gives intellectual assent to Marx's doctrine. One is also not a committed Marxist if, believing that Marx was basically mis-

taken, one hypocritically pretends to others that one is so committed; or if one self-deceptively takes oneself to be so committed.
Moreover, someone who professes to be committed to something
but repeatedly succumbs to temptation and fails to do it is not
committed, and someone who has made a commitment can lose
integrity if he or she is weak-willed and abandons that commitment. Accordingly, I propose to look more closely at the different
kinds of behavior that can show lack of integrity. A person can
have integrity, of course, even if he or she sometimes behaves in
less than honorable ways; additionally, integrity might be exhibited
in some areas of life but not in others.

Wantonness

A minimal and basic requirement of the possession of integrity is
that individuals be capable of assessing their motivations and of
forming what Harry Frankfurt calls "second-order volitions" to
govern their first-order desires.[7] They must be capable of wanting
certain of their first-order desires to be effective and of rejecting
others. Those that they want to be effective, they identify with,
assimilate to themselves; they want to be the kind of people who
are motivated in these ways. Those desires that are rejected and
that they do not want to be effective in moving them, they regard
as not being expressive of their true selves, the selves whose wishes
they want to see carried out. Such persons do not just act on those
desires that happen to be the strongest, indifferent to what these
are. They may in fact decide to act on some desire that is weaker
than a competing one, weaker, that is, relative to some subjective
criterion like the extent to which a desire absorbs one's attention.
(If "strongest desire" means "causally strongest desire," then an
agent's action is necessarily determined by his or her strongest
desire.)

Some feminists, it should be noted, have faulted the conception of
superior moral–psychological functioning that Frankfurt presents.
They regard it as an example of value-hierarchical or "up–down"
thinking that attributes greater value to what is "up" (viz., reason)
than to what is "down" (viz., emotion).[8] But this criticism does not
diminish the value of Frankfurt's insight. Surely there is a crucial

evaluative difference between the case where all that disposes a person to act upon desires is the strength of the hold they happen to have upon this individual, and the case where the causal efficacy of a person's desires is affected by reflective self-evaluation.

An agent acts with integrity only if the desires motivating that action are of a certain kind, namely, those that are supported by second-order volitions. The person who lacks second-order volitions Frankfurt calls a "wanton." If there is a conflict between the agent's desires, then this individual does not care which of them proves to be the more effective. The agent is a passive spectator of what moves him or her, for none of the agent's desires is made peculiarly his or her own by willing it to be effective. Since the wanton does not have a stake in the outcome of any conflict between desires, the outcome of such conflict cannot be either a victory or a defeat for that individual. The wanton is only a kind of battleground on which desires of varying strengths contend with each other as brute natural forces, not a self that compares and orders desires in terms of some conception of the sort of person the agent wants to be or some conception of how the agent's life should be lived if it is to be satisfactorily lived. We might construct a parallel here to Kant's claim that the relatedness of subjective representations is a necessary condition of theoretical knowledge:

If each representation were completely foreign to every other, standing apart in isolation, no such thing as knowledge would ever arise. For knowledge is (essentially) a whole in which representations stand compared and connected.[9]

Without the ability to group fragments of experience according to principles, an ability that Kant calls a transcendental power of synthesis and which is accompanied by an awareness of one consciousness in which these fragments are united, experience would be chaotic and unintelligible. Analogously, if each desire "were completely foreign to every other, standing apart in isolation," as it is in the wanton's case, agency would be incoherent, no desire could come to be specially constitutive of oneself, and principled action would therefore be impossible. It cannot be true of the person of integrity, as it is of the wanton, that he or she confers no particular legitimacy upon any of his or her desires.

Very young children are thoroughgoing wantons in this sense. But even if a more mature person does engage in reflective self-evaluation manifested in the formation of second-order volitions, this person may be, as Frankfurt observes, "capricious and irresponsible in forming his second-order volitions and give no serious consideration to what is at stake."[10] That is, a person with second-order volitions may be no less wanton with respect to them than a wholly unreflective individual is with respect to first-order desires.[11] The former reflects on and evaluates the prereflective self, but does not give serious consideration to the self who is doing the first reflecting and evaluating. If and when his second-order volitions change, it will not be because there is sufficient reason for changing them, but because the individual merely feels inclined to do so or because, holding personal values in a compliantly second-hand way, this person passively and thoughtlessly follows the lead of others. The individual's second-order volitions seem to give his or her motivational structure the stamp of authenticity, but the second-order volitions themselves are not validated by the agent's reflective powers and so are inauthentic.

Without second-order volitions, individuals cannot act with integrity. Even with them individuals may not be acting with integrity, for the kind of valuing that consists in identification with some desires and rejection of others is not sufficient for commitment. Someone with second-order volitions may only be what Gabriele Taylor calls "shallowly sincere,"[12] perhaps a kind of chameleon who is quick to modify or abandon previously expressed evaluations depending on the company being kept. This is frequently true of adolescents, for example, who have developed second-order volitions but who are quite prepared, without further thought, to change their values if they should be unpopular with their peer group. (This phenomenon is not confined to adolescents, of course.) The truly shallowly sincere are not committed to being so and they do not act this way on principle, so we cannot say that they are acting with integrity when they fail to take seriously consistency of evaluation from one situation to another. Rather, they lack commitment, even a general commitment to have no particular commitments. Their evaluations do not express commitments because they are liable to be changed or shaken at the first breath of criticism or the first urging of a contrary inclination. If they deny this, they might lack integrity for another reason as well: they may be self-deceived.

Some existentialists actually seem to valorize wantonness with respect to one's evaluations. Sartre, for example, argues that each self constitutes itself as a "fundamental project," the product of a choice that is absolutely free, entirely without antecedents to which it can refer itself. The sole restriction on free choice is that it cannot choose to be incapable of choice, which is to say that a human being cannot choose to be a being of another kind—a material thing, for instance. As Sartre puts it, "No limits to my freedom can be found except freedom itself or, if you prefer . . . we are not free to cease to be free."[13] Accordingly, every "conviction" or allegiance has to be examined afresh each time the need for choice arises. This is not just, as I read Sartre, to keep our commitments from becoming unreflective habits, but because nothing, not even our own antecedent choices, ever commits us to, or even provides us with any reason for, choosing one way rather than another. To be absolutely free means that the choice of values on a particular occasion is arbitrary and reasonless, having no roots in the past and no implications for the future.[14] Were a person to take refuge in the belief that decisions of principle or commitments on prior occasions hold sway over present choices, then this person would be guilty of self-deception because this would be denying the truth about ourselves, namely that we are what we make ourselves ("existence precedes essence") and that we make ourselves anew on each occasion of choice. The person who is in "authenticity," Sartre's term for integrity, understands that the appeal to commitment is no more than "bad faith," a lie we tell ourselves in the futile attempt to disclaim self-responsibility. This reflective affirmation of one's own absolute freedom may be rarer and more difficult than bad faith and we may have a tendency to evade its acknowledgment (indeed Sartre labels the reflective consciousness of freedom "anguish"[15]), but presumably the former is possible as well.

It may be argued, in rejoinder to Sartre, that a free being does not make choices in the void of arbitrariness or that if this is what freedom is, it is not worth having. In any case, integrity does not require the affirmation of Sartrean freedom. The distinction between authenticity and bad faith cannot be identified with the distinction I am trying to draw between integrity and the lack thereof, for those who possess the Sartrean virtue of self-truth repudiate commitments rather than hold firm to them.

Weakness of Will

When we think of persons showing integrity, we typically have situations in mind in which they hold firm to their principles or commitments in the face of dangers or enticements of various sorts. Related to this, individuals might lack integrity because they freely and intentionally act contrary to their principles or commitments when it is difficult for these individuals to remain true to them. They are not wantons with respect to their first-order desires or, we may suppose, with respect to their second-order volitions, but they act akratically in that they fail intentionally to do an action that they believe it would be better or best for them to do, and which is psychologically and physically within their power. Not every instance of weakness of will, of acting contrary to one's better judgment, and not even repeated akratic failure, necessarily indicates a lack of integrity, for what individuals fail to do might not be very important to them. There must be a deficiency in self-control with respect to commitments or principles that have some bearing on the agent's broad conception of his or her life's direction or sense of self-identity. Moreover, agents do not lack integrity merely because they freely and intentionally act contrary to a particular personal commitment, for example, a moral commitment. For they may have made other commitments besides moral ones, and they may have judged that all things considered (moral and otherwise) it was better for them to act as they did, even though it was not morally better. What is required for akratic lack of integrity is that the commitment or principle against which agents freely and intentionally act be taken by them to provide sufficient reason for doing otherwise under the circumstances.

Though weakness of will seems to be a common occurrence, something that all normal people are subject to to some degree, various philosophers have sought to rule out cases of weakness of will by arguing that it is either incoherent or incompatible with acting freely.[16] These arguments certainly merit serious consideration and cannot just be dismissed with the observation that they fly in the face of experience. What is needed is an adequate explanation of the possibility of akratic action.[17] It would take us too far from the topic of integrity to pursue this matter here, however. Suffice it to say that the phenomenon of weakness of will merely illustrates, what is in any case pretty obvious, that judging x to be a better course of action than y neither entails nor is entailed by wanting to do x more than wanting to do y. Moreover, the long-standing charge that an agent who acts weak-willedly cannot be acting freely is unpersuasive. An agent who believes that there are good and sufficient reasons for not acting on a desire but who does not successfully resist the desire, may still be able to successfully resist acting on it. The desires in accordance with which an agent acts akratically need not *compel* that agent to act in a particular way.

Persons who, because of weakness of will, act contrary to their commitments must obviously have made commitments to begin with and acted in accordance with them to some extent. They have second-order volitions and do not abandon them merely for a whim. But their actions exhibit a deficiency in the exercise of self-control: they are not, under the circumstances, able to master motivation that is contrary to better judgment. They judge that there are good and sufficient reasons for doing x rather than y, but their better judgment is rendered ineffective by opposing motivations and they do y. Those who have and exhibit the power to master motivation that is contrary to their better judgment might still lack self-control in a broader sense, however. The values on which their better judgments rest might be generated and maintained by brainwashing, for example, in which case they seem not to be fully in control of themselves, but are instead controlled by their brainwasher. Moreover, brainwashing is plainly not a way of ensuring that persons remain true to their commitments and maintain their integrity. On the contrary, it undermines integrity.

The explanation for a person's failure to act according to his or her commitments might be that he or she succumbs to self-indulgence and so yields to temptation. ("Yielding to temptation," as I am discussing it here, is one possible explanation of the lack of integrity. Suppose, however, that a person makes it a principle to yield to temptation and acts according to it. Should we say in this case that the *failure* to succumb to temptation might evidence a lack of integrity?[18]) Another might be that the person is overcome by fear, anger, or repulsion. These cases are perhaps not best described as ones of succumbing to temptation. For example, fear, according to James Wallace, can sometimes "force or drive a person to do something" against better judgment, but the coward is not seduced by fear.[19] Yet another sort of weakness of will is what Ronald Milo calls "irresolution."[20] In such cases, a person does not make a sufficient effort to preserve strength of resolve even though this could have successfully been done had the person exercised powers of self-control in ways open to that individual at the time.

In short, weak-willed persons might lack integrity either because they fail to mount a successful resistance against some particularly strong desire or emotion that prompts them to act contrary to their commitments (for example, they yield to temptation or are overcome by fear) or because they fail to take adequate steps or precautions to ensure that their resolve to act according to their commitments remains intact (for example, they are indecisive or they repeatedly find excuses for not living up to their commitments). In both cases, the agents commonly feel remorse or blame themselves for failing to act as they believed they ought; often, this feeling is accompanied by the intention of agents to mend their ways and repair their integrity. Unlike wantons, who take no evaluative stand toward the desires that incline them to act, weak-willed agents who do not act in accordance with their basic commitments when it is difficult to do so regard their wayward desires and the actions that stem from them as somehow disfiguring their true selves, and they may succeed in removing the discrepancy between these desires and their core values.

Persons might not find it easy to stick to their commitments and may need to actively resist competing desires if they are to act with integrity, but it is not always the case that those who act with integrity rely on a special effort of self-control to act as they judge best. Sometimes what we admire in persons of integrity is the firmness of their intentions that does not require the assistance of such an effort. In these cases, the agents' knowledge of what their life is about, their commitments and the actions that flow from them, are second nature. They are living according to their commitments and merely doing what comes naturally to them, and they do not need to make an effort to bring their motivations into line with their commitments. In addition, the contrary of this exceptionally resolute person—the individual who has habitually to exercise self-restraint over his desires and emotions in order to act according to his commitments—can plausibly be regarded as having a defective sort of integrity. They must keep a tight rein on themselves, for they know that if they were ever to "let themselves go," then they would act badly. Their commitment, we might say, is never strong enough to carry the day without the support of an exercise of self-control.

Exceptional resoluteness is an ideal species of integrity. But how is this to be reconciled with Kekes' observation that a man is called upon to act with integrity "only if it is difficult to act in accordance with his commitments?"[21] If it must be difficult to act in accordance with one's commitments, then it seems that the person for whom it comes easily does not act with integrity. We can avoid this conclusion if we distinguish, as Aristotle did in connection with courage, between something that is difficult for the agent to do (i.e., subjectively experienced as difficult) and something that is difficult for most people to do (i.e., objectively difficult):

> [W]hat is formidable to the majority of men or to human nature, that we call absolutely formidable . . . the brave man shows himself fearless towards these and endures such things, they being to him formidable in one sense but in another not—formidable to him *qua* man, but not formidable to him except slightly so, or not at all, *qua* brave.[22]

The exceptionally resolute person will act with integrity, therefore, even when it is not difficult for him or her to act in accordance with personal commitments, if most people would find it difficult to stick to their commitments in the same circumstances. For example, most people would find it difficult to hold fast to their principles and values when put to the test of death; Socrates, apparently, did not.

Ordinarily we do not say that people act with integrity if they sticks to their commitments or principles despite some difficulty that most people would not find it hard in the circumstances to overcome. If persons adhere to their commitments, for example, at the cost of what most people would regard as a minor inconvenience or embarrassment, we assume that it cannot be difficult for them to act as they do either, and we do not see integrity involved in that act. But a problem arises in those cases where we learn that agents do feel their act to be difficult, even though most people would not. Perhaps through an effort of self-control they manage to master some strong desire or emotion that prompts them to act against their commitments, but the desire or emotion itself (relative to the experience of most people) is excessive. Here we seem to be pulled in two directions on the question of whether they act with integrity, focusing alternately on the difficulty for the agents of acting according to their commitments and on the normal lack of difficulty in doing so.

Persons of exceptional integrity have no tendency at all to succumb to fear or temptation or to be irresolute, and so need no exertion of will in order to remain true to their commitments. Such persons might still change their mind about their commitments, however. Indeed, an account of integrity would be seriously flawed if it maintained that persons of integrity only regularly act in accordance with their present commitments and are incapable of change or development in this regard. People might fail to act according to their commitments because they change their minds about them, and not every action in accordance with a change of mind about one's commitments exhibits akrasia. Sometimes circumstances are such that we think a change of mind is reasonable. For example, suppose that a man who has committed himself to a career in medicine discovers, perhaps painfully, that he does not have the talent or temperament to make a go of it as a doctor. As a result of this realization he turns his energies to other work that is more realistic for someone with his capacities. In this case we are disinclined to count his change of mind as a loss of integrity. On the other hand, there are cases in which, given a person's values and beliefs, his change of mind seems to us unreasonable, and we are inclined to say that he changes his life plan or ground project out of weakness. If he had only gotten a grip on himself, we think, if he had exercised self-control, he would have retained his initial commitments. Weakness of will, whether exhibited with respect to the commitments one retains or with respect to a change of mind about one's commitments, is one contrary to integrity. But it is not weakness of will to be open to reason and persuasive argument and to be moved by them to revise or abandon one's commitments.

Personal integrity, in one of its senses, is the consistency that obtains when people act according to their commitments, and these who display integrity have virtues that enable them to do this. One such virtue is courage. (One can of course act courageously in situations where one's principles or commitments are not at stake.) Agents of courageous behavior do not have to feel fear themselves and overcome it, but they must at least believe that it is dangerous for them to act as they do and appreciate the value of life and safety. The difficulty or danger might be a threat to their physical well-being, in which case they exhibit physical courage; or the danger might not be directly or primarily physical, but rather a threat to social standing, financial prospects, relations with colleagues, popularity among constituents, and so forth. In this case, they exhibit what might be called moral courage. Correspondingly, a person's lack of integrity is sometimes explained by physical or moral cowardice.

Consider the behavior of various Hollywood actors, writers, and directors who were summoned before the House Committee on Un-American Activities in the 1950s and asked to identify present or former Communists in the entertainment industry. Lillian Hellman castigates those who, lacking the courage of their convictions and failing to stand up for what she calls "the right of each man to his own convictions,"[23] sold out to the Committee because they did not want to destroy their film careers (a probable consequence of refusing to answer the Committee's questions). On the other hand, cooperation might not in all cases have been the result of moral cowardice. Elia Kazan's basic argument for cooperating with the Committee, for instance, was that he did not want to ruin his film career for the sake of a cause he did *not* believe in, namely, protecting the anonymity of Communists or former Communists.[24] He regarded cooperation as a necessary, if painful, duty of good citizenship. To be sure, rationalization and self-deception may have been at work here. But perhaps some of those who cooperated actually exhibited moral courage in doing so: they stuck to their principles in the face of opposition from other members of the entertainment world and pressure from them not to cooperate.

Courage is only one of the virtues that enables persons to act with integrity because danger is not the only difficulty that persons who remain true to their commitments and principles confront. In

general, the virtues that involve rational self-control over our desires and emotions preserve practical reasoning and enable it to
issue in action in the face of various sorts of difficulties, and in
different circumstances different virtues may be exercised by those
who display integrity. Integrity itself is a virtue as well, but not of
the same type as courage or temperance. According to Andreas
Esheté, integrity belongs to a distinctive class of virtues, different
from the self-regarding virtues of courage and temperance—what
he calls the class of "master-virtues." I do not possess integrity, he
argues, "in maintaining a hierarchy of desires against the unsettling
impact of specific contrary desires," as in the case of courage or
temperance. Instead, "I acquire the master-virtues in possessing
and actively maintaining a settled hierarchy of desires."[25] When
faced with temptation, my concern for my own integrity may motivate me to make an effort to resist it. But properly speaking,
integrity does not enable me to stick to my commitments and principles in the face of some difficulty. It is rather what I show when, for
example, I display temperance and hold fast to my principles
against temptation.

Self-Deception

Weakness of will is one explanation of lack of integrity; self-
deception is another. For Gabriele Taylor, in fact, "the case of self-
deception is the most important and indeed fundamental case of
lack of integrity."[26] Not all instances of self-deception involve the
loss or lack of integrity, of course, any more than do all instances of
weakness of will. The self-deception must be serious, that is, bound
up with one's self-image: one must be self-deceived in thinking of
oneself as a certain sort of person or with respect to what one takes
to be the basic goals and concerns of one's life. The character of
Mr. Casaubon in George Eliot's *Middlemarch,* for example, is seriously self-deceived. As Taylor describes him, Casaubon "values
creative scholarship above all, and the only worthwhile life for him
to lead is the life of the creative scholar . . . everything else in his
life . . . is subordinated to this task."[27] His wife Dorothea serves as
his dutiful secretary, spending seemingly endless hours copying her
husband's notes for the masterpiece he has dedicated himself to

producing and that will, he believes, win him his immortality. But the masterpiece remains unwritten and as his trust in his own authorship wavers and his doubts about his scholarly commitment grow, he takes steps to protect himself from his anxieties. He buries himself in his library, abruptly turns aside his wife's searching questions, refuses to learn German (the language in which the most important works in his field had been written), and so on. Gradually and painfully Dorothea becomes disillusioned with the man she had looked up to; she comes to see him (correctly) as a man who is more concerned about maintaining his flattering image of himself as a dedicated scholar than about the values he still professes to believe in. He clings obstinately to the false belief that he is leading a scholar's life and thereby avoids the trauma of having to reassess himself and the life he leads.

Though we frequently apply the expression "self-deception" to both real and fictional cases, the most common characterizations of the phenomenon leave us wondering how self-deception is possible at all. Thus, it is often said that those who deceive themselves into believing that p know or believe that not-p while causing themselves to believe that p; or that they persuade themselves to believe what they know ("in their heart") is not so.[28] These formulations use interpersonal deception as a model for self-deception, and this seems to lead to incoherence: how can a person simultaneously believe p and believe not-p? However, most philosophers have not been skeptics about self-deception and have instead adopted one, or some combination, of two types of strategy to either resolve or avoid the paradox. In one, the analogy with interpersonal deception is taken seriously and mental partitioning, or some variation of this, is introduced. In the other, the analogy or some aspect(s) of the analogy with interpersonal deception is rejected, at least in typical cases, and self-deception is redescribed as wishful thinking, self-delusion and the like. Alfred Mele, for example, in an important recent discussion of irrationality, adopts the second strategy. For Mele, self-deception essentially arises through the operation of a person's desires for certain beliefs: self-deceived persons acquire or cling to a false belief that p because their wanting it to be the case that p leads them to manipulate or treat inappropriately evidence that bears on the truth of p.[29] Here the supposition that the self-deceived person simultaneously has the true belief that not-p is dropped. Neither of these strategies simply dismisses self-deception as impossible.[30]

Casaubon's case is one to which the expression "self-deception" paradigmatically applies, and as it illustrates, there may be a discrepancy between the self-deceiver's avowed values and principles and conduct that is motivated by quite different, incompatible interests and desires. Such individuals lack understanding of their own lives or parts of them, and if the self-deception is deep-seated enough, they cannot be brought to take the evidence for p (whatever it might be) at face value. We do not have to suppose that the individuals set out to deceive themselves, but the result of self-deception is that they are able to preserve their desired self-conception while indulging incompatible interests and desires. In this way, they retain at least the internal appearance of integrity.[31] Casaubon believes that his life is dedicated to creative scholarship because he wants to believe it. However, he does not only want to: he needs to believe it in order to preserve his self-respect. At the same time, the discrepancy between the avowed values of self-deceivers and conduct motivated by unacknowledged incompatible desires may be quite apparent to others, for at least the former do not set out to mislead others into thinking they are something they know they are not. Will Ladislaw, Casaubon's bohemian cousin, saw much earlier than Dorothea that Casaubon was not the man he professed to be, and Casaubon's inhospitality toward him served a protective or defensive role: it kept Casaubon from having to confront Will's damaging accusations.

Self-deception can also be related to integrity in a different way. There are less extreme cases of self-deception than Casaubon's that are not so obviously at odds with the possession of integrity, even though the self-deception concerns matters of deep importance to the individual. Imagine a man who, unlike Casaubon, is actually committed to a scholarly life and who identifies with the life and ideals of the scholar in a way that his integrity is bound up with them. Further, he hopes to become a first-rate scholar but does not have it in himself to be other than mediocre. Were he to admit this to himself, were he to admit that his expectations for himself as a scholar are too high, he would not be able to sustain his scholarly endeavors and his dedication to the scholarly life would be shattered. So he deceives himself into thinking that he is a better scholar than he is and thereby averts disheartenment. In this case, self-deception seems to be a way of protecting one's integrity, not just of disguising its absence.

Though the concepts of self-deception and weakness of will are not coextensive, they are similar in one respect: there is desire-influenced irrationality in both cases. Weakness of will, or acting against one's better judgment, can also pass over into self-deception, into believing against one's better evidence. A person who fails to live up to his or her values in a particularly grievous way, for example, might form the desire to believe that he or she has not done so because of a desire that it be the case that he or she has not done so. This person might then try to rationalize away evidence that, in the absence of this desire, would easily be recognized to count against self-control. In this case, self-deception covers up a loss of integrity that is due to weakness of will.[32]

Hypocrisy

Hypocrites are those who present themselves to others as they know or suspect they are not, in situations where they are not presumed to be role-playing and with respect to matters where sincerity is valued in itself.[33] In the most familiar case, they cynically and calculatingly practice what Erving Goffman calls "the arts of impression management,"[34] exploiting for self-serving reasons the fact that others will interpret their behavior to imply certain commitments that they have not in fact made. The success of the hypocrite's charade depends crucially on getting *others* to believe that he or she is sincere; the most adept hypocrites have learned how hypocrites are detected and are systematically on their guard against any misstep that might expose them and baldly contradict what they have openly avowed. By contrast, self-deceivers actually believe that they are committed to what they profess to be committed to because they want it to be the case that they are so committed. Their wanting this leads them, for example, to ignore or rationalize away their audience's reactions to their behavior, and this enables them to hold on to their false belief in their integrity. When Casaubon professes to be committed to a life of creative scholarship, others may be fooled. (Or they may not. Behaviorally self-deception may also look like hypocrisy because of an incongruity between what is said and what is done.) But he is not simply conveying false impressions to take others in, for as he presents himself to others, so he presents himself to himself.

A good example of a self-serving hypocrite is Gilbert Osmond in Henry James' *The Portrait of a Lady*. Osmond, an expatriate American living in Italy on a very meagre income, presents himself to his future wife Isabel as a man who spurns convention and is indifferent to poverty. Isabel is initially charmed by what she perceives as "a noble indifference, an exquisite independence" (Chap. 42), and sees her marriage to a man of Osmond's refined taste and limited means as an opportunity to do some good with the vast fortune she recently acquired from her uncle. But Osmond is in fact quite different from the image he succeeds in conveying to Isabel. As Ralph, Isabel's clever cousin, comes to realize:

> Under the guise of caring only for intrinsic values, Osmond lived exclusively for the world. Far from being its master, as he pretended to be, he was its very humble servant, and the degree of its attention was his only measure of success. He lived with his eye on it, from morning til night, and the world was so stupid it never suspected the trick. Everything he did was *pose—pose* so deeply calculated that if one were not on the look-out one mistook it for impulse. (Chap. 39)

Osmond's unacknowledged "ideal was a conception of high prosperity and propriety, of the aristocratic life" (Chap. 42), and it was only to gain the resources that Isabel could afford him to live such a life that he professed contempt for worldly success. Once he achieves his purpose, he shows a chilling insensitivity to the satisfactions and aspirations of those who are dependent on him for emotional and personal support.

Hypocrites like Osmond are plainly not persons of integrity, and they do not act with integrity even if, outwardly, their behavior often appears to cohere with their professed values. People who act hypocritically are not always self-serving, however, and in these cases we may hesitate to accuse them of lacking integrity. Consider, for example, the German agent in Ken Follett's novel, *Eye of the Needle*. In order to pave the way for a Nazi invasion of Britain, she takes up residence in a strategically important village on an island off the coast of Britain. In time, by living and working among its inhabitants and passing herself off as an ardent supporter of the Allied cause, she manages to become a respected and trusted member of the community. Yet she never loses sight of her mission and never wavers in her commitment to Nazi world domination. Her behavior toward the villagers is that of a hypocrite; however, it is not for self-serving reasons that she risks exposure and reprisals from those whose trust she has abused. She is above all the loyal Nazi who dutifully takes her orders from her superiors in Berlin and she eagerly looks forward to the day when she can openly acknowledge to the world her true values. Perhaps in her case we will say that deceiving others does not indicate a lack of integrity.

One of the reasons we think hypocrites like Osmond are not persons of integrity seems to be that they are so completely self-serving. Integrity, we believe, cannot be displayed in the selfish pursuit of our own good, even if our selfishness is openly acknowledged. But there is as well something especially disturbing about their hypocrisy itself: such hypocrites typically (and this is certainly true of Osmond) do not have the attitude toward their own deception that we expect persons of integrity to have. For Osmond, for example, the fact that his behavior constitutes systematic deception of Isabel is not itself a reason against behaving in this way; he is not distressed that he must have recourse to *hypocrisy* in order to satisfy the desires that are actually motivating his behavior and with which he most strongly identifies. Persons of integrity who act hypocritically, on the other hand, are deeply troubled by their having to pretend to others that they are what they know they are not and deplore being in a situation that calls for deception. They are disposed to openness about their basic commitments, motivations, and character. While this does not entail that they will never use hypocritical means to accomplish certain ends, they will not take their hypocrisy lightly. Even if persons of integrity do not feel remorse for a particular episode of deception, because they believe it was so overwhelmingly right to act as they did, it cannot fit comfortably with their conception of themselves.[35]

Hypocrites cannot publicly acknowledge the values they actually live by and cannot allow themselves to be identified by others as a person with these values. In this state of isolation it will be difficult for those who extensively and successfully mislead others to maintain a clear distinction in their own minds between the values and principles of their public personas and the values and principles that they keep hidden. For our sense of who we are is fixed by reference points in other people's reactions to us, and to hypocrites the reactions of others are quite useless as evidence about themselves. Hypocrites, therefore, do not just separate their inner from their outer lives: this way of speaking suggests that one will continue to be clear about what is inner and that the outer will remain outer even if they are systematically separated. If they deny themselves a public forum for the expression of what they take themselves to value most and rely only or mainly on internal monitoring, they are very likely to lose their objectivity about what they are doing. Perhaps, as Taylor observes, they "will slide into self-deception."[36] Another possibility is that hypocrites will eventually become attached to the principles and values they had earlier only professed to live by and that their unsure grasp of their identities will lead to genuine conversion. Their outward behavior, at one time carefully orchestrated to convey a false impression of genuine commitment, may eventually affect what they inwardly value in such a way that there is no longer any significant discrepancy between what their actions are taken by others to imply and what they take their purpose to be.[37]

Hypocrites are not committed to what they only pretend to others that they are committed to. What they lack, it might be said, is only external integrity, not internal integrity, because they have a coherent rationale for what they are doing and are guided in their conduct by certain core values (kept hidden from others, but not from themselves, and clearly operative whenever they believe it unnecessary to make a false impression). There are two problems with this. First, purely internal integrity seems to me to be an incoherent notion. Second, if what I have just been arguing is correct, whatever "internal integrity" the hypocrite has may be extremely tenuous.

10

Integrity and Practical Necessity

Among persons of integrity, there are those who, though strongly tempted to abandon their principles or commitments, succeed in resisting temptation either by sheer effort of will or by active manipulation of their motivational condition. They achieve coherence between principle and action by exercising their powers of self-control. There are also those whose wills are so strong and whose intentions are so firm that they do not need to make an *effort* of self-control in order not to act against their principles or commitments, even in the face of strong competing desires. These persons, we might say, have exceptional self-control and therefore exceptional integrity. What I want to focus on in this chapter is the phenomenon of volitional or practical necessity: what is experienced by these who do what they are committed to doing because, to quote Luther, they "can do no other." What they care about, are dedicated to, is felt to urge itself upon them with such peremptory force as to make forbearance from a certain course of action practically impossible. Such persons feel they "must" do what they do, but since there is more than one explanation for a person's inability to do other than he or she does, we need to clarify the particular sense of "must" being used here. Moreover, we sometimes ascribe integrity to persons precisely because of this inability, and say they are acting with integrity because they are acting in accordance with a commitment that is felt as practical necessity.

To begin with, we are not talking of physical inability nor, more interestingly, of the sorts of cases where "I can do no other" is an avowal of frailty. One of these is the unwilling drug addict who hates being addicted and struggles desperately to be rid of the addiction. This addict tries brute resistance and various strategies to increase the motivation for refraining from taking the drug (or to decrease the motivation for taking it), but the craving gets the upper hand. The addict takes the drug because he or she can do no other. Another is the phobic person who, because of irrational and debilitating fears, always avoids the object of those fears. Like the addict, this phobic wants to be rid of the phobia and tries everything that he or she thinks might help overcome it. But the phobic's rational control faculty is impaired, and in the end the fears win out. The phobic avoids being alone or in public places (agoraphobia), say, because he or she can do no other. In these cases, desires and fears are too powerful for the individual to resist even though this person wants to resist and, as Frankfurt puts it, wants this want "to be effective and to provide the purpose that he will seek to realize in what he actually does."[1]

Unwilling addicts or phobic persons act contrary to their better judgment and, because they cannot muster the power to forbear, they cannot bring the motivational force of their wants into alignment with their evaluative ranking of the objects of their wants. If we suppose that what people *really* want is what (unequivocally) accords with their better judgment, and that it is only what one really wants that is fully one's own, then we may view the addicts or phobic persons as being moved to act by something other than what they really want and by a force that is not fully their own. Further, addiction and phobia normally function as excusing conditions: persons suffering from them are relieved of responsibility for their actions while in the "grip" of these conditions. The sense of "must" or "has to" that Luther's statement exemplifies can be clarified in relation to these features of the more familiar cases of psychological impossibility.[2] The phenomenon in question, first, is one in which what the agents do does not conflict with what they judge it best to do and in which they do not dissociate themselves from what they believe they must do. They might concede that they could have led more secure or comfortable lives were their characters not such that there is something they feel they have no choice but to do, but it is not against their will that they accede to the force that constrains them. They have no sense that they are in the grip of some alien force to whose operations they must remain helpless bystanders. They identify themselves with their desire to do what they must and are expressing their authentic selves in the actions that they have no choice but to do.

Examples of this sort of necessity are not difficult to come by. In addition to Luther, who claimed (I suppose this is the truth about him) that his conscience made it impossible for him to recant, there are persons whose commitment to some moral principle (e.g., "Do not torture innocent human beings") is such that they cannot bring themselves to do what the principle proscribes. We also think of Gauguin, whose all-consuming devotion to his art made it impossible (on some accounts of his life) for him to remain with his family. Gauguin can serve as an example here even if he suffered remorse for deserting his family, as long as he also believed himself to be justified in doing what he felt he had to do. In some cases, it is not conscience or dedication to a cause that constrains choice in this way, but commitment to one's deepest impulses or to another person.[3] The important point is that such constraint is not a sign of weakness and passivity: the agent endorses it and it constitutes this person's will. Moreover, by doing what, on this explanation, the agent must do, the agent may display integrity.

These cases where a person cannot help doing what he or she does also call into question the widely held view that "a necessary condition for holding an agent responsible for an act is believing that the agent *could have* refrained from performing that act."[4] Luther's refusal to recant and Gauguin's foresaking his family for the South Seas are acts for which we can hold them responsible even though they could not have done otherwise in the situations in which they found themselves, and persons with such an incapacity typically *take* responsibility for what they find it impossible not to do. This claim (as well as the claim that they display integrity) might be denied in the following way: if it is right that they cannot do otherwise than they do, then they must be some sort of zombie, "programmed" always to follow their consciences or pursue their ideals without any consideration of the pros and cons of their doing so. Genuinely responsible agents must be able to see both sides, and they are able to do this only if in any particular situation in which they act it is true of them that they could have done otherwise than they do. This argument does not succeed, however.[5] From the fact that a person cannot do otherwise than he or she does in a particular case it does not follow that under some variation in the circumstances of action he or she would not do otherwise, and all that seems to be required for responsible agency is that there be some circumstances in which one would with reason do otherwise. If it had become apparent to Gauguin, for example, that abandoning his family and going off to the South Seas to paint would have precipitated some worldwide catastrophe, it is quite possible that he would not have found it impossible not to go. So Luther or Gauguin does not have to be depicted as unable to listen to reason, or as being so constituted that he will do what he is doing "let the heavens fall," merely because he cannot do other than he does in the particular circumstances in which he acts. What's more, if being able to listen to reason is a necessary condition of integrity, then integrity is not necessarily compromised by the sort of practical impossibility being discussed here.

Persons sometimes betray their identity-conferring commitments, that is, the commitments that reflect what they take to be most important and so determine to a large extent their identities. For some, it may be all too easy to do so and they must make an effort of self-control in order to be true to themselves. But if there is a commitment to something that matters to us in such a way that it is impossible for us to forbear from a certain course of action, like Gauguin's commitment to his art or Luther's commitment to preaching his message of salvation, then it will count as identity-conferring. (It should be remembered here that a person is not committed to something if that person self-deceptively takes him or herself to be so committed.) Such an incapacity is constitutive of one's core self, and the actions one cannot forbear from performing are governed by desires that are governed by and expressive of this core self. We might want to ask how much control Luther or Gauguin had over the *formation* of their core selves, how much it was up to them that they are the sort of person who "can do no other." But even if we do not see them as responsible for their incapacities, they can still properly be accorded responsibility for the decisions and actions that flow from these incapacities. For one thing, it cannot plausibly be maintained that though Luther's or

Gauguin's actions express their core selves, these selves are deeply flawed because they are not responsive to reason. It is not that a Luther or a Gauguin cannot do otherwise because his rational control faculty is impaired, but rather because he sees so clearly what the situation is that he finds himself in and because that faculty is *not* impaired.[6]

I have been discussing how the particular kind of necessity someone like Luther or Gauguin is subject to is different from more familiar cases in which one is driven to act by some desire or fear that one is too weak to overcome, but more needs to be said about the character of this necessity. Frankfurt offers a promising suggestion: "An encounter with necessity of this sort characteristically affects a person . . . by somehow making it apparent to him that every apparent alternative to that course is unthinkable."[7] One "must" do what one does in part because alternatives are unavailable to that person in the special sense that they are unthinkable (by that person). The unthinkableness by S of alternatives to x can be explicated as follows: alternatives to x are not entertainable as serious options by S. Thus "unthinkableness" does not mean that S is literally unable to think of alternatives to x. Luther could certainly have the thought of his recanting and Gauguin of his staying with his family. Indeed, it may be precisely as a result of thinking about alternatives to x and finding that they are "unthinkable" that S must do x. (The reverse might also happen: it may be that S must do x because he or she attaches such overwhelming importance to x and that as a result all apparent alternatives to it become unthinkable.[9]) Rather, y is not entertainable as a serious option by S if S would regard doing y as going against his or her character.[9] What is or is not a serious option for S is thus relativized to features of S that are deep-seated and more or less long-lasting. Alternatively, we might say that y is not entertainable as a serious option by S if S, imaginatively trying on y for size, so to speak, could not bear to be the sort of person who does y. Alternatives to x that one cannot consider oneself doing without experiencing a grave loss of self-respect cannot be seriously entertained. The drug addict in my example can certainly envision being the sort of person who is not addicted to drugs without doing violence to a sense of self-identity (indeed this is what this addict really wants), and so does not "have" to take drugs in the sense that alternatives to this are unthinkable. But for someone like Luther or Gauguin, he could not live with himself were he to do other than he does and he cannot bring himself to act in any other way than as he acts.

There are some individuals for whom virtually nothing is unthinkable and who are prepared to do anything as long as the consequences are desirable enough. But for Luther or Gaugin (and for those of us similarly constituted), there are certain actions he cannot perform, and this not because he has too much self-control to let this happen, but because he cannot help doing what he does, because his acting in the way he acts is not within the scope of his voluntary control. I do not want to claim that persons will never do what is unthinkable by them in the preceding sense, that they will never do what they are unable to bring themselves to do. On the contrary, one can, because of forces that one is too weak to overcome, do something that is so disgusting or offensive to oneself that one cannot entertain it as a serious option.[10] Further, I do not propose that persons are acting with integrity whenever all apparent alternatives to what they are doing are unthinkable by them, and they act in the face of difficulty. One reason this is not so is that it is possible for someone's sense of self-identity to be based on perceived features of oneself that, owing to self-deception, one believes oneself to possess. Alternatives to what one is doing might be regarded by that person as incompatible with his or her (compromised) self-respect and so be unthinkable. That is, given that someone self-deceptively identifies him or herself with a certain type of person, these alternatives are rendered unavailable to this person as serious options. If a person who "can do no other" is to give evidence of integrity by doing what one must, it is not merely because the sort of person this person identifies him or herself as being leaves him or her with no alternative. It must also be the case that this person's integrity is not vitiated by self-deception about what he or she is really like, by having an image of self that, owing to self-deception, is a false one.

We should not conceive of the situation of Luther or Gauguin as one in which he is attempting to maximize the good of self-respect through actions that are means to a goal. Such persons do not canvass the alternatives open to them, test each one in terms of its conduciveness to the further good of self-respect, and then choose the one that leads to the most of this good. Nor is it because alternative *y leads to* a grave loss of self-respect that it is unthinkable as a serious option by them. Instrumental thinking is not at work here. When they say (as I am imagining they do) that "I couldn't live with myself if I didn't do *x* or if I did *y*" or "I should be worth nothing if I gave *x* up," they are not just pointing to something further that their action will produce, but are indicating the way in which their lives are bound up with the action and the sort of intrinsic importance it has to them. Instrumental thinking may enter at another point, however. For if, not being able to live with oneself if one does *y*, one avoids doing *y*, and doing *y* is a matter of bringing about some outcome, avoiding it may require thinking how not to produce that outcome.

Frankfurt also observes that cases like those of Luther "differ from situations in which it is clear to the person that he must reject the possibility of forbearing because he has such good reason for rejecting it."[11] For one thing, it can be clear to a person that the weight of reasons overwhelmingly comes down on the side of rejecting alternative *y* to a certain course of action *x*, and that person may intentionally and freely do *y* nonetheless. And even if he or she does *x*, holding a judgment that *x* is very markedly favored over all apparent alternatives to *x* (and undertaking to follow this judgment with implementation) is not the same phenomenon as Luther's having to act as he does.[12] What I "must" do, in the sense of having such good reason for rejecting the possibility of not doing it, should not be confused with what I "must" do, where the possibility of not doing it is excluded from the range of my serious alternatives. For example, I may deliberate about whether I should invest in the stock-market at this time and decide, in light of the current favorable situation on the stock-market, the unattractiveness of other available investment options, and my desire for wealth, that I must buy stock now. This is not the same as saying, however, that passing up the opportunity to invest in the stock-market does not fit in with the sort of person I am, or that I could not live with myself if I did so. (The accumulation of wealth may just not be that important to me.) Now I do not want to suggest that people like Luther and Gauguin do not deliberate. Indeed, it is sometimes through deliberation that one recognizes that one cannot do certain things and must do others.[13] But what one recognizes in these cases is not that, relative to some objective one has, a certain course of action is very clearly singled out from a number of possible alternatives. Rather, one discovers a fact about oneself, namely, an incapacity in oneself to forbear from a certain course of action. Moreover, this fact about oneself is something that one endorses: one does not want to change, to be a person who does not have this incapacity.

As I suggested earlier, it may be some *moral* principle the transgressing of which one could not knowingly live with oneself for doing. For example, come what may (barring outlandish circumstances), torturing innocent people might not be a serious option for a person. But as the case of Gauguin shows, practical necessity can involve other sorts of commitment as well. Sometimes the impossibility of doing other than one does obtains for nonmoral reasons, and sometimes the integrity one displays in so acting is not specifically moral integrity (taking "moral" here in the familiar sense as concerning our relations to other people). Further, as Bernard Williams observes, "practical necessity, even when grounded in ethical considerations, does not necessarily signal an obligation."[14] What an agent feels he or she must do, and what in fact he or she must do, may or may not be an obligation, that is, a universal and inescapable demand on action that must be met on penalty of blame. What Gaugin "had" to do was arguably not an obligation in this sense—in fact, as Michael Slote tells the story, it ran counter to his obligations[15]—and not something that applied to him even if he did not want it to. And people may "have" to do things that, though morally praiseworthy, are supererogatory.[16] If we are going to use the language of "obligation" here at all, we should recognize that it is often a very personal sort of obligation.

11

Integrity: Form and Content

I have argued that a person who has integrity is not a wanton and is not seriously weak-willed, self-deceived, or hypocritical. These are necessary conditions for the possession of integrity. Are there, in addition, constraints on the content of the principles or commitments a person of integrity may hold? Can persons have integrity no matter what their principles or commitments, so long as they generally hold firm to them in the face of temptations and dangers, they are reflected in the reasons that actually cause these persons to act in the way they do (on the relevant occasions), and as a rule they publicly acknowledge the standards they live by? Intuitions here are often pulled in opposite directions. Samuel Scheffler expresses this ambivalence:

> A person whose deepest and most powerful desire is to inflict pain on others, and who acts accordingly, may succeed in establishing a coherent personality. Here as elsewhere, coherence is not enough. I do not know whether to say that a coherent relationship between motivation and action is not enough for *personal integrity,* or alternatively, to say that coherence is enough for integrity and that therefore integrity is not enough.[1]

If we build into the notion of personal integrity certain substantive moral constraints, then the sadist will probably be disqualified as a candidate for integrity and we will not have to inquire further whether this person is genuinely and openly committed to cruelty and would act accordingly even in the face of difficulty. On the other hand, if we are willing to ascribe integrity even to persons who act in accordance with principles or commitments that we find morally abhorrent, then the fact that someone has acted with integrity may be an additional count against that person rather than a point in his or her favor.[2]

According to Rawls, the virtues associated with integrity, namely "truthfulness and sincerity, lucidity, and commitment, or as some say, authenticity," are "virtues of form," and as such, are compatible with almost any content:

> [A] tyrant might display these attributes to a high degree, and by doing so exhibit a certain charm, not deceiving himself by political pretenses and excuses of fortune.[3]

Rawls does not say whether these virtues are sufficient for ascriptions of integrity, but if they are, then even particularly revolting and vicious people can have and exhibit integrity.

Moral constraints are not the only ones to be considered. Lynne McFall asks us to think about the following claim: "The connoisseur showed real integrity in preferring the Montrachet to the Mountain Dew."[4] As she sees it, even if connoisseurs are strongly tempted to drink the Mountain Dew and force themselves to drink the wine instead through a strenuous exertion of will power, and even if being a drinker of fine wines ranks highly in their hierarchy of values and concerns, we would not say that the connoisseurs show integrity in preferring the wine. This is because the commitments in accordance with which a person acts with integrity must be *important* ones, and most of us just do not regard drinking fine wines as important, or important enough to justify the ascription of integrity. As McFall puts it, "we must at least recognize [a person's principles or commitments] as ones a reasonable person might take to be of great importance and ones that a reasonable person might be tempted to sacrifice to some lesser yet still recognizable goods" (p. 11). But even here our judgments show an ambivalence that McFall does not acknowledge. On the one hand, we, "the enlightened majority" (p. 10), regard consuming fine wines as a relatively trivial pursuit and might therefore hesitate to ascribe integrity to the committed connoisseur. On the other hand, we might allow that what strikes us as unreasonable, given our values and beliefs, might not be unreasonable from the point of view of the agent, and in focusing on what is important to that agent, might say he or she shows integrity even though we have great difficulty appreciating how anything so trivial (to us) could be of such importance to someone. Sometimes we grant or deny integrity on the basis of our own conceptions of importance, and sometimes we see integrity involved in an act on the basis of the role some commitment plays in a person's life.

Ordinary language may pull us in two directions on the question of whether a sadist can have *personal* integrity, but there is little hesitation when it comes to deciding whether that person has *moral* integrity. Further, though we may accept that a ruthless tyrant can display personal integrity in acting ruthlessly, or that a connoisseur can show personal integrity in acting to satisfy refined tastes, ascriptions of integrity are sometimes of a more qualified sort, and here there are definite constraints on the content of the principles or commitments a person of integrity can hold.

For example, consider what I will call intellectual integrity. Persons of intellectual integrity are committed to the pursuit of truth, and because they have integrity, they pursue the truth in certain characteristic ways. We expect them, for example, to be open to the ideas of others, to be willing to exchange ideas with and learn from them, to lack jealousy and personal bias directed at their ideas, and to have a lively sense of their own fallibility. That is, we expect them to have qualities of impartiality. In addition, they must be willing to conceive and examine alternatives to popularly held beliefs, they must persevere in the face of opposing views until they are convinced that their own are mistaken, and they must be willing to examine and even actively seek out evidence that would refute the hypotheses they presently adopt. In short, they must have qualities of intellectual courage. These traits of impartiality and intellectual courage are ways of being a conscientious or responsible epistemic agent, and the person of intellectual integrity possesses these epistemic virtues. These qualities do not have to be displayed to the same extent on all relevant occasions by the person of intellectual integrity. Perseverance may predominate over impartiality, as in the case of persons who propose radically new theories and need to temporarily blind themselves to or dismiss ideas that are contrary to their own in order to be able to follow out their vision. Though dogmatic, such persons do not necessarily betray a lack of desire for truth. But dogmatism, if occasionally admirable, surely evidences an intellectual vice when it systematically precludes openness to opposing viewpoints. In an overall judgment of the intellectual personality of one who has intellectual integrity, impartiality and courage complement each other and balance each other out. In addition, the person of intellectual integrity continuingly reflects on the appropriate balancing of perseverance in his or her own beliefs against openness to those of others.[5]

In persons of intellectual integrity, the formal virtues of personal integrity combine with specifically epistemic virtues of intellectual courage and impartiality and the disposition to reflect critically on their proper balancing in different situations. They hold fast to their commitments to the truth despite the temptation of self-aggrandizement and the risk of ostracism or censure. They do not merely pretend to others that they are committed to the truth, or self-deceptively take themselves to be so committed (to do so is not to be *committed*), and their commitments to the truth are filled out in terms of the epistemic virtues. On the other hand, motivations that conflict with and undermine the impartial and courageous pursuit of truth disqualify their adherents as candidates for intellectual integrity.

An example will help clarify how the pursuit of certain ends can corrupt a person's intellectual integrity, or at least call it into question. The example concerns scientific integrity, a type of intellectual integrity, and its background is the shift in the role of faculty members at this nation's large research universities from teacher/investigator to entrepreneur. As universities search for new sources of funds to replace dwindling federal support, and as private capital moves aggressively into disciplines like biotechnology, the ties between research universities and private industry expand and deepen. One question researchers at these institutions ought to be asking, and increasing numbers are, is whether they can enter into consulting contracts with outside businesses and maintain their integrity as scientists. Leon Wofsky, professor of immunology at Berkeley, puts the conflict this way:

The business of business is to make money, to beat the competition, and the mode is secrecy, a proprietary control of information and the fruits of research. The motive force of the university is the pursuit of knowledge, and the mode is open exchange of ideas and unrestricted publication of the results of the research.[6]

The fear of Wofsky and others within the academy is that the norms governing scientific investigation—open and free sharing of information, a disinterested approach to research that puts the advancement of science first—are being eroded as the pull for commercial application of research and consequent profits intensifies.

The person of intellectual integrity is a person who possesses certain epistemic virtues, and similarly, a person of artistic integrity possesses certain specifically artistic virtues. This individual does not, for example, imitatively follow past or existing aesthetic styles and traditions, but modifies, amplifies, and possibly even rejects them in accordance with the demands of a personal vision. This person also does not indulge in capricious and undisciplined outpourings of emotion, but exercises skill and expends intellectual effort in transforming the materials provided by an inner sensibility so that they do not remain private and confused. Someone with artistic integrity is conscientious and prizes mastery of a chosen craft as a virtue, yet this individual eschews mere technical perfection displayed without regard to what it contributes to the work of art (i.e., virtuosity for its own sake). These artistic virtues, and the earlier epistemic ones, are characteristics that make a person an admirable and responsible participant in a particular practice, the practice of art in the one case, that of, say, scientific inquiry in the other. Following Alasdair MacIntyre, a practice is

[A]ny coherent and complex form of socially established cooperative human activity through which goods internal to that form of activity are realized in the course of trying to achieve those standards of excellence which are appropriate to, and partially definitive of, that form of activity.[7]

The standards of excellence that partly define the practice of art or science are maintained by persons of artistic or intellectual integrity. In general, persons who are participants in a certain practice have integrity relative to that practice only if they have the virtues that aim at excellence in that practice and subordinate themselves to its standards of excellence.

Moral integrity, like intellectual or artistic integrity, adds a substantive requirement to personal integrity.[8] A person of moral integrity has moral commitments and acts according to them, but what makes something a *moral* commitment? Neil Cooper observes that we sometimes describe the goals or ideals to which a person single-mindedly devotes him or herself as that person's "morality":

> Aestheticists think that one human activity, Art, is more important than any other. . . . We could describe them as "subordinating" . . . morality to Art. But we could also say that their own autonomous morality consisted of putting Art first. As Gaunt says of the Bohemians, "They had one law, one morality, one devotion and that was Art."[9]

In the same sense we might say that a person's "morality" consists in making money, if that person is single-mindedly, passionately devoted to it. But surely this use of "morality" is metaphorical only, and it is not even a very good metaphor at that. (A better word to use to refer to the object of maximal devotion is "religion," for it is the nature of religious devotion to be all-consuming.) Further, it is especially clear that this is metaphor when we note that even the unalloyed and all-consuming wickedness of an Iago or of Milton's Satan would count as a moral stance on this view. Those who rejoice in the suffering of others and seek it as an end in itself, knowing it to be an evil, could hardly be candidates for (literal) moral integrity. Nor could the less extraordinarily wicked who only do what they, mistakenly, believe is good.

Of course, people often disagree among themselves to some extent about the right principles of behavior without accusing each other of lacking moral integrity. I might not fully endorse another's moral commitments or principles—for example, I might fault consequentialist principles on the ground that they absolve the individual of any special responsibility for his or her own moral integrity—but I might nevertheless see us both as condemning certain acts that ignore or interfere with the interests of others, as belonging to the same moral community by virtue of an underlying consensus on the goods that ought to be taken account of and criteria of membership in the community, and as disagreeing only in our particular interpretations of what our common standards require or allow. In this way, the other's commitments are still recognizable to me as genuinely *moral* ones, and this makes it possible for me to acknowledge the other's moral integrity even as I disagree about what is right.[10] This ability to recognize other people's acts as expressing a moral stance even when we do not endorse that stance ourselves, and as displaying integrity based on their moral outlook, is an important part of our more general ability to treat others with respect.[11]

In addition, persons of moral integrity possess certain traits of character that (following James Wallace) may be labeled "forms of conscientiousness": honesty, fairness, truthfulness, and being a person of one's word.[12] Such persons are committed to being worthy of the trust of their fellow human beings, and each of these virtues of moral conscientiousness is a specific form of that commitment. (Consider in this context Webster's definition of "trust" as "the assured reliance on another's integrity."[13]) They are committed to the avoidance of deceitful violations of trust, they characteristically shoulder their fair share of the burdens of joint enterprises with others, and they are trustworthy in their agreements. Further, like the examples of artistic and scientific integrity discussed earlier, moral integrity can also be related to practices, only now it is practices in general rather than any specific one. Practices, being "socially established cooperative human activit[ies]," depend for their availability on the trustworthiness of their participants. Without honesty, fairness, truthfulness, and fidelity to agreements if agreements are made, practices degenerate into a free-for-all in which there are no rules, no sense of shared enterprise, and no cooperation. By contrast, persons of moral integrity possess those socially useful traits that make possible and sustain patterns of cooperation in a broad range of circumstances. They are trustworthy persons in general and as such reliable partners in practices of all sorts.

Plainly persons can have intellectual or artistic integrity and lack moral integrity. They might have the virtues that make them admirable participants in a particular practice and yet when not functioning in their capacity as scholar or artist, or the like, abuse the trust of their fellow human beings. In addition, some practices, like that of organized crime, are themselves defined by vice, and the participants in these practices, though perhaps excellent in them, do not qualify as possessors of moral integrity. We might feel some admiration for the integrity they show as criminals, for their commitment to the principle "honor among thieves," but we do not admire the practice itself and the integrity of the participants is morally revolting.

Let us now turn from the preceding forms of consciousness to conscientiousness itself, that is, conscientiousness about not doing what one regards as wrong, whatever this may be. The conscientious person follows the dictates of conscience, experienced as an inner "voice" and a severe taskmaster: he or she is "driven by conscience" to do something, or his or her conscience "won't let him (or her)" do something, or he or she is "punished by his (or her) conscience" if he or she acts wrongly. Those who follow their consciences, particularly in situations that threaten grave personal harm, are also commonly described as acting with integrity. A case often cited in this connection is that of Thomas More. Prior to his confrontation with Henry VIII over an act of Parliament ordering him to take an oath in support of Henry's divorce of Catherine of Aragon, More was the honest and loyal civil servant, dedicated to his king and country. But he was also a deeply religious man committed to the teachings of the Roman Catholic Church, and since the pope had refused to grant the divorce, More felt he could not take the oath without perjuring himself before God and sacrificing his own immortal soul. For More, his conscience, as developed and tempered by the teachings of his church, was the overriding authority with regard to his behavior and preempted all other obligations. So he refused to swear the oath, knowing that his act of conscience would incur the charge of treason, and, as we might say, his integrity cost him his life.[14]

What is the role of conscience? Conscience is plainly not an infallible source of moral direction: persons can believe in the moral rightness of what they are doing, and act in furtherance of what they believe with the utmost vigor, perseverance and wholehearted dedication, and yet still be acting immorally. Conscientiousness, or the active concern to behave in a moral fashion, can add to our estimation of an agent when it is enlisted in the service of certain ends, but the conscientious commitment to monstrous moral principles is pernicious rather than admirable. The reliability of conscience is thus not self-certifying; support is needed from some source external to conscience itself. Alternatively, we might think of conscience's role the way Peter Fuss does, as *reinforcer* of "an individual's felt sense of the need to conduct himself in accordance with whatever moral convictions he happens to possess, regardless of their source."[15] The explanation for this seems to be that conscience introduces into the agent's practical deliberations a concern for the self. When people feel bound to obey or follow the judgment of conscience, they consider how they will view themselves after they have done that which is seen by them to be wrong. Because they fear or worry that they will experience guilt or remorse if they do this, because they are concerned about the future condition of themselves and disvalue the disruption of inner harmony that the contemplated act will cause if it is done, they feel they should obey this judgment. The authority or bindingness of conscience comes from within each person and reflects the importance one attaches to one's own future inner harmony.[16]

Persons of conscience are not necessarily conscientious: they might never critically reflect on the dictates of their conscience and only unquestioningly obey them. (Such a person of conscience would not have integrity.) I would not characterize them, however, as Nicholas Fotion does, as people who are "undeterred by reason and facts from continuing to hold the views" they hold, or as people who lack or are unable "to participate in self-criticism."[17] They may in fact come to see the dictates of their conscience in a new light and conscientiously defy the conscience they have hitherto followed. The anxiety they anticipate as a result of defying their conscience will not dissuade them from doing so.

12

Integrity and the Unity of a Life

Persons of integrity are not wanton, nor are they seriously weak willed, self-deceived, or hypocritical. They have their commitments or principles and normally hold firm to them in the face of dangers or enticements to do otherwise, and there is no systematic discrepancy between the principles or commitments they profess (to themselves or others) to live by and the desires and interests that actually motivate them to act as they do. These are necessary conditions of authentic commitment. Lack of integrity may, however, be due to something else as well—lack of what John Kekes calls "wholeness":

> A principled man may not be a whole man, he may not be all of a piece, for his commitments may be incompatible, or he may punctiliously adhere to one commitment after another. [To have integrity in this sense] is to act authentically in accordance with coherent commitments.[1]

In this chapter, I will discuss integrity in terms of the *structure* of principles and commitments to which the individual adheres.

Edmund Gosse's eloquent and moving study of his father in *Father and Son* vividly depicts a man who lacks wholeness in this sense. The elder Gosse was a man of impeccable scientific credentials, a respected marine zoologist known for his intellectual honesty and painstaking research, as well as a man of severely funda-

130

mentalist religious principles. Until the advent of the theory of natural selection, his scientific and religious commitments, his devotion to the truth in science and in Scripture, co-existed harmoniously. But the harmony did not last, and in 1857 the elder Gosse suffered an intellectual crisis:

> [T]hrough my Father's brain . . . there rushed two kinds of thought, each absorbing, each convincing, yet totally irreconcilable. . . . It was this discovery, that there were two theories of physical life, each of which was true, but the truth of each incompatible with the truth of the other, which shook the spirit of my Father with perturbation.[2]

On the one side was evolutionary theory, which "every instinct in his intelligence went out at first to greet" (p. 86); on the other was his Christian fundamentalism with its literal reading of the Genesis account of creation. As Edmund saw it, the antagonism his father perceived between evolutionary theory and religion "was not, really, a paradox, it was a fallacy" (p. 84), but for his father they could not simply be alternative, mutually reinforcing, ways of explaining the same set of events. Moreover, the rigorously high standards the elder Gosse set for himself in his relation to the natural world, when put to the test by the new biology, were in conflict with his particular religious convictions. Gosse the dedicated scientist and Gosse the fundamentalist Christian could not cohere with each other in a unified life of commitment. And though he might have been able to integrate his conflicting theories and keep his religious belief substantially intact, he could not do so.

Gosse's intellectual crisis was precipitated by his awareness of incompatible commitments, but the incoherence is not always recognized as such by the agent. For example, Robert Jay Lifton, in his book *The Nazi Doctors,* identifies a psychodynamic process that he believes partly explains the SS physician's complicity in mass destruction: the process of "doubling."[3] SS physicians had sworn allegiance to Hitler as well as taken the Hippocratic oath, had dedicated themselves to working for the Fatherland as well as their patients, and these commitments were in conflict with each other. But as a result of doubling, the self was radically compartmentalized into two semi-autonomous, functioning wholes and the conflict was not acknowledged. One, the "Auschwitz self," was

committed to Nazi ideology, which defined the doctor as the ultimate biological warrior in the battle to purify the German Volk.
This double protected the other original self, the self committed to
benefiting the sick and keeping them from harm, from a shattering
realization of its dealings with death. The development of an autonomous Auschwitz self with a separate identity allowed the individual doctor to repudiate his death-dealing double by insisting
upon his true identity as a genuine doctor and healer. From the
standpoint of the original self, it was another self who collaborated
with the Nazi regime, and this splitting off of the Auschwitz self
enabled the physician to continue to believe in his own integrity as
a physician. From the standpoint of the Nazi doctor's double, it
was another self who would have qualms, for instance, about cur-
ing a patient only to get him well enough to be sent to the gas
chamber. But there was no standpoint from which the agent saw
his incompatible commitments as commitments of a single self.

Ascribing incompatible commitments to different selves may preserve the appearance of integrity, but it undermines wholeness.
For the person of integrity, incoherence among one's principles or
commitments cannot be dealt with in this way. Commitments must
be experienced as internally related, as bearing on each other, and
their inconsistencies worked out within the framework of a single,
unified life. A "whole person" takes responsibility for such inconsistencies and lives by a personal standard of coherent commitment
by which that person is prepared to judge him or herself. In other
words, this individual has a second-order commitment to conduct-
ing life in accordance with coherent first-order commitments and
principles, and is true to this commitment.[4]

Lives of coherent commitment can take different forms. They
might be conducted on the basis of a more or less stable and long-
range life plan and achieve coherence by virtue of steadfast adherence to some final end or vision of how one should lead one's life
overall. In some, perhaps rare, instances, persons live their lives
under the domination of a single end to which they dedicate themselves; their lives are organized to achieve the satisfaction of some
one ruling passion. We might offer as examples of this Disraeli's
political ambition or Henry James' self-dedication to the art of the
novel or Loyola's commitment to promoting the glory of God. In
each case, commitment to one dominant end takes absolute prece-

dence over the agent's other aims and commitments. Persons might also have a more complex ideal, consisting of a plurality of well-ordered ends, which they strive to realize and around which their lives are organized. However, not everyone plans his or her life to this extent or, if so, adheres to this plan over a large stretch of his or her life. Some people might even repudiate such far-reaching plans, preferring instead to take life as it comes and not to tie themselves down in advance by adopting a particular direction for their lives. In many cases there is no predetermined, explicitly worked out goal commitment to which organizes one's life. Nevertheless, individuals who have not planned out their lives in this way are not necessarily ones who simply pursue their various commitments and hope for the best (i.e., that they do not come into conflict with each other). They may be committed to coherence, believing that it is important for them to be "all of a piece" in terms of the commitments they presently have. Deliberately establishing and maintaining coherence without some regulative final vision or comprehensive ideal to which one aspires is another way of achieving wholeness.[5]

Further, there is a tension between wholeness and well-roundedness. Persons who are single-mindedly committed to a comparatively small number of closely related and coherent values and principles are likely to have less difficulty maintaining wholeness than persons with a large number of diverse commitments. Thus, we could perhaps maximize wholeness by minimizing our commitments. But if we do minimize them, it might be argued, we may miss the invigorating effect of variety, as well as the chance to enrich our lives by being open to feelings, attachments, and values that incline us in different directions. These are the costs of fixation on wholeness: by giving greatest weight to wholeness in the conduct of our lives we neglect an important dimension along which lives may be evaluated. Of course, this does not show that wholeness or integrity is without value. It can still count for something, though perhaps it counts for more in some cases than others. A well-rounded life of coherent commitment may be a better life for a person to live than a life that sacrifices well-roundedness for wholeness, despite the greater difficulty of achieving and maintaining integrity in these circumstances.

In order to have integrity or be a whole person, Kekes asserts, one must "adhere to the pattern of hierarchically organized commitments that compose one's life."[6] (This way of speaking may suggest a degree of preplanning that is often not found, but I do not think the language of hierarchy necessarily imports this.) A commitment's ranking in this hierarchy is a function of the status the agent accords it so far as core identity or life-plan is concerned. Those commitments that reflect what a person takes to be most important and that constitute a sense of self-identity are "unconditional" [Kekes' expression (p. 514)] or "identity-conferring" (Lynne McFall's expression[7]). The other commitments, which involve a personal dedication to the actions implied by them but which are less crucially bound up with the individual's conception of self, are "defeasible." A person of integrity will normally act according to defeasible commitments only if doing so does not conflict with or threaten disruption to identity-conferring ones. Further, if the individual has a plurality of identity-conferring commitments, integrity requires that these too be ordered or integrated in some way in order for there not to be ruinous conflicts between them and to better prepare the individual for difficult situations that may occur in the future. For example, one or more of the commitments might be amended so as to render them consistent with each other, or a higher-order principle might be found that establishes which of the commitments is to prevail (and under what circumstances) when a conflict arises.[8] Commitments derived from a single identity-conferring commitment must also be ranked or otherwise rendered consistent. However, if a person's defeasible commitments conflict, this does not by itself damage that person's integrity the way inconsistency with respect to identity-conferring commitments does.

Kekes cites Montaigne as an example of a man who keeps his integrity by maintaining a proper balance between his unconditional and his defeasible commitments. Montaigne, choosing to give up his life of reflection and writing for the public life of mayor of Bordeaux—a life that he acknowledged necessarily involves the commission of vicious acts—nevertheless regarded himself as a good man. He came to terms with the problematic aspects of his official role as follows:

> I have been able to take part in public office without departing one nail's breadth from myself, and to give myself to others without taking

myself from myself. . . . The mayor and Montaigne have always been two, with a very clear separation. For all of being a lawyer or a financier, we must not ignore the knavery there is in such callings.[9]

One way to interpret these remarks is that they refer to something like the process of "doubling" discussed earlier.[10] Kekes, however, argues that Montaigne accepted the commitments of the mayor as his (Montaigne's) commitments, but that they were only defeasible ones, and that he never departed "one nail's breadth" from himself in the sense that he was never untrue to his identity-conferring commitments. He will soil himself by participating in public life, but only up to a point: he will stop short of those actions that corrupt his basic goodness and decency. We are asked to think of Montaigne not as a knave who refused to accept responsibility for the morally problematic aspects of his political activity, but as a good man who was able to integrate the activities of mayor into a coherent conception of his moral life and keep his conscience clear.

Conflicts might arise between a person's identity-conferring commitments, and integrity requires that this person have or find some way of rendering them consistent. This individual may add exception clauses to commitments or give priority to one over another. But even where exceptions and priorities are clear and the individual is convinced he or she has acted for the best, persons of integrity will not evade acknowledging to themselves when they have had to give up or limit or frustrate one basic commitment for the sake of another, and a sense of loss or some sort of distress because of this is still appropriate. The feeling here is not merely disappointment in the wake of unfulfilled desire, but has, or has something akin to, a moral dimension. As well, integrity involves more than just responding appropriately to predicaments of conflict that one finds oneself in. For whether or not conflicts of commitment arise in the first place is to some extent in a person's control, and persons of integrity take seriously whether they are inviting inconsistency by engaging in a certain course of action. They regard themselves as having some control over the conditions for the compatibility of their commitments, and though they do not shield themselves from the contingencies of the world and thereby from the possibility of personal growth, they also show imaginative and practical resourcefulness in avoiding situations that threaten to set their core commit-

ments in opposition to each other.[11] In contrast, people who avoid-
ably and without due care conduct themselves in such a way that
they are confronted with a serious conflict between their identity-
conferring commitments, lack some integrity, even if they then re-
move the inconsistency by prioritizing them.[12]

A person's commitments not only might conflict with each
other; they might also conflict with someone else's commitments.
If such interpersonal conflicts threaten the realization of their respective commitments, some sort of mutual accommodation or
compromise might be considered by them. But can a person of
integrity compromise his or her commitments without compromising his or her integrity? For Ayn Rand, this depends on the importance of the commitment to the prospective compromiser:

> It is only in regard to concretes or particulars, implementing a mutually
> accepted basic principle, that one may compromise. . . . There can be
> no compromise on basic principles or on fundamental issues.[13]

In order to remain true to the commitments that rank most highly
in our hierarchy of values and concerns, that are most central to
our overall identity, it may be necessary to refrain, at least temporarily, from acting in accord with commitments that are more lowly
ranked and more peripheral. Abandonment of these commitments, but not even partial abandonment of "basic principles," is
compatible with the maintenance of integrity, and may actually be
required by integrity. There need be nothing dishonorable about
compromise so long as it is confined to compromising conflicts of
interest or conflicts of relatively peripheral commitments.

There will no doubt be some people who will admire Rand's
intransigence when it comes to compromise on basic principles.
From another point of view, however, refusal to compromise on
these might mean in practice abandoning entirely the hope of seeing them realized or realizing them to a lesser extent than would
otherwise have been possible. For example, suppose that there is a
group of legislators with conflicting basic commitments to justice,
and that they put forward competing policies or programs that are
backed up by these commitments. If they reject any compromise,
holding firm to their respective principles, each will do worse, as
measured by the extent to which each one's principle is realized,

than each would have done had the compromise been adopted. In such a case, we may ask, as Ronald Dworkin does:

> if each member of the legislature who votes for a . . . compromise does so not because he himself has no principles but because he wants to give the maximum possible effect to the principles he thinks right, then how has anyone behaved irresponsibly?[14]

We can ask the same question about compromise in nonpolitical situations. Perhaps there is no loss of integrity if one compromises on one's basic principles when, under the circumstances, this is the only way to give "maximum possible effect" to them. Yet presumably Rand would claim that one should still refuse to compromise on them, that integrity demands not giving an inch when one's basic commitments are involved.

It might be argued that those who categorically refuse to compromise on their basic commitments in a particular instance, even to secure their greater realization, must be acting irresponsibly or inconsistently, but I do not see how to make a convincing case for this. It is not that they do not care very much whether or not these commitments are realized, but rather that in reflecting on the justifiability of compromise, they do not think only or chiefly in terms of what will give "maximum possible effect" to their commitments. They would rather abandon hope of seeing them more fully realized than partially abandon them themselves. On the other hand, I do not see how a convincing case can be made that persons who agree to compromise a conflict of principles because they want to maximize the effects of their principles must be acting irresponsibly or lacking in integrity. They are not weak-willed or hypocritical or irrational, and they compromise their principles on principled grounds.

For persons of integrity, there are always limits to compromise, but what these limits are is not the same for all of them.[15] One explanation for the variation in limits has to do with the decisiveness of one's commitment. Persons who are willing to allow that they might be mistaken about their principles, who are not entirely confident of them, are more likely to agree to compromise on them than those who are committed to them without reservation. The limits also vary depending on the capacities that are constitutive of character. For example, some people are just capable of standing firmer in the face of serious personal adversity than are others. If the refusal to compromise threatens their safety or well-being, they will be able to hold out against compromise to a greater extent. And then there is the explanation suggested in the previous paragraph. Some might agree to compromise on their principles because they place greatest weight on consequentialist consider-ations. What matters most to them, for example, is how much justice there is in the world, and they are willing to settle for what they regard as less than optimal because the alternative would be a world containing even less justice. Others, however, might refuse to compromise despite this because adherence to their principles has a significance *for them* that is not exhausted by its probable overall consequences and because their sense of self-identity would be devastated were they to agree to compromise.

13

Integrity and Self-Transformation

When the commitments that reflect what people take to be most important change, they become in a sense different people. This transformation of self, if it is something over which the individual has control, will not be sudden. Because of the particularly profound investment of personality in the objects of one's identity-conferring commitments, the severance of attachment to them must allow time for retrenchment, adjustment, and eventual acceptance of new priorities. But once the transformation is complete, residual feelings of guilt with respect to the commitments one has abandoned and negative self-assessment may be inappropriate. Things that one formerly could not do without self-betrayal one may now be able to do without it, for the commitments departure from which would have constituted self-betrayal might no longer be identity-conferring and one's change of mind might not have been unreasonable.

Change of basic allegiances does not always come about as a result of rational reflection on the circumstances of one's life. One may experience a sudden conversion (it need not be a religious conversion, literally speaking). In such cases, change of core commitments is not a step-by-step process involving deliberation on the direction one's life has taken, but a relatively sudden and unstructured event like a gestalt switch. One simply comes, in a "lightning flash," to see oneself and one's relation to others in a fundamentally different way, and this change in commitment is not a rational procedure. Further, while the preconversion and postconversion selves may each have integrity relative to their respective commitments, the shift in allegiance from one core commitment to another does not itself display integrity. More common than such conversion experiences, however, are cases of self-transformation in which individuals change basic commitments for what are taken to be good reasons. They do not cast off or take up a commitment at will, of course, for commitment is not under a person's direct voluntary control. But as a result of a reevaluation of existing commitments, they take measures to loosen the grip of some and to nurture new ones. Setbacks or hindrances, mishaps, unfortunate events, unfulfilled expectations, and so forth can provide occasions for such reevaluation. And unlike nonrational conversion, persons who thus transfer their allegiance from one basic commitment to another may only be doing what they have done all along and will continue to do: ordering and shaping their lives by their practically rational judgment. In this sense, they remain true to themselves even as their lives take a fundamentally new direction.

Self-transformation is not always a matter of shifting allegiance from one core commitment to another. A person might lack a core, the kind of commitment that gives a person character and that makes a loss of integrity possible, and then acquire one. A (somewhat ambiguous[1]) example of this is Major Jones in Graham Greene's novel, *The Comedians*. Jones is a hypocrite and pleasure-seeker who, at the book's end, redeems himself by joining forces with rebels fighting against the regime of Papa Doc. Sometimes a person of integrity only adds a basic commitment to other existing ones. Self-transformation might also be a change from an integrated life to a life of dissolution or, in less extreme cases, it might just involve the loss of a basic commitment without its replacement by a new one. For example, the only change may be that a formerly basic commitment becomes a nonbasic one. Whether commitments are added or eliminated, persons of integrity will make readjustments in their lives. New commitments will have to be ranked relative to or integrated with continuing ones, or their lives will have to be reorganized around a smaller set of basic commitments. Further, transformation of self may be a matter not so much of no longer having a core commitment as gaining a deeper understanding of what it is to be so committed. John Kekes explains the latter, as it relates to moral commitment, as a process in which one "discover[s] hitherto unknown possibilities in one's own view" and comes to appreciate "the complexities inherent in the tradition which was already [one's] own."[2] Personal growth through the discovery of new possibilities for oneself in one's commitments can occur as well in other areas of life besides the moral, and an adequate account of integrity would allow for change of this kind.

III

INTIMACY

14

Caring About Others

In Chapter 2, I drew a number of distinctions with respect to caring, focusing on what I called "caring about." The objects of such care are extremely diverse, including persons (oneself and others), communities and traditions, ideas and ideals, material objects, and personal projects. In addition, caring about can be positive (when one makes oneself vulnerable to losses as the object of one's care is diminished and susceptible to benefits as the object of one's care is enhanced) or negative (when one makes oneself vulnerable to losses as the object of one's care is enhanced and susceptible to benefits as the object of one's care is diminished). And finally, caring about can be disinterested of self-interested: disinterested care is not directed toward my own satisfaction or advantage and is not a means to some further end of mine, while care that is aimed at the realization of something pleasurable or profitable to myself is self-interested. One can, quite disinterestedly, either negatively or positively care about someone or something, and both positive and negative caring can stem primarily from self-concern.

In this chapter, however, I will be concerned with only one type of caring about: caring about that is positive and disinterested, and only as it is directed at other persons. Within this category, I will distinguish impersonal from personal care, and within the latter, between caring that does and caring that does not involve certain desires whose content essentially refers back to the one with the desires. Love of particular others and friendship are instances of personal care, and it is often critical to the agent that he or she be the one to extend personal care to a friend or loved one.

Sometimes caring about others takes the form of embracing the good of humanity, or a significant number of people, as one's personal cause or calling (as with Mother Theresa, for example). With attachment to causes, however, comes the possibility of fanaticism, the promotion of one's cause for its own sake, purely as an abstraction, at the expense of the concrete interests of the people whose condition one is supposedly trying to ameliorate.[1] In addition, there are ways of living that are consistent with really caring about the welfare of others and which do not involve the sacrifices of time and energy that those who commit themselves to humanitarian causes make. For example, I see a person who is in pain, or who experiences some hardship or affliction, and I feel compassion for that person. I care about this person's suffering and desire its alleviation, and when I can do something appropriate and not overly burdensome to relieve this condition, I am disposed to attempt to help. I do not turn my back on needy people, but I also do not go out of my way to involve myself in good causes. Compassion, whether occasional in this way or the ruling passion of one's life or something in between, involves viewing other persons in a certain way, as fellow human beings. Compassionate persons see the others' suffering as the sort of thing that could happen to anyone, including themselves insofar as they are human beings, and not just as a particular affliction occurring to these particular individuals; and though they give special attention to the individuals they are trying to help, they do not give preferential consideration to the needs of these persons as against those of others. Involving as it does a conceptualization of the sufferer as a member of the human community,[2] compassionate concern is nonparticularistic and nonpreferential caring.

There is a kind of anonymity of response in disinterested, positive caring about another individual under the description "a human being, like you and I, who needs assistance," and it is an instance of what I call *impersonal* care. So, too, though perhaps less obviously, is caring about another individual under the description "a friend of mine who stands to benefit." Impersonal care does not *overlook* the person who is the object of goodwill; it does not disregard the particular features of other persons, their particular capacities, desires, and ends. But it is also not directly targeted on any particular individual. That is, the person who cares impersonally about others is only motivated by reasons that refer him or her to others just so far as they satisfy certain identifying descriptions (e.g., a person who is in need or a friend who stands to benefit). This is the sense in which impersonal care is nonparticularistic.[3] Impersonal care is also nonpreferential in that it does not give priority to the needs or interests of some particular person over those of others who satisfy the same identifying description. By contrast, in the activity of *personal care* the individual is motivated by reasons that cannot be replaced without motivational loss by other reasons that fail to refer that individual directly to the potential beneficiary of an action. That it is this friend, for example, rather than some other person who fits the description of being a friend, is not a matter only of incidental interest to the agent. (If it were only this, there might be a commitment to friendship but there would be no real friendship with this person.) In personal care, the one cared about is independently individuated for the one who cares, independently of that person's (the former's) satisfying certain general conditions. Moreover, as we normally think of personal care, those we care about are special to us in the sense that we give special weight to their interests and needs in deciding how to act.

Nonparticularistic, impersonal care may or may not involve the having of personal feelings of liking or affection for the individuals cared about (what I have called "caring for"). I may be moved by compassion to help a fellow human being in need for whom I do not feel any particular affection; I may not be personally drawn to this individual, I may have no particular desire to get to know this person better or to spend time with him or her, and I may not find this person particularly appealing or pleasant as an individual. On the other hand, caring about a friend impersonally, that is, caring about someone, whoever he or she may be, as my friend, does involve such feelings, for friendship is not merely a matter of mutual disinterested well-wishing and well-doing. So, too, therefore, does caring about a friend where the identity of the particular friend *is* of essential importance. But while caring about a friend (personally or impersonally) is accompanied by some liking or affection for someone that is absent from typical cases of caring about strangers in need, it is not the having of these feelings that constitutes my caring about an individual. As I noted earlier, I can like or be personally drawn to someone I do not care about. Liking or having affection for my friend may explain why I do things for the friend that I do not do for others and why I give preference to that person's interests over those of others. But caring about my friend involves the desire and willingness to act on behalf of my friend's good, whereas personal feelings are not similarly directed toward others in regard to their weal or woe.

Caring about another for his or her own sake, as an end, is necessary (though not sufficient) for friendship. But is it necessary for personal love? Here we must proceed more slowly, for it is notoriously difficult to extract a common meaning for the term from its varied uses. Sometimes love is conceived on the model of personal feelings, as only a particularly intense liking or affection directed toward another in virtue of personal qualities or features. (We use the expression "x is in love with y" to indicate the presence of such strong feelings, and sometimes by "x loves y" we mean "x is in love with y.") On this view, the difference between liking someone and loving someone is a matter of degree. Alternatively, it may be viewed as a difference of kind. It is not possible for one person to love another and yet not be actively concerned with the good of the beloved, indeed not be inclined to act toward the beloved in ways that one is not inclined to act toward arbitrary strangers or mere acquaintances. Love, we might also say, involves commitment to (the well-being of) the beloved, and unlike relations of liking and being attracted to, we should retract our characterization of a relation as a love relation if the so-called lover never hesitated to sacrifice the one beloved to some other personal commitment. This way of regarding love, as a species of disinterested care[4] and not merely as strong attraction and the like, is the one I will adopt.

Further, personal care may include personal desires on the part of the one who cares that *he* or *she* be the one to do the caring. Such care is doubly personal, personal with respect both to its object and its subject: special importance is attached by the one who cares to the particular other's receiving care by the former's own hand. To explain, consider two ways in which a mother might conceive of her own involvement in the care of her children. In the first case, she desires that she take care of her children, but this desire is entirely derived from a desire that her children be taken care of by someone or other. Her thinking can be represented as follows:

1. I desire that my children receive as good an upbringing as possible;
2. I believe that I can provide them with this upbringing;
3. Therefore, I desire that I care for my children.

Perhaps she believes that her children's sense of being taken care of by their own parent is itself a benefit for them, and that when this benefit is added to the other possibly somewhat meagre benefits she can bestow, the resulting total is greater than the total of benefits her children can receive from other caretakers. But the main point is that she desires to be the one to take care of her own children only because there happens to be no one else who can do as good a job or a better job of raising them, and that therefore she should have no reason not to prefer another caretaker for her children if that person could do a better job than she rearing them. Following Jennifer Whiting, we can say that this makes her desire to take care of her own children "impersonal."[5] (Taken literally, the common idea that parents are just "guardians" of their children's well-being suggests that parents should be entirely self-effacing and that their desires to take care of their children should be impersonal.)

In the second case, the mother's being the one to do the caring of her children is not desired only accidentally, but essentially. That is, she attaches some nonderivative, noninstrumental value to its being *her* who takes care of them. Perhaps if she found somebody else who could clearly do a much better job raising her children than she could and who was willing to undertake the responsibility, she would want to and would relinquish her children. But in doing so, she would still feel that she has given up something of value, namely, the possibility of her continuing to be the one to do the caring. Following Jennifer Whiting again, we can say that she has "personal"[6] desires to care for her children, personal because the content of her desires essentially includes a first-person indexical. She desires to care for her children under the description "my caring for my children" and not just under the description "the person who can provide my children with as good an upbringing as possible." In either case, however, I suppose that each of the children who are hers is him/herself the target of her concern, and not just indirectly the target of her concern by virtue of satisfying some identifying description (e.g., "a child of mine who needs to be looked after.")

We can use the distinction between impersonal and personal desires to get a better understanding of the nature of friendship. Suppose a man x has an impersonal desire that the person best able to meet the needs or satisfy the interests of his friend y attempt to do so, and x, as he sees, happens to be that person. So he, derivatively, desires to be the one to care for his friend. X never attaches any independent value to its being *him* who does this. I do not believe that this is a case of true friendship, even if x cares about y and even if the particular identity of y matters to x's motivation.

If I am another's friend, I sometimes want to be the one to do things for that other, and not just because the other stands to gain the most if I am the one to do them. (The nonderivative desire to be the one who benefits the other need not indicate that I am ultimately egoistic.) My friend stands in a particular relation to *me* such that in *my* promoting my friend's interests I am doing something that has value for me in itself. One is not a friend just because I feel responsible for that individual's well-being, for this way of putting it does not capture the essential self-referential character of friendship. This is also true of the caring of personal love. Here, too, I do not just benefit my beloved for the more or less incidental reason that I happen to fit the description "the person who is in the best position to promote this particular other's good." Love for a person does not require that I always have the desire to care for that person by my own hand, or that I desire to be the one and only person who benefits that person. I might realize that I am too anxious or angry or guilty to give my beloved what she now needs and decide that it would be better for her if I let someone else assist her. Indeed, part of personal love is being sensitive to one's limitations in this regard, to one's limitations as caregiver. But when the desire to extend personal care to my beloved is present, it cannot just be impersonal.

Personal desires should not be confused with the desire to promote one's own self-interest, and the personal desires of friendship
and love are not just of this sort. I am not being self-serving, in the
derogatory sense, when I do things for my friend out of a desire
that I particularly be the one to do them. There is a value for me in
my being the one to do the caring, but the boundaries of my self
have been extended and redefined through my friendship or love
relationship in such a way that my happiness comes to include the
happiness of the other. The interweaving of lives in friendship does
not involve an identification with the other in which I fail to retain
my own separate ends: my self, to whose caregiving I attach independent value, is not submerged in but enlarged by the other. Nor,
to return to an earlier point, is the particular interweaving of lives
in friendship and personal love the same as the sense of shared
humanity that compassion involves.

Personal desires are also implicated in the pursuit of personal
projects and personal commitments generally. My personal project
to win a gold medal for the United States in the Olympics, for
example, is not entirely derivative from the impersonal desire that
someone or other win a gold for the United States. I may partly or
even mostly want to do this for my country, out of a sense of
patriotism, but I do not automatically drop my project upon learning that there are others who stand a better chance than I do of
succeeding. Indeed, in the case of some personal projects, I may
have no desire at all that someone or other do what I have set out
to do. Again, I am impersonally committed to a principle, say, the
principle of promise-keeping, if I am dedicated to the actions implied by it but my desire to do what the principle prescribes is
entirely derivative from my desire that promises be kept; I am
personally committed if to some extent it nonderivatively matters
to me that *I* carry out the principle. I might put my concern this
way: it matters to me that *I* do so because it is my integrity that is at
stake; maintaining or repairing my integrity is specially important
to me simply in virtue of its being mine.[7]

Personal care is not only directed toward our intimates. We may
care about other people because they are the particular people they
are, we may have personal feelings of liking or affection for them,
and be motivated by personal desires to act on their behalf, and yet
circumstances or our own personalities may prevent us from becom-

ing or remaining intimate with each other. We are not always on intimate terms with those we love, nor do we even always wish to be.[8] Some degree of intimacy, as well as being disposed to intimacy, are necessary for friendship, however. Friends confide in one another, tell each other things about themselves, and show each other sides of their personalities that they would not show to just anyone. It is not merely knowing intimate details of another's personal history that is of primary significance to me as someone's friend, but rather the fact that I come to know them because he or she cared to reveal them to *me* and that my knowing them facilitates my caring about that person.

Before turning to a closer examination of the nature of personal relations, I want to say a word about the widely held view that intimate relationships of personal care depend for their existence on privacy. For example, Charles Fried argues that the defining mark of intimacy is the sharing of information about and allowing of observation of oneself that is not shared with or allowed to the rest of the world, and that this would be impossible without privacy. If there were nothing about myself that the world at large did not have access to, I would have nothing special left to give to or share with my intimates, no way to mark off my intimate from my nonintimate relationships. As Fried says,

> Intimacy is the sharing of information about one's actions, beliefs, or emotions, which one does not share with all, and which one has the right not to share with anyone. By conferring this right, privacy creates the moral capital which we spend in friendship and love.[9]

For Fried, the information we share about ourselves is made valuable because it is made scarce by privacy, and this valuable commodity is the stuff of intimacy. But as Jeffrey Reiman argues, the possession of intimate information is surely not sufficient for intimacy.[10] What makes a relationship intimate, Reiman points out, is not the sharing of otherwise withheld personal information, but the context of mutual caring that gives this sharing special significance for the parties involved. It is caring about those to whom we disclose and from whom we receive personal information that makes this information relevant to intimacy. My intimate is one to whom I care to reveal information about myself so that this person can share "intense experiences" with me, and who I believe cares to know this so that this person can do so; the exchange of personal information enables us to care more sensitively about each other and deepens our emotional commitment to each other. Reiman maintains further that even if intimate details of my life and personal history were known to strangers, I could still share this information with those about whom I care and who care about me. And since it is the caring that makes the information valuable, I could still "enter into a meaningful friendship or love relationship." But this part of Reiman's thesis (viz., that the loss or lack of privacy does not diminish our capacity for intimacy) is more dubious than his criticism of Fried's proprietary conception of intimacy,[11] and one can make a case for the importance of privacy for intimacy without relying on that conception.[12]

15

Personal and Nonpersonal Relations

Personal care is focused on particular persons, not on persons as instances of a type; sometimes, but not always, we are on intimate terms with the persons we care about in this way. I shall characterize a *personal relation* as an intimate relationship that persists over some more or less extended period of time, in which the parties engage in a range of shared activities, and each is predominantly moved by considerations that make the other matter in his or her own right, as the particular person he or she is.[1]

Friendship is a personal relation in this sense, as are some cases of personal love. (There are, of course, different degrees of friendship, depending on the level of intimacy, care, and concern at which the friendship operates. Some of my friends I may not care about very deeply: I wish them well, hope for good things for them, and act to protect and promote their good, but I do not give much of myself to them. I may be willing to go to great lengths to help out other friends, and I may identify quite closely with their good.)

The typical psychotherapist–patient relationship does not fit my conception of a personal relation, however. It is characteristic of such relationships that patients and therapists participate in them in fundamentally different ways. Though patients are intimate with their therapists in that they share profound information about their history, values, strengths and weaknesses, idiosyncracies, and hopes and fears with their therapists, the intimacy is not reciprocated, as it is in an intimate relationship. Interaction is localized to the therapist's office where communication is controlled and often manipulated by the therapist, and while deep familiarity with the individual patient is required for adequate diagnosis and treatment, personal involvement with the patient is strictly limited and professional distance is maintained.[2] Further, personal relations are not always animated just by positive personal care, by a desire to promote the other's good for his or her own sake. It is possible to have an enduring intimate relationship largely dependent for its maintenance on mutual and particularized ill-will.

Though personal care can exist without intimacy, intimacy nurtures and deepens personal care in friendships and intimate love relations. In addition, intimacy enhances particularity and provides directions for personal care: the particular identity of my friend or loved one is filled out by the context of intimacy and intimacy helps to keep my personal care tightly targeted on the beneficiary of my concern. I shall have much more to say about the nature of love and friendship in the next chapter, but first we need to get clearer on how relationships can fail to be personal. I consider three kinds of relationships: those of strangers, of role occupants, and of acquaintances.

Strangers

The word *stranger* is sometimes used in the sociological literature to refer to anyone with whom we are not acquainted, whom we have never met. I may possess a great deal of biographical information about a person, perhaps even more than some of that person's friends and loved ones, but this individual remains a stranger to me as long as we have never been face-to-face. Alternatively, "stranger" has been defined as any person who is personally unknown to me, where personal knowing may but need not involve actual acquaintance. To know someone personally is to have knowledge of that person "based on information not only about his roles and statuses, his categories, but on information, however slight, about his biography as well. To know another personally is always to apprehend him as a unique historical event."[3] On the first construal, Sigmund Freud is, and will remain, a stranger to me because I have never been and never will be directly and immediately aware of him; according to the second, a person is not a stranger to me if I can associate bits and pieces of accumulated personal material with a name or face or some other identifying marker. For example, I can do this with Freud by reading his letters or memoirs by colleagues and patients.

As I use the term, absence of actual acquaintance with someone is sufficient for that person to be a stranger to me. Even if someone is personally known to me, in the previous sense, this individual may still be a stranger. But absence of actual acquaintance is not necessary: people can interact with each other and remain strangers. Further, I do not consider lack of personal knowing to be sufficient for someone to be a stranger, and as I shall shortly discuss, there is another type of relationship where personal knowledge plays at most a subsidiary or instrumental role. This is the relationship of role occupants, and I distinguish it from the relationship of strangers.

What is the character of the interaction between strangers, supposing that they do interact? Strangers, when they meet, typically do so by accident, and do not associate with each other over a long period of time. Each gets a fix on the other by attending to age, sex, dress, and other general identifying features. Where there is no particular cause for fear or suspicion, each observes the rules of etiquette and common moral decencies toward the other. Among themselves, strangers normally engage in what Erving Goffman calls "unfocused interaction," that is, "the kind of communication that occurs when one gleans information about another person by glancing at him, if only momentarily, as he passes into and then out of one's view."[4] One form of unfocused interaction, the maintenance of which is increasingly becoming a problem in some places in our society, is "civil inattention," by means of which "the individual implies that he has no reason to suspect the intentions of the others present and no reason to fear the others, be hostile to them, or wish to avoid them" (p. 84). Rules of social intercourse, however, do recognize circumstances in which strangers may properly approach each other and initiate encounters, in which the normal presumption against face-to-face involvement is overridden. In these circumstances, according to Goffman, the stranger opens him or herself up to contact with certain others by virtue of being in an "exposed position" (pp. 125–26). One such exposed position that usually provides a nonsuspect basis for approaching a stranger is when the individual "is in patent need of help" (p. 127).

The particular conventions governing appropriate forms of interaction among strangers are not the same in all societies, and they may vary even within a given society, but in general we can say the following. Civil inattention among strangers—what Goffman calls "the slightest of interpersonal rituals" (p. 84)—normally gives way to more focused interaction only under socially prescribed conditions[5]; strangers require a reason to enter into face-to-face engagements with each other rather than a reason not to; their encounters are not circumscribed by specific role requirements; during the course of the engagements, participants commonly stand in readiness to invoke their rights to be free of inopportune overtures and requests; and even in focused interactions, strangers have at most only slight personal knowledge of each other.

In many ways, relationships among strangers clearly fail to be intimate. Moreover, unlike the care given to friends and loved ones, it is possible for strangers to be the recipients of no more than impersonal care from one another. In fact, in the thoughts that move me to help a stranger in need, the identity of this particular stranger is standardly only of incidental interest, and the ties between strangers are usually too tenuous to support personal care.[6]

Role Relations

Participants in this second type of nonpersonal relationship are not strangers to each other, or at least not strangers in the specific sense of the word just explained. Interactions between role relations are not primarily unfocused. What distinguishes them is their institutionally defined character: persons relate to each other as occupants of particular jobs or offices within a relatively well-defined and determinate system of roles making up an institution. The content and structure of their face-to-face engagements is constrained by public institutional rules that attach specific rights and duties to their positions and designate certain forms of behavior as permissible and others as impermissible to them. Penalties and defenses are also provided for when violations of the rules occur, and conditions for assuming and relinquishing roles are fixed.[7] Common to all sorts of role relations is the fact that their content and shape are not entirely or mainly under the control of the participants themselves, but are regulated by the requirements of the larger institution within which they function. In addition, personal knowledge that one role occupant has of another is either of relatively minor importance in their relationship or enlisted in the pursuit of some end external to the relating, and to a greater or lesser extent, their interactions are routinized.

Persons who relate to each other primarily as occupants of certain roles engage in narrowly prescribed reciprocal behaviors between segments of themselves. Role relationships are relatively inflexible and limited interactions that engage only well-delineated segments of persons. The role need not be thought of pejoratively as a mask that disguises one's "real self," and it would be a mistake to suppose that role players must somehow be insincere or inauthentic in their role relations. Their role behavior might not be a way of hiding something about themselves from others, or a kind of contrived performance or con game, but a very personal form of self-expression that is central to their self-conception. (We often say that it is the self that emerges in intimacy that is most real, but I think there are better, less question-begging, ways of drawing the distinction between intimate and nonintimate relationships.) Moreover, the occupants of roles are replaceable. Roles, as the term is used in sociology, are socially identified patterns of behavior and attitude that enable us to identify and place persons in society. Once stabilized, the role structure defined by an institution tends to persist, regardless of changes in the actors.[8] The relationship between, say, a lawyer and a client, as a role relationship, is not materially affected by changes in the individuals who occupy these positions. What is of central importance is that the integrity of the roles be preserved, that whoever occupies the role of lawyer and the role of client learn what obligations, privileges, rights, and duties are the defining characteristics of their positions, and that they enact role behaviors that are congruent with the expectations held by participants in the social system. One lawyer will do as well as another, as a lawyer, if their job qualifications—their knowledge, argumentative skill, motivation, ability to inspire trust—are the same.

Of course, a client may value certain personal qualities of a particular lawyer that are unrelated to the main task of lawyering, and may even choose a lawyer on the basis of these qualities. The lawyer might also add certain intimate behaviors to the basic core activities, as when giving a "personal touch" to relations with a client. But in role relationships, these expressions of individuality are kept to a minimum and have only secondary importance as compared with the actions or qualities regularly expected of anyone occupying the roles. The lawyer and the client may be on friendly terms with each other, but theirs is, after all, primarily a professional relationship, not a friendship. (Evidence for this is the fact that if the lawyer does not fulfill his or her role function well, the personal touches are little consolation to the client.)

A role occupant might be expected to be warm, friendly, and caring. Unlike, say, the way in which employers treat workers in modern economies, people in the so-called helping professions are expected to display such qualities. This is, so to speak, part of the job description, not just more or less incidental to the main task: it is crucial that clients be made to feel that they are specially important to the professionals, that they are not being treated "by the book." And in such cases it is not very surprising if the institutional character of the relationship should remain in the background for the client. However, professionals do not lose sight of the fact that a particular client is only one of many actual and possible beneficiaries of their attention, and if they are doing their job well, they make *every* client feel special.

Though institutional relationships are not personal ones, it is of course possible to have both sorts of relationship nonconcurrently with the same person. Your lawyer can also be your best friend, your co-worker can be your spouse (here thinking of husband–wife as a personal and not an institutional relation), and so forth. These combinations frequently pose difficult and delicate problems of mutual adjustment for the parties involved and could lead to conflicts of interest; in some cases there may be strong professional or social pressures against such doubling-up. Often less problematic are those situations in which role occupants do not associate with each other "after hours" at all or are only acquaintances.

Role relationships are not intimate. Deep and detailed knowledge of the other's life, character, and desires is commonly not available to the parties involved, and if intimate knowledge is required at all, it is because the role demands it. Moreover, the participants in role relations do not matter to each other in their own right, as particular persons, but insofar as they fulfill certain functional norms. They encounter one another as segmental persons, and are more or less easily replaceable by others who fulfill the same norms as well or better.

Acquaintances

Acquaintances may like or have affection for each other; they may also care about each other to some extent as the particular persons they are. They do not relate to each other mainly according to general social conventions or the pre-established requirements of a role. Yet acquaintanceships, or perhaps better, casual acquaintanceships, are not personal relations, for they lack intimacy. (Admittedly, there is no sharp line separating mere acquaintances from friendships that are not especially close. The contrast between acquaintanceships and intimate relations becomes more evident the farther we move away from marginal friendships.)

One of the ways we differentiate between acquaintances and intimates is in terms of the depth and thoroughness of the knowledge each acquires of the other over the course of their association. Acquaintances become familiar with each other's manner of behavior, and gain knowledge of each other's attitudes, tastes, interests, values, and goals. Among other things, each discovers what the other thinks, feels, likes, and dislikes about him or her. They also learn something about each other's biographies, which show how their personal features accumulated and developed. But the portrait each constructs of the other lacks depth, density, and definition, and since acquaintances have no strong desire to apprise themselves of any changes in the other's features and fortunes, the knowledge each has of the other, such as it is, can easily become obsolete as well. Each usually intends for the other to learn only matters of middling importancce to him or herself. Self-disclosure at either extreme, of one's deepest concerns and core aims and attitudes and of the minutiae of one's life, is not the norm for their relationship. (Sometimes one acquaintance may reveal something weighty about him or herself to another as a first step toward establishing an intimate relation.) Further, the pieces of information acquaintances obtain about each other are relatively discrete and disordered. Each has but a poor grasp of the particular connections between the other's behavioral and psychological elements.[9] The fragmentary and shallow character of the knowledge acquaintances have of one another is related to the depth of affect in these relationships. It is because they care about each other only slightly that the information revealed or collected by acquaintances is such that strong personal differentiation and a high degree of individualization of the acquaintances does not occur.

Psychological closeness to others is not just a matter of how much one knows about them but of one's emotional tie to them. There is no closeness, however, without knowledge of what it is like to have the experiences another person is having or of what it is like to be that other person. I am speaking here about a way of knowing that consists in empathic identification with another, and though such identification is possible with someone with whom I am not on intimate terms, it occurs most readily and regularly in intimate relationships. Acquaintances in particular often know well enough *that* the other feels a certain way, and often feel sorry or happy that the other is in a certain situation; it is less common for acquaintances to know *how* the other feels, how the other finds being in a certain situation. What is lacking is the imaginative projection of the self into the other person's place and the adoption of the other's particular perspective on his or her own experience. Intimates are more or less routinely capable of this, but acquaintances do not constitute and define themselves as a unit through empathic identification.

There are other features, relating to the frequency and nature of the interaction, as well as to how it is initiated, that set acquaintanceships apart from intimate relations. Acquaintances seek each other out only occasionally, for joint activities in which they are oriented predominantly to something outside their mutual interaction. We find acquaintances to help us enjoy ourselves while we engage in activities that we have an interest in pursuing independently of them, and our enjoyment and interest in what we are doing with an acquaintance are largely limited to what we directly do ourselves. The interactions of acquaintances are also frequently less open-ended in regard to their duration than the interactions of intimates, and in contrast to these, the former are usually initiated only by explicit invitation or by a request for permission to join in. Further, the encounters of acquaintances flow less spontaneously than do those of intimates, and except when intimates experience difficulties or are engaged in resolving problems in their relationship, interactions between acquaintances that are sustained for a long period of time are more tiring psychologically than are similar interactions between intimates.[10]

*

Putting all this together, the following characteristics of personal relations emerge from the discussion of strangers, role relations, and acquaintances. At the very least, the parties to a personal relation must have met and interacted with each other, and must sustain this interaction for some length of time.[11] Their approaches to and departures from one another are not governed only or mainly by conventions of social intercourse, nor does their relationship primarily depend on a common understanding of what each owes the other in the way of forbearances and positive services. In addition, in a personal relation individuals do not just encounter one another as general persons: it is not just what is common between people, the facts about human nature that make each person one among others, that each is focused on and in light of which each responds to the other as he or she does. In these ways, personal relations differ from relations among strangers. In contrast to role relations, the parties in a personal relationship do not interact with one another primarily as occupants of offices or positions within an institution. Each is strongly individuated for the other and is chiefly important to the other apart from occupying a specific place in a social organization, and the character of their relationship is inseparable for each from their particular identities. Their interactions are holistic, not segmental, and multifaceted. And unlike acquaintances, those who have a personal relation with each other acquire deep and detailed knowledge of each other's lives, characters, and desires, and each is regularly in touch with the subjective side of the other's experience. Their lives and interests are closely intertwined, and this knowledge offers them special possibilities of mutual support and concern (as well as frustration of the other's desires) lacking to acquaintances.

These attributes of personal relations are not only found in friendships and pure love relationships. (It should be noted that a loving relationship between parent and very young child is not a personal one in my sense, for a parent cannot share his or her life with an infant.) There are personal relations in which malice and hatred are closely intertwined with love, as in the case of Martha and George in Edward Albee's play, *Who's Afraid of Virginia Woolf?* The hatred surfaces in the following exchange:

> MARTHA: You can't come together with nothing, and you're nothing. . . . And I'm going to howl it out.
> GEORGE: You try it and I'll beat you at your own game.
> MARTHA: Is that a threat, George? Hunh?
> GEORGE: That's a threat, Martha.
> MARTHA: You're going to get it, baby.
> GEORGE: Be careful, Martha . . . I'll rip you to pieces.
> MARTHA: You aren't man enough . . . you haven't got the guts.
> GEORGE: Total war?
> MARTHA: Total.

Yet after the war is fought, there are still tender feelings:

> GEORGE: It will be better.
> MARTHA: I don't . . . know.
> GEORGE: It will be . . . maybe.
> MARTHA: I'm . . . not . . . sure.
> GEORGE: No.
> MARTHA: Just . . . us?
> GEORGE: Yes.[12]

It might be claimed that another defining feature of personal relations, of personal love–hate relations as well as of friendships and personal love relations, is that the parties to them intend their relationship to continue indefinitely and do not place any definite time limit on it. Persons may enter into role relations with others or choose to maintain acquaintanceships for a specific amount of time only, but personal relations are, to use Michael Bayles' expression, "intentionally of indefinite duration."[13] On this view, marriage, though it frequently expresses an especially close personal relation, does not itself qualify as a personal relation, for it is possible to set a time limit to a marriage. (A couple who enters a trial marriage may already have a personal relation and intend only to limit the marriage, not the relation.) Or suppose two people form a friendship, but mutually agree that it will be limited to a certain number of years, at which time they will reassess it in order to decide whether it should continue. Again, on this view, as long as the agreement remains in effect, their relationship is not a personal one and not a friendship in the proper sense at all. Now it might be admitted that personal relations need not be completely unconditional—x may not be prepared to maintain a relationship with y no matter what y does or becomes. But (the view continues) it is one thing to be realistic about the limits of one's constancy or even—if, say, serious and insurmountable problems develop in the relationship—to expect it not to endure, and quite another to enter into or to remain in a relationship intending that it will continue only for a specific length of time. The former is not incompatible with a truly personal relation. I feel uncomfortable, however, maintaining that the intention to continue a relationship indefinitely is part of the concept of a personal relation. We can, of course, pack as much into the concept of a personal relation as we wish, but I worry that the definition will become too remote from our ordinary understanding of the phenomenon if we make this particular stipulation.[14]

I do not think this is the case with another requirement, viz., that personal relations involve a conception of interests that is essentially collectivist. Sometimes a relationship is only formed to serve as means to the satisfaction of certain antecedently identifiable interests of the parties involved, and once these interests are satisfied the relationship lapses. Each of the parties has the particular interests he or she does regardless of whether anyone else in the relationship has them. The interests might be based on distinct objectives that are all of the same kind or they might converge on the same specific thing, as in the case of a neighborhood association organized to protest inadequate police protection in the area. But even in the latter situation the interests are private in the sense that each of the members of the association would continue to have an interest in better police protection even if no one else in the neighborhood does or would have it. By contrast, in personal relations persons come to define themselves as a unit, not merely as individuals interacting with other individuals. Their interests (or rather some of them) remain the interests of individual persons, yet they are not private, neither congruent nor just convergent, but common and interdependent. When I have a personal relation with you, I do not just regard my interests as *mine* and your interests as *yours*. Personal relationships do not merely serve as means to the satisfaction of the varied interests of the participants in them. On the contrary, some of my and your important interests concern matters of *our* way of life. I regard these interests as mine insofar as I regard myself as being associated with you, and you regard the same interests as yours insofar as you regard yourself as associated with me. In this way we as a community can be said to have an interest in certain states of affairs. These interests, which constitute a shared life, are collective.[15]

These collective interests are embedded in the ongoing practices and traditions of particular personal relationships. Each personal relation has its own customary patterns of behavior, involving shared religious, moral, artistic, recreational, and other activities. Collective interests are not mainly chosen or adopted in personal relations, but are more typically uncovered or constructed through reflection on the practices and traditions in which one finds one has already been participating. As a young child, for example, I simply live in the midst of my parents' way of life and come to share in it; later I discover what interests I have as a member of this family by reflecting on how I have lived my life with my parents. Consensual associations, too, such as friendships, develop through a series of choices and events the full implications of which, in terms of the friends' collective interests, are rarely appreciated as the relationship unfolds. Friends first live all or part of their lives together and then come to recognize fully what (some of) their aims and interests are by reflecting on what they have done. In addition, the collective interests of personal relations include an interest in the preservation or enhancement of the relationship itself.

Within this shared life, the members of a personal relation remain oriented primarily toward each other in his or her own right. Preoccupation with the demands of friendship is often a sign that the relationship is in danger of dissolving or on the verge of some major transformation, and it may prevent one from responding appropriately to the demands of a particular friend.[16]

16

Love and Friendship

"Tell me, you who know, what is this thing, love?" asks Cherubino in Mozart's *Marriage of Figaro*. The question is incapable of any fully satisfactory answer as long as it implies that there is but a single entity. First, the objects of love are enormously varied. Second, even if we restrict ourselves to the love that is directly targeted on a particular person and set aside the love of inanimate objects, of God, of humanity in general, and so on, there is more than one kind of personal love. There is the love of a parent for a child, of a sibling for a sibling, of a friend for a friend, of a lover for a lover. All of these have much in common, but there are also crucial differences relating to the appropriateness of sexual relations between the parties involved, the centrality of personal choice in the love, and the extent of equality in status and power of the interacting individuals. Friendship in particular is neither necessary nor sufficient for love, but in close friendships the depth of concern and care amounts to love, and the love of friends, unlike parental love, is a love that insists on equality and does not preclude sexuality. As well, some kinds of personal love are more constrained by circumstances than are others. Friendship, we say, is an expression of choice,[1] but we do not say this about the love of children for their parents or the love of a mother for her offspring.

In order to clarify the focus of my concerns in this and subsequent chapters, I begin with Platonic love. On some accounts,[2]

Plato in the *Symposium* describes a process of idealization in which love seeks release from human finitude through progressive abstraction from particular instances of beauty, culminating in the lover's losing sight of these instances altogether. Passionate attachment to an individual, on this reading of Plato, is not a thing of intrinsic value and beauty at all, not contributory to the good life but destructive of it. It is only a way station toward the good, properly valued only as a step in the lover's ascent from attachment to beautiful people and things, which come to be seen as replaceable, as valuable not in themselves but as instances of the universal, to absorption in the universal itself. As Irving Singer observes of Plato's strictures on emotional attachment to an individual, "no search for *natural* goods could possibly satisfy the definition of love. That requires a highly intellectual, purely rational, nonsensuous striving for a transcendent insight, a love of wisdom which may have little or no relation to a love of life."[3] In the *Symposium* Plato does indeed allow that the erotic impulse is necessary even to motivate the philosopher's attachment to the world of Forms; but in that dialogue the proper development of the impulse consists in the perfection of one's rational nature by detachment from "the pollutions of mortality, and all the colors and vanities of human life."[4] From the transcendent standpoint that the trained lover of beauty attains, a particular person will be seen as nothing more than a congeries of accidental properties thrown together by nature and chance, whose beauty is exactly the same in quality as the beauty of other particular persons or laws or institutions or sciences and differs from it only with respect to contingent spatio-temporal location and amount. All beautiful persons and things are only instances of beauty, swallowed up in a vast homogeneous "sea of beauty" (p. 353).[5]

Thus understood, the Platonic lover of the *Symposium* turns away from responsive intercourse with persons in their particularity: as he sees them, they are just so many pieces of the Form. He devotes himself to "the contemplation of beauty absolute" (p. 354) and leaves no room in his life for ongoing devotion to individuals.[6] In so doing, we might further suppose Plato to be suggesting, the lover manages to avoid the problems that plague our earthly loves.[7] Unlike our particular loves, the contemplative love for all beauty is directed toward an unvarying object, "without diminution and without increase, or any change" (ibid.), and so the activity itself is stable. Beauty is also pure, "not fair in one point of view and foul in another" (ibid.), whereas particular individuals have uglinesses and faults that render them unsuitable as objects of wholehearted devotion. Beauty fully satisfies the lover's longing for possession of the object of love: there is no danger of rejection or frustration or loss as there is with our mundane loves, for beauty is always available and its presence is not dependent on factors over which the lover has little or no control. Moreover, the lover of beauty rises above the deeply troubling conflicts of value that our particular attachments invite. There will be no agonizing choices of the sort E. M. Forster described, between love of friend and love of country.[8]

There is always, with the love of particular persons, the risk of alteration and conflict with other plans and commitments, the possibility of estrangement and misplaced affections. Yet the above vision of the best human life, as one in which the intellect dissociates itself from intense love for particular persons and rises to a more general appreciation of beauty, omits something deeply important to ordinary human beings. In treating the person as a locus of valuable properties and taking the object of love to be these repeatable properties, rather than (to quote Gregory Vlastos) "the individual in the uniqueness and integrity of his or her individuality,"[9] something fundamental to our experience of love is missed. Plato's conception of the best life for humans, on the present account, is not derived from an examination of the peculiarities of our complex nature and the way of life conditioned by it, but is modeled after divine activity. From this transcendent point of view, ordinary personal love ultimately has nothing to recommend it. By contrast, a theory of love for human beings specifically will not denigrate the physical and emotional side of humans, and will not regard absolute beauty alone as the proper object of love, whose instantiation in an individual's life is but an unfortunate entanglement. It will defend the worth of close and intimate relationships with particular persons and tell us why it is good to give them a prominent place in our lives.

Romantic love is one type of personal love much celebrated in the contemporary West, looked for and longed for by many. There is, however, much disagreement among theorists concerning its definition, and this has led to significant disagreement about its value. According to Morton Hunt, there are four "articles of faith in [our society's] credo of romanticism."[10] First, for each person, there is some "Mr. Right" or "Ms. Right" out there in the world waiting to be found, and he or she is the only one in the world for that person. Second, love is a kind of superior force that renders those who are caught in its grasp helpless. Generally people are "swept off their feet" by love, unsuspecting of and unprepared for its sudden attack. Third, love is blind to the imperfections of the beloved and will not admit them even if they are pointed out. And finally, love can conquer all obstacles, such as those erected by differences in social class, religion, or race, and by adversity of all sorts.

It would not be fair to romantic love, however, to tie it necessarily to these tenets. Romantic love, if it is a form of personal love, has a particularistic focus; that is, we love a particular person and not some property or properties that person happens to possess or some role or office that person happens to fill. Hence, in personal love the loved one is not replaceable: even when we lose a loved one and come to love another, it is not accurate to think of the new as replacing the old. It is an additional condition, not required of romantic love, that the one who loves believe that he or she could never have truly loved anyone other than the particular person now loved and that he or she has been drawn to this person by some kind of preexisting affinity. Regarding the second tenet, it confuses the beginning of the emotional process of love with love itself, and defenders of romantic love may be well aware of the difference. The initial phase of romantic love is "falling in love," a process that, as Robert Brown describes it,

> resembles the onset of sexual desire and hunger in not requiring the agent to hold any specific beliefs about the person or thing except that he or she or it is a fitting object of the agent's desire. . . . The agent becomes a patient, and is overcome by desire for the object: that is, does not critically examine, and intervene in, the process of seeking it. The process is nonrational.[11]

Persons who come together by falling in love do not always come to love each other or succeed in establishing a love relationship; the failure to appreciate this can have quite destructive consequences for the parties involved. Hunt's third tenet is also just a defining feature of a particular conception of romantic love. It is not necessary for romantic love that lovers fail to recognize faults in each other, or that they be indiscriminately enthusiastic about every facet of each other's personalities.

These last remarks bring us to one type of fraudulent love: love that excessively idealizes the beloved. The lover sees the beloved as being, potentially if not actually, ideal, the very embodiment of perfection. Here the lover does not really love another person but rather some imaginary creation based on, but usually bearing scant resemblance to, the flesh-and-blood person he or she appears to love. William Hazlitt, the literary critic, is a case in point. Hunt gives the following account:

> In 1820, when [Hazlitt] was forty-two and separated from his wife, he fell in love with his landlord's twenty-year-old daughter, a pretty, uncommunicative, uneducated girl. Each morning when she brought up his breakfast, Hazlitt would speak extravagantly and at length of his love for her, uttering innumerable statements like this: "Ah! enchanting little trembler! You are an angel, and I will spend my life, if you will let me, in paying you the homage that my heart feels toward you." He attributed to her every virtue, every beauty, every uplifting influence, and assured her that she could, if she would, remake his life for him. . . . Hazlitt supplied her with all the qualities he wanted her to have. . . . His friends were not so ecstatic. . . . Benjamin Haydon . . . considered her nothing but a "lodging-house hussy" who would be the death of Hazlitt, and he wrote to a mutual friend: "He is really downright in love with an ideal perfection which has no existence but in his own head." (p. 311)

Hazlitt was mistaken in attributing to the landlord's daughter the ideal attributes he did, but it was not just because he misunderstood the sort of person she was that he did not love her. (Love does not require that we have only true beliefs about the persons we love.) It was rather because he did not "let himself" see her as she really was: prompted by some deep-seated emotional need to see her as an ideal woman, he misinterpreted data and overlooked evidence that, in the absence of the need, could easily have been recognized to count against her perfection, and so he could believe that she had "every virtue, every beauty, every uplifting influence." Hazlitt overvalued the landlord's daughter and willfully persisted in his erroneous belief in the face of good grounds for thinking that she was not really extraordinary. He was not open to testing his picture of his beloved against the reality of her qualities and actions and to revising his expectations of her and of their relationship accordingly.

Overvaluation of the beloved need not be so radically mistaken as Hazlitt's. The lover might selectively focus on certain qualities of the beloved, those that support his or her favorable impression of the other, and fail to focus on evidence about the beloved that counts against it. Further, the overvaluation or excessive idealization that only mimics love should not be confused with the sort of exaggeration of the loved one's virtues that those who love commonly indulge in. The mother who says of her child, "my boy is the most wonderful child in the world," or the husband who boasts, "I have the best, most beautiful wife one can possibly have," is not necessarily exhibiting bad judgment or being undiscriminating. (Of course, in some circumstances these boasts might also reflect self-deception.) They might not lack the ability to make sound appraisals of their loved ones, if called upon to do so. And despite the comparative language that is used, such extravagant claims typically signify quite the opposite, namely, that the one who loves is not basing his or her love on a comparison between the qualities possessed by the loved one and others. Any standards in terms of which the one who loves assesses the loved one's qualities are such as to be satisfiable by the loved one alone, or what amounts to the same thing, objective measurement of the loved one's qualities is not what the one who loves is engaged in.[12]

Hazlitt's willful folly is an example of infatuation. Before stating how I understand this phenomenon, I want to mention two other views about it that I believe are promising. According to one, what we might call "being in love with love" is a state of readiness for infatuation. In this state, *what* the object is to which a person will become attached is of less importance than that there should be one to match the state; and when an infatuation develops, to quote D. W. Hamlyn, "the object is, at it were, found or invented for the state rather than the other way around."[13] Gabriele Taylor offers a more elaborate characterization, drawing on a distinction between two sorts of wants.[14] One sort requires the agent to evaluate favorably what the agent wants: "his wanting *a* is based on the thought that *a* is of some value to do or have" (p. 155). Some of the wants of the loving person are of this sort. With the other sort of want, the agent

> may not evaluate *a* at all; or he may think that no value or even that a dis-value attaches to doing or having *a;* and finally he may think it worth while to do or have *a,* but if so then not because *a* as such is worth doing or having, but because he thinks it worth while to satisfy his desires, either on this occasion or as a general policy. (p. 155)

These are the wants of the infatuated person. Taylor also admits that this distinction is "a highly theoretical one" (p. 155), in part because the two sorts of wants exist together and one often turns into the other.

Taylor claims that infatuation "is very suitably linked with a type of desire which may lead a man to act against his better judgment" (p. 156); a person in this situation is foolishly infatuated because of a weak will. But the infatuated person, according to Taylor, cannot be moved by desires that are based on the thought that *a* as such is worth doing or having. Yet if an analysis of infatuation is to conform to our view of it "as a state which we do not even attempt to link with anything that is accessible to rational . . . evaluation" (p. 154), as Taylor believes her analysis does, then it is arbitrary not to allow the infatuated person to have such desires. For even if a person's wants are based on the thought that it is worthwhile, for example, to be with and cherish another, that person's positive evaluations might be formed capriciously or irresponsibly and the individual might not be able to scrutinize the wants based on such evaluations critically. The distinction between the loving person and the infatuated person, in my view, is not a distinction among their wants according to the content of these wants (this is Taylor's view as well); nor is love distinguished from infatuation in terms of the presence or absence of favorable evaluation (this is not Taylor's view). Rather, what distinguishes them is the presence or absence of the ability to exercise rational control with respect to one's wants, on the level of judgment or action or both. Favorable evaluation is thus compatible with infatuation because such evaluation does not necessarily reflect sound judgment. According to the first view about infatuation

(Hamlyn's), the infatuated person directs his or her attention to or at someone, but is not really focused on that person. Defining infatuation in terms of the inability to make sound appraisals of what one wants, or the inability to put one's considered judgment into practice, helps make sense of the suggestion that the identity of the object is not of primary importance in infatuation.

A wanton, who either does not assess desires or gives no serious consideration to assessments, lacks commitments and so cannot be a person of integrity. A person who does not at all evaluate desires to benefit and cherish another, or to keep company and communicate with another, is also not a loving person, even though that person wants the same sorts of things that people who love want. (This is one type of infatuated person.) If these desires are based on the thought that benefiting, keeping company, and so on, are worth doing, but the individual is not able to critically reflect on these desires, then this is still not a loving person. (This is another type of infatuated person.) Though the individual thinks that benefiting, keeping company, and so on, are of some value, and wants to do these things because he or she thinks this, this individual's positive evaluations have no implications beyond the present occasion because this person is not guided by considered evaluation. By contrast, the wants involved in love are based on favorable evaluations that the individual must act on with some consistency. We do not require consistency of infatuation, whether or not the desires involved in it are based on the thought that benefiting, keeping company, and so on, are worth doing—indeed, it is a commonplace that infatuations often follow one another in rapid succession or that an infatuation may come to an end as a result of some capricious change of mind or circumstance. Like infatuation, genuine love can cease (contrary to the suggestion of some that if x's emotion toward y ceases, x never really loved y[15]); but unlike infatuations, we cannot abandon our loves merely for a whim.

I now want to turn to sexual intimacy and sexual love. Arguably, the Platonic lover, who aspires to a position of understanding that transcends empirical contingencies in general and any sort of personal intimacy, need not eschew sexuality. Lovemaking, if indiscriminate, might help liberate him from the particular.[16] Another sort of lover might oppose sexuality because he or she cherishes personal love. This person may believe that sexuality interferes with other elements of a close relationship with another individual, such as respect and tenderness, and that because personal love is a thing worth preserving and its value is so easily corrupted by sexuality, sexual feelings must be repressed and sexual activity renounced. But this renunciation of sexuality for the sake of the deep and lasting values of personal love may reflect an impoverished view of human sexuality. It may be rooted in the misconception that human sexual appetite is only some blind animal force reaching out for its objects without discrimination or selectivity, or more plausibly in the still erroneous view that sexual desire is simply the desire for pleasurable bodily contact with any person who happens to have certain physical characteristics one finds attractive. Perhaps the thought is that whereas personal love has a particularistic orientation, sexual desire is only for sexually arousing physical contact with anyone indifferently or with any presentable specimen of a physical type. Either way, sexuality is not focused on the particular person, not responsive to another in his or her particularity. And assuming that sexual feelings must be held in check or they will lead to a thoroughgoing depersonalization of the other, the specialness of the loved one can only be preserved if sexuality is kept out of the relationship with him or her.

Human sexual desire is not merely desire for contact with some *body* or with anyone who has specific kinds of physical features. It is considerably more complicated than this. Persons sometimes find specific features to be sexually stimulating only in those with whom they have a close and prolonged relationship. Perhaps some physical attribute of the person I love is sexually appealing to me precisely because I love this person and not because it is a feature to which I am generally attracted.[17] Sexuality also derives much of its deep psychological significance for us from its connection with love, from the fact that sexual intimacy can be an expression and consummation of a love relationship. What makes sexual contact an expression of love is the context of caring within which this contact takes place. The quality of sexual intimacy is altered by the knowledge that it is being shared with someone one cares deeply about because one cares deeply, even if outwardly the sexual acts look a lot like sexual acts in other sorts of contexts. Further, it is a commonplace that among persons whose love relationship includes sexual intimacy, lovemaking is enjoyable in large part because it is continuous with other (nonsexual) ways they have of conveying their feelings of love and tenderness for and to one another.

Nothing said so far supports the claim that sexual intimacy should be reserved to and shared with only those for whom we have very great affection; or that a love relationship cannot survive if one (or both) of the parties to it regularly engages in sexual activity outside the relationship and they know this; or that we cannot at the same time have multiple sex-partners who are also love-partners. For most people in our culture, being sexually intimate with another expresses love for that person only if the sexual behaviors one allows the other person, or shares with that person, are not allowed or shared with others. Love or affection is measured by the exclusivity of the sexual relation. As well, in most cases, the loved one will feel betrayed and inadequate if he or she finds out that his or her partner has been sexually intimate with another; even if the person does not find out, the unfaithful partner will be guilt-ridden and will withdraw emotionally from the relationship. But some advocates of sexual liberation maintain that the demand for sexual exclusivity as proof of sexual love is merely a product of our possessive, market-oriented culture, and that we can and should be socialized differently. It is not an a priori truth that nonexclusivity breeds jealousy; in a society that no longer operated on the assumption that the special delights of a sexual love relationship can only be experienced with the context of a sexually exclusive relationship, our emotional lives would be richer. Naturally, even in this case there would still be a limit on the number of sexual love relationships a person could have at a given time. But this would be because love relationships of any kind make tremendous emotional and psychological demands of us, and not because of stifling social conventions.

The issues raised by this position are surely worth exploring in detail and with care, but I shall not take them up here. Instead I want to say something more about sexual love itself, apart from whatever links it might have with feelings of exclusivity and possession.

Sexual relationships or encounters that fail to comply with the Kantian principle never to use other persons as mere means, but always at the same time as ends in themselves, do not express love. One person uses another sexually as a mere means when acting in ways that make consent to or dissent from the sexual contact impossible. Sexual coercion (e.g., rape and other forms of sexual assault) and deception (e.g., seduction and breach of promise) preclude genuine consent and are obvious ways of violating Kant's principle. The Kantian notion of treating others as persons involves more than this, however. There is also a positive requirement to treat others as ends in themselves, and to do this we must act on maxims of sharing and furthering their ends. When we undercut another's pursuit of ends through manipulation, or paternalistically impose our conception of another person's interests on a person with ends of his or her own, we fail to share that person's ends. Coercion and deception might be absent, but we have nevertheless failed to respect that person's ends. Moreover, intimate relations lend themselves especially easily to manipulative and paternalistic failures of respect, because intimates develop deep dependencies on and reveal their points of vulnerability to one another, and because they identify so closely with one another. When sexual intimacy is part of the relationship, the manipulator might use it to strengthen a hold over a victim, making it even more difficult for an individual not to succumb to manipulation of his or her dependency and vulnerability.

Lack of respect entails lack of love (sexual or otherwise), but lack of love does not entail lack of respect. Failures of love can occur, Onora O'Neill notes, "when the other's ends are indeed respected, and he or she is left the "space" in which to pursue them, yet no positive encouragement, assistance, or support for their pursuit is given."[18] By giving those we love encouragement and support, we do not just share their ends by taking them into account: we share their ends by actively promoting them. (How this is to be done cannot be determined in abstraction from the particular character, abilities and weaknesses, interests and desires of the person we love and the particular history we have with him or her.) Thus, physical intimacy does not express love merely because the lover is respectful of the sex-partner's ends: he or she must also be engaged in furthering the partner's ends. Sexual intimacy frequently serves to confirm and sustain a relationship that is supportive of the particular partner's ends generally, and it is only when it does so that we may properly speak of a relationship of sexual *love*.

Romantic love is a certain kind of love that is intimately tied to sexuality: there is, if not actual sexual contact, at least a prolonged, active, and intense desire for sexual relations. In the case of parental love, to which I turn next, whatever sexual feelings may exist must be repressed and denied. What takes place in a romantic love relationship between two adults is not appropriate, and is even perverse, in a love relationship between a parent and his or her child. Yet romantic love and purely parental love have elements in common with each other, as well as with other forms of personal love.

Parents usually feel an unconditional love for their children. They love their children as soon as they are born and delight in their very existence, and there is no type of personal love that is less affected than is parental love by changes in the loved one's qualities. (Parental love is the model of love that alters not when it alteration finds.) What explains this love? According to Aristotle, parents have a special concern for their own children in part for the same reason that craftsmen have a preferential attitude toward their products:

> The producer is fond of the product, because he loves his own being. And this is natural, since what he is potentially is what the product indicates in actualization.[19]

Parents are causally responsible for their children's being and love their children as the actualization of their own being. However, children are not only products of their parents, as the poem is the product of the poet, but products that share the *same* being as their parents (parent and child both being human). A parent loves a child as being *of* the parent, or as "a sort of other himself" (1161b28), loves the child not only because the parent has made the child, but also because the creature he or she has made has the same being as the parent.[20]

Hegel advances our understanding of parental love beyond what we learn from Aristotle. Aristotle relates parental love to self-love: "a parent loves his children as [he loves] himself" (1161b27). Hegel focuses instead on the connection between parental love and the mutual love of parents:

> In substance marriage is a unity, though only a unity of inwardness of disposition; in outward existence, however, the unity is sundered in the

two parties. It is only in the children that the unity itself exists externally, objectively, and explicitly as a unity, because the parents love the
children as their love, as the embodiment of their own substance.[21]

On this sort of account (the specific reference to marriage is not
essential), children are valued as tangible expressions of the love
that parents have for one another, and also as new bonds of love
linking the parents more tightly to each other. What matters to
many parents is not just that they have a son or daughter—
someone on whom they can shower affection, or who will support
them in their old age, or who will extend the blood line or carry on
the family name, and the like—but crucially that this child is *theirs,*
in the sense that he or she is a product of their commitment to and
concern for one another. Indeed, having a child with another person with whom one intends to raise it is widely regarded as one of
the most serious steps that adults can take to show how much they
care about each other. (Of course, adopting a child, no less than
having one, can be an outgrowth of the love parents have for one
another.)

Parental love can thus arise from a combination of factors. Consider next the character of this love. Extreme parental overprotec-
tion or overindulgence of children, well-intentioned though it
might be, is a failure of parental love. The main outcome of over-
protectiveness is the child's failure to become self-sufficient and to
take responsibility for his or her actions. When so much is done for
children and they are hedged about by so many protections, they
are deprived of the opportunity of learning to fend for themselves
and they are taught to depend on other persons to help them with
their tasks and to assist them with their difficulties. It is these
others who are to be responsible for their actions, opinions,
thoughts, and achievements, not the children themselves. Overindulgence has similar consequences. Overindulgent parents, who
may also be overprotective, are unable to refuse the demands and
requests of their children and repeatedly give in to their importuni-
ties. These children become tyrannical in forcing compliance to
their wishes from their parents and shirk responsibility in their
constant pursuit of self-gratification. Because both parental over-
protectiveness and overindulgence undermine development of children's capacities for autonomous action, put obstacles in the way

of their becoming adults who can lead lives that do not require the continued attendance of others, they only masquerade as parental love. (Perhaps someone will want to say that in these cases children are loved badly or too much, rather than not at all. I have described these cases differently: certain modes of childrearing exhibit a fundamental lack of respect, and love is incompatible with this. But I do not want to insist on this formulation.)

Loving parents, on the other hand, encourage their children's autonomous and independent strivings. They show pleasure at their successes in growing from dependents into self-reliant adults and praise them for their achievements. Mistakes and failures due to lack of knowledge and other developmental deficiencies are patiently accepted by such parents as an integral part of learning, and they sympathize with their children's struggles to master the tasks of growing up. And when restraint and discipline are used, as they must sometimes be, children of loving parents retain their self-esteem and are not made to feel that their parents' love for them is dependent on their conformity to their parents' wishes.

The way parents relate to their *grown* children can show a lack of love even if the way they were treated while young did not, and there is a special explanation for this having to do with the particular nature of the parent–child relationship. Parents generally, even those who were not overprotective or overindulgent of their children as they were growing up, often have difficulty dealing with adult children without images of the child's former dependency imposing themselves. Parents do not meet their children for the first time as fully formed adults. The child grows to adulthood under the influence of parents who see themselves as authorities on the child, experts on the child's development and temperament. Long before the adult emerges and the child takes charge of his or her own life, the discerning parent will have foreseen the options that are open to the child, given that child's natural talents and temperamental propensities. Further, it is rare that parents do not at least occasionally continue to think of themselves as experts about their children even after their children have reached adulthood. The image of the young, unformed child, and memories of the role the parents played in their offspring's development, remain and color the parents' present perceptions of the adult the child has become. In the extreme case, if the parent is blinded from seeing and appreciating who the child is as an adult and fails to accord the child's ends and decisions an equal status with his or her own, then the parent's professions of parental love are spurious: the character of the love has not changed to reflect fundamental changes in the object of this love.[22]

As developmental psychologists tell us, the presence or absence of parental love has a major bearing on the child's self-esteem and self-love, as well as on the capacity to form loving attachments to other particular persons in adulthood. According to Elizabeth Newson, the child "*needs* to perceive itself as especially valuable to somebody: 'needs to know that to someone it matters more than other children; that someone will go to unreasonable lengths, not just reasonable ones, for its sake'."[23] This need is met by parental love, whose defining characteristic is its special "*partiality* for the individual child," whereas the best that community or institutional care can offer the child is fair and even-handed treatment. When children realize that they are the object of parental love, that they are uniquely precious to those who rear them, they acquire a sense of their own value as individuals and respond to their parents with love and trust because they connect the parents with their sense of their own worth. The children's capacity for love is activated and, equipped with a basic trust and sustained by self-love, they have a solid psychological foundation on which to build intimate relations of love and trust with persons outside the family. On the other hand, when children are not made to feel that they are loved by their parents or parent-surrogates as irreplaceable persons, that they are the objects of intense personal concern on the part of those who take care of them, they will have an enormous handicap to overcome if they are to have any close personal loves in their lives.

The final sort of personal love I want to discuss is the love of friends: the deepest kind of friendship or, as we commonly say, friendship that is more than *just* friendship. Aristotle, whose writings on friendship are among the richest and most sugggestive on this topic, distinguishes between three kinds of friendship: pleasure-friendship, which is based on shared pleasure, utility-friendship, based on mutual usefulness, and virtue-friendship. It is only virtue-friendship, however, that Aristotle takes to be genuine friendship:

Those who love each other for utility love the other not in himself, but in so far as they gain some good for themselves from him. The same is true of those who love for pleasure; for they like a witty person not because of his character, but because he is pleasant to themselves.[24]

True friends love each other in themselves, and unlike those who love others for the good they can do them or the pleasure they can give them, those who love others for their virtue love them in this way. For those who befriend others for their virtue are befriending them for traits that are central to their character, and one's identity is largely a matter of one's character. But if, in relationships based on pleasure or utility, the parties wish each other well and act in the interests of the other's good, for the other's sake, then such relationships may be considered friendships of a sort. And in fact, associating with people because they are pleasant or useful to me is no bar to my also wishing them well and doing them good for their own sake, rather than only as a means to my own good. Still, my well-wishing and well-doing will be more restricted in these relationships than in virtue-friendships because above all I do not want the others to stop being a source of pleasure or utility to me, and so I will not seek to promote their good in ways that could jeopardize their continuing to be pleasurable or useful and will stop befriending them if they lose those features that make them pleasurable or useful.[25] By contrast, virtue-friends do not make the promotion of their own self-interest a condition of the friendship and do not impose narrow self-regarding limits on their well-wishing and well-doing.

Commentators on Aristotle disagree on whether his account of friendship does violence to the intuition that in true friendship the object of love is a person in his or her individuality, and thus on whether he actually understands friendship the way we do. Gregory Vlastos[26], and following him Julia Annas[27] and Ferdinand Schoeman,[28] claim that a major weakness of Aristotle's analysis of friendship is its conflation of loving someone in or for him or herself with admiring that person's qualities:

[Aristotle's] intuition takes him as far as seeing that (a) *disinterested affection for the person* we love . . . must be built into love at its best, but not as far as sorting this out from (b) *appreciation of the excellences instantiated by that person.* (Vlastos, p. 33 n. 100)

Vlastos' criticism of Aristotle seems to be, in part, that if we con-
centrate on the excellences we lose sight of the individual with
these qualities: if one loves a friend for the friend's virtue, then
since one virtuous person is, qua virtuous person, like another,
friends must be, as it were, fungible commodities. One can simply
replace a virtuous friend with some other equally virtuous person.
But in a true friendship, as we understand it, my friend is not just
someone who is at best only irreplaceable because I have not yet
become acquainted with anybody who shares that friend's admirable properties.

Vlastos thinks that Aristotle "does not repudiate—does not
even notice . . . 'the cardinal flaw' in Platonic love."[29] For both
Aristotle and Plato, the best kind of love focuses on what is essential in an individual, either as an end in itself or as a stage in an
ascent to the ultimate object of love, and what is essential in an
individual are certain qualities that can be abstracted from their
mode of expression in a particular life. Moreover, though Aristotle
does not make this point, if these features are reinstantiated in
other individuals, then one has just as much reason to love them as
the original object of love. But this lumping together of Plato and
Aristotle overlooks at least two important points. First, Aristotle
rejects Plato's transcendental metaphysics, according to which particulars are only instantiations of abstract, preexisting qualities,
and his conception of ethics as a deductive science primarily concerned with universals. Second, an account of genuine friendship
that renders friends interchangeable and replaceable violates a
psychological condition of attachment that Aristotle himself sets
out in *Politics,* book II. Here Aristotle formulates two psychological principles in the context of arguing against Plato's radical claim
in *Republic* V that political harmony and unity require the aboli-
tion of the family:

> There are two things above all that make persons love and care: They
> are a sense that something is one's very own or proper to oneself and a
> sense that that object is all one has, i.e. it must do. (1262a8)

It is not an essential part of pleasure or utility friendships that the
friend be unique or irreplaceable for me. Instrumental friendship is
compatible with replaceability of the friend: the loss of an old

friend might for the most part be made up by my acquiring a new one who serves my needs or ends. But if pleasure and utility friends do not necessarily love and care about each other, for the particular persons they are, true friends, those who befriend each other for their virtue, do. Here the object of attachment is all one has, which implies that he or she is not substitutable[30]; and the loss of an old friend is a distinct loss that cannot be made up, the gain of a new one a distinct gain.

Aristotle's emphasis on the relational and historical character of friendship also suggests an argument that true friends, or perhaps more accurately, friendships, are not easily replaceable. "Good-will," Aristotle observes, "would seem to be a feature of friendship, but still it is not friendship." Goodwill is only "inactive friendship," and "when it lasts some time and they [the friends] grow accustomed to each other, it becomes friendship" (*Nicomachean Ethics,* 1166b30, 1167a12). The love of friends develops through long association and a history of shared activities, and their involvements have a history of understandings that contribute to each friend's perception of present interactions. Though it may be possible for other relationships to have the same history or career as theirs, this possibility need not seriously concern us. Since our love for our friends is based in part on our history together and this history is practically unrepeatable, the replaceability and interchangeability of friends is (as a matter of contingent fact) ruled out. Perhaps before forming a friendship with either *B* or *C*, *A* will think that since *B* and *C* are equally virtuous, there is an equally good reason to befriend either. But this is very different from saying that the friendship *A* forms with *B* is replaceable by a friendship with *C*.[31]

For Aristotle, the love of the best sort of friends presupposes a deeply shared conception of human value, of what is ultimately good in living. Persons who come together as true friends share virtue as an overall end, and each esteems the other for the admirable qualities the other possesses. In maintaining that the love of true friends is the love of persons similar in character, Aristotle does not commit himself to the view that true friends must express their common commitment to virtue in exactly the same ways. Indeed, if true friends had to be exactly similar, had to express the particular virtues to the same degree and in the same manner, then it is hard to see how they could learn from each other and grow in the relationship, as Aristotle insists they do:

> The friendship of decent people is decent, and increases the more often they meet. And they seem to become still better from their activities and their mutual correction. (*Nicomachean Ethics,* 1172a10–13)

In addition, Aristotle's picture of true friendship does not entail that friends must approve of or admire all the qualities the other exemplifies. Certain qualities might not be admired, but if they are not central to making one the kind of person one is, their presence would not undermine the basic unity of purpose that genuine friendship requires. At a deep level there could still be a general agreement about ends and pursuits, and a consensus about how and what sort of life to live together, even though one finds fault with some of one's friend's qualities and behavior. Only when this basis of common virtue is absent, as when a once-virtuous friend of a virtuous person becomes incurably vicious (see *Nicomachean Ethics* 1165b12–23), is true friendship impossible.

Aristotle's account of friendship agrees with much that we want to say about friendship. In particular, a good case can be made that it does not conflict with our pretheoretic understanding of friendship in the way that Vlastos would have us believe. Friendship goes beyond goodwill in that it arises in specific contexts and with specific persons over long periods of time, persons who, because of their embeddedness in relationships with particular histories, are not easily substituted by others. Aristotle also tells us, what we already believe, that true friends are not primarily concerned with their own pleasure or advantage, but extend care to each other simply because it appears to benefit the recipient. I wish my friend well not for my own sake but for my friend's. (Mutual disinterested well-wishing is not sufficient for friendship, however:

> Many a one has goodwill to people whom he has not seen but supposes to be decent or useful, and one of these might have the same goodwill towards him. These people, then, apparently have goodwill to each other, but how could we call them friends when they are unaware of their attitude to each other? [*Nicomachean Ethics* 1156a1–4])

Again, that true friends have a common commitment to virtue does not preclude their recognizing and living with certain short-comings in each other, nor does it mean that their values are such that they will never disagree about what would be best to do in specific cases. True friends do not have to agree on all things, only on what matters most, namely, their broad conceptions of living well. And finally, friendship is an essential part of Aristotle's conception of the good life for human beings, having both instrumental and intrinsic value.[32]

Disinterested care is a defining feature of all personal love, not just friendly love. I can care disinterestedly about a particular person, however, without loving him or her; even with respect to those friends on whom we bestow disinterested care, we frequently distinguish between those we love and those we do not. Not all friendships exist on the same level of caring and commitment. At the lowest level, friendship fades into acquaintanceship; above this, some friendships are closer than others, are more affectionate than others, involve deeper and stronger concern and commitment than others, a greater willingness to go out of one's way to help, and so forth. Aristotle claims that true friends spend their lives together, that they "live together and share conversation and thought" (*Nicomachean Ethics* 1170b11), and lives may intermingle to greater or lesser degrees. It is usually only the especially deep and intimate friendship of an essentially noninstrumental nature that is said to be a kind of love.

Living together is a requirement of friendly love but not of all personal love. I can love another whose tastes, opinions, and values are so dissimilar from or uncomplementary to my own that rewarding companionship with him or her is impossible, and I may not wish to share the most intimate and important parts of my life with that other. Perhaps this is what is sometimes meant by the claim that I can love someone I do not like: I can love someone even though I do not desire to unite my daily activities with that person's, even though I do not want us to pursue many of our most intimate activities together. Another feature of friendly love, but not of all personal love (consider parental love, for example), is that the loved one is not under the authority of the one who loves.[33] This does not mean that friends do not influence one another, for surely they do. And while friends are not entitled to deference from one another, they may have wide latitude to influence or control the other's behavior for his or her own good. Expressions of concern that would be overly intrusive or the mark of a busybody in public contexts might not be such in a particular friendship, because one friend has made it clear to the other during the course of their relationship that such concern is welcome or even expected.

It might be objected at this point that friendship, no matter how deep and intimate it may be, cannot properly speaking be a kind of *love:* love is somehow always more than friendship, more even than the best and closest friendship. Love involves a complete union with or symbiotic attachment to another person in which one has no clear sense of a self separate from the other and in which one lives through the other. In friendship, by contrast, and Aristotle insists on this as well, the boundaries of the self are expanded to include the other without negating the separateness of those who come together as friends. Thus the picture of love that explains the exclusion of friendship is one in which love cancels out what friendship preserves and indeed what friendship thrives on. But this conception of love is plainly not unproblematic. Some degree of critical detachment from the desires of the person I love is compatible with the deepest commitment to that person's well-being. Indeed, love requires that I seek the good for the one I love, but if I so closely identify with someone that I lose a sense of my otherness from that person, and that person is not aware of what is good for him or her, how can I be in a position to help him or her achieve it?[34] In my view, personal love does extend and redefine the boundaries of the self. The person who is loved becomes psychologically part of the identity of the person who loves, and the latter arranges his or her life with the other's flourishing in mind. This does not mean, however, that the one who loves no longer has any individual identity or that his or her sole identity is as part of a new union with the loved one.

It is not only the flourishing of the irreplaceable other person that the parties to a friendship value: they also value the friendship itself, their association, the life they jointly pursue (or their living of this life).[35] Friends often try to maintain the integrity of their relationship against changes in residence, social circumstances, and other factors external to the relationship.[36] Because the relationship matters to them, they have a higher tolerance for irritations and annoyances than do those who are not close, and they take steps to keep the relationship from breaking down when it is threatened from without and within. They might also move to broaden their friendship by including more parts of their lives within it or to deepen their friendship by becoming more intimate with each other. Though the primary concern of friends is the good of the other for his or her own sake, and this is distinct from concern for the friendship itself, it is clearly possible to be motivated by both considerations. I may do something both out of care for my friend and to maintain or strengthen the bond between us. Indeed, since the relationship between us is also a constituent of my friend's good, and I know this, concern for the friendship cannot be entirely separated from concern for the friend. But sometimes the friend may be faced with a choice: for the sake of a friend, one may have to risk or even end the friendship.

In one sort of case, my friend is engaged in a course of action to which he is committed but that, in my view, seriously threatens his long-term welfare and most important interests. I will not make an issue of what I regard as only minor failings in my friend, but this is clearly different. My friend, I know further, does not take criticism easily, as least with respect to something that he is so invested in, and he would not welcome my interference. Yet for his sake I cannot stand by idly, even though I realize that I am inviting his anger and risking a rupture in our relationship by letting him know how deeply disturbing his project is to me. Another sort of case is illustrated by an episode in Dickens' *Nicholas Nickelby*.[37] Ralph, the uncle of Nicholas and his sister Kate, has made it a condition of her receiving an inheritance that Nicholas leave her. Without the uncle's inheritance, Kate faces a life of poverty; but she cannot get the inheritance unless Nicholas ends his relationship with her, a relationship of deep and loving friendship. Nicholas chooses Kate's welfare over the continuance of their companionship:

> "You will be helped when I am away," replied Nicholas hurriedly. "I am no help to you, no protector; I should bring you nothing but sorrow, and want, and suffering. My own mother sees it, and her fondness and fears for you, point to the course that I should take. . . . Do not keep me here, but let me go at once. There. Dear girl—dear girl."

Nicholas leaves, convinced that he has acted for the best, but depressed, too, that he is now "so entirely alone in the world . . . separated from the only persons he loved."

Though friends are mainly concerned about each other, not their relationship, the character of the relationship over time can undermine this primary concern. Cynics like La Rochefoucauld are wrong to claim that friendship is nothing but the exchange of material and psychological benefits for individual profit: "What men call friendship is just an arrangement for mutual gain and an exchange of favors; in short, a business where self-interest always sets out to obtain something."[38] True friends are motivated by disinterested caring and not by the prospect of repayment. On the other hand, it is also wrong to maintain that friends never attend to the balance of giving and taking that exists between them. Friends are more willing than business associates to tolerate imbalances in their relationship for a longer period of time. However, serious and prolonged imbalance in how much each in the friendship does to sustain the goods of friendship, in the emotional support, favors, services, and gifts that each gives the other, can threaten the survival of a friendship and the loyalty that has been shown a friend. At the same time, not every friendship is an equitable one in the sense that the participants perceive that they are receiving, over the long run, equal net gains from the relationship. Each friendship has its own shape, determined in part by the rules regarding reciprocity that the friends have set in the development of their friendship. Which rules they set depends on their personalities and circumstances, and so the rules vary considerably. Some friends expect more or less symmetrical exchanges of acts of kindness and assistance, while in some cases it is understood between them that one will do much more than the other. It is when the terms of their interaction are violated, terms that are mutually agreed upon and subject to renegotiation, that their friendship is in jeopardy.

*

Intimacy, I have argued, is neither necessary nor sufficient for personal care. It is not necessary because I can care positively and disinterestedly about a particular individual even if we are not prepared and do not wish to share intimate parts of our lives with each other. And one reason intimacy is not sufficient is the possibility of hostile intimacy, which involves desires for the frustration, rather than the fulfillment, of the desires of another person whom one knows well and deeply. But intimate self-disclosure often does function as a sign of the very special regard that I have for another person: in these cases I show another person that I care deeply by revealing intimate and important parts of my life to that person. I enable someone to get closer to me, not primarily so that I can profit from some assistance that person is then in a position to provide me (as a patient might with his or her therapist), but so that this individual can share my life, and I have reason to believe that this person's happiness is to a significant extent dependent on being able to do so. Moreover, when someone I care about is intimate with me, I am better able to minister to that person's needs and to identify with that person's joys and sorrows. The sentiments of sympathy and empathy are heightened as the intimacy of a caring relationship grows.

Personal relations of love and friendship are intimate: the intimacy both expresses and strengthens the caring and the caring gives special meaning to the intimacy. In all cases of personal love, whether or not there is intimacy, the one who loves has affection for or is fond of the loved one, wishes the loved one to prosper because of feelings of goodwill for that person, and reacts with special pleasure at that person's good fortune and pain at misfortune. And the object of this well-wishing and consequent well-doing is the irreplaceable and noninterchangeable person. (I will say more in the next chapter about what this irreplaceability consists of.) Further, the one who loves has a deep personal commitment to the loved one, and this commitment imposes serious bounds on the former's choices and behavior. This is not to suggest that in practical deliberations affecting a loved one's welfare, commitment to the loved one must always have the greatest normative significance for one's decisions. Commitment to a loved one may come into conflict with other, weightier considerations. Personal love is not threatened simply because there are occasions in which one is prepared to choose against a loved one's welfare. But there can hardly be a *commitment* to a loved one if the choice to act against that person's welfare becomes the norm. (This is true of commitments in general. We can refrain from acting on our commitments under certain circumstances, but these must be extreme and out of the ordinary.) And if such a decision is made, it cannot be an easy one: it will be preceded by careful deliberation and felt keenly as grave and possibly fateful.

17

Particularity and Irreplaceability

According to John McTaggart, love, "as we find it in present experience," may be "because of qualities," but it is "never in respect of qualities":

> To love one person above all the world for all one's life because her eyes are beautiful when she is young, is to be determined to a very great thing by a very small cause. But if what is caused is really love— and this is sometimes the case—it is not condemned on that ground. It is there, and that is enough. This would seem to indicate that the emotion is directed to the person, independently of his qualities, and that the determining qualities are not the justification of that emotion, but only the means by which it arises.[1]

One way of interpreting the claim that love is "never in respect of qualities" is that no reasons at all are involved in personal love. Less sweepingly, D. W. Hamlyn argues that it is possible "to be loved full-stop," that is, "without there being anything that the love is for" even though "there is likely to be some explanation why the love came into being." All that is required is the "merely formal condition" that the lover "must see the beloved as an object for love."[2] Someone might advance a thesis like this because of a belief in the irreplaceability of the object of personal love. If love were "in respect of qualities," it might be said, it would not be of the person him or herself. We would be cherishing the qualities

191

that happen to be exemplified in this person, loving this person only as an exemplification of a type and not as a particular instance as distinct from other instances. Moreover, it might be argued, once we admit that "love is for" a person's qualities, the move to the more impersonal stages of Diotima's account of love in the *Symposium* is difficult to block. Thus, if the loved one is to be irreplaceable and to be loved for him or herself alone, he or she must be loved "independently of his [or her] qualities."

The McTaggart–Hamlyn thesis strikes a familiar chord, and read as a repudiation of the Platonic conception of love, it points to something important in our understanding of love. But on closer inspection, there are serious problems conceiving of love the way McTaggart does. McTaggart is not so unrealistic as to deny that love can be changed by a perceived alteration of the qualities in the beloved. He claims, however, that love "justifies itself" independently of these qualities, and that if one really loves another person, alterations in the beloved's qualities can never provide one with a "reason why [love] ought to cease." "Admiration, hope, trust, ought to yield," perhaps, if there are such changes. "But love, if it were strong enough, could have resisted, and ought to have resisted" (ibid.). True love, therefore, is unconditional in a very strong sense: love is never for another in respect of qualities, and once love has arisen, no alteration in the beloved's qualities can be a reason that justifies the cessation of love.

This holds as well, presumably, if we extend the notion of "qualities" to include relational properties like "father of" or "child of." It might be argued that a mother's love for her child is unconditional in the sense that she loves the child in virtue of her belief that the description "the person I brought into the world" is true of that child, and not in virtue of a belief that descriptions mentioning nonrelational properties are so. But this move does not seem to be available to McTaggart, for her love would still be in respect of empirical facts about the object of her love. Love can and should survive even the discovery that this is not my child.

Now there is at least this much truth in the claim that "love justifies itself": in the normal course of events, a lover does not have to justify love of another, to defend or support it, by pointing to qualities in the beloved for which one loves another. The demand that one somehow provide evidence or arguments in favor of one's love strikes us in many cases as impertinent. But McTaggart's thesis goes beyond this: it is not just that we normally do not have to justify our loves, but that love is not at all for a person's characteristics and that it is independent of justificatory reasons.

This is not how I think of personal love, however. If *x*'s love for *y* is not in respect of any of *y*'s characteristics, then *y* is likely to feel incidental to the occurrence of *x*'s emotion. *X*'s love would be directed to or at the particular, numerical individual with whom *x* happened to come into contact, but the love would not be focused on *y* as a person with an identity distinct from that of others.³ In addition, contrary to McTaggart's suggestion about the permanence of love, a love that is genuinely attuned to another person in his or her particularity should not necessarily be condemned if it does not survive a change in the beloved's qualities. We sometimes regard ourselves as being justified in trying to end our love because the loved one has changed in some unacceptable direction, and if our love wanes this is not always to be taken as a flaw in our love, something that we would have resisted if only we had loved enough or in the right way. Indeed, there is a sense in which a person who would never believe that there is good cause to cease loving me, whose love for me is as unconditional as McTaggart believes it ought to be, does not really love *me* at all.

McTaggart's conception of love, then, is not where we should look for an alternative to the Platonic. Again, however, this much can be said for the former: it draws our attention to a feature of what are, for us, vitally important forms of love (viz., their essentially personal character). The challenge now is to make sense of this. What we need is an account of personal love that avoids both extremes, one according to which (1) we love a person for him or herself alone and not merely as an exemplification of a type, and (2) a person's characteristics are relevant to loving that person for him or herself alone.⁴ (1) is necessary for the irreplaceability of the loved one, but the irreplaceability must have something to do with the beloved's qualities.

In the case of a Don Juan, what the individual is "loved" for is a common general property (viz., roughly the property of being female). The recipient of his attentions is often seduced into believing that when he says "I love you" he is focused on her as a particular woman distinct from others. But as Leporello sings of his master in Mozart's *Don Giovanni,* "he never thinks of whether she's rich, ugly or beautiful—as long as she wears a skirt, you know very well what he does!"[5] He loves *woman,* and the particular person his love is directed at only as an instance of woman.

The object of personal love is not just a person's qualities but a whole person. One's attractive or valuable qualities (or combination of such qualities) are what one is loved for, or why one is loved, not all that is loved. We might put it this way: particular persons are vitally significant to us not because they exhibit certain *qualities,* but because *they* exhibit certain qualities. Thus, I love my wife for her high-spiritedness, charm, consideration and her other qualities, and not just the high-spiritedness and other qualities she exemplifies. If it were some abstract repeatable quality that I loved, then I would feel no tremendous loss if my wife was replaced by someone else who possessed this quality to the same degree. But obviously I would care enormously about this exchange. Again, the reason is that I love *my wife* for her high-spiritedness, and so on, not high-spiritedness in general.

It is still obscure exactly what "loving my wife for her high-spiritedness, etc." means and how this differs from "loving my wife as an exemplification of the type 'high-spirited'." Clarifying this will tell us just what irreplaceability amounts to. But let me make two preliminary points. First, though the object of my love is a unique and irreplaceable individual, I do not just love this person as a bearer of the property "being a unique and irreplaceable individual" or as an exemplification of the type "unique and irreplaceable individual." Here we are building into the property the very irreplaceability that we are trying to account for, but the impression that we have thereby accounted for it is erroneous. For it is not just as *some* irreplaceable individual or other that this person is loved, but as this particular irreplaceable individual. As Robert Nozick puts it in a related discussion, "any old unique and individual self would do just as well. There is a difference between valuing something for being unique, and valuing it for the (particular) uniqueness it has."[6] Personal love attaches to the particular way in which a person instantiates the possibilities of being unique and irreplaceable.

Second, I want to sharpen my claims about irreplaceability by considering some thought-experiments. When I stated earlier that I would feel a sense of loss if my wife's place was taken by someone who shared her high-spiritedness, and so on, I was assuming that the properties in question are not *sui generis,* that is, that they are the same in all their instances and are abstractable from their mode of expression in my wife's life. (As I shall argue, I believe we can block this abstraction without giving up point 2, earlier.) If properties are indexed in a particular person, then the substitution of one person by another with literally the *same* properties would be conceptually impossible. We can, however, imagine a case in which one person is replaced by another with indistinguishable indexed properties. Suppose that, unbeknownst to me, my wife is replaced by a clone, qualitatively indistinguishable from her. The clone will not just be as high-spirited, and so on, as my wife (as when we say, for example, that my son is as intelligent as my daughter); that is, she will not just have some general property to the same degree as my wife. Rather, she will be high-spirited in the precise way that my wife is high-spirited: the clone's very particular high-spiritedness, and so on, colored by her particular existence, will be indistinguishable from my wife's very particular high-spiritedness, and so on. Under these circumstances, plainly, I would not be upset at the switch and would transfer my love to the clone.

Love could not be transferred so readily from my wife to my wife's identical twin. My love for my wife is not only love for this individual with these qualities, but also love for this individual with whom I have been through so much, with whom I have shared intense and important experiences over some more or less extended period of time. Our sense of our history and our shared history, of what we have done for each other and what we have done together, informs our continuing interactions. My wife's clone will have full quasi-memories of this history: the memories of this history will exist in her as if she had lived it herself. (I assume here that the clone does not know that she is a clone.) My wife's identical twin will not, however, and her behavior will soon make it apparent to me that I have lost my wife.

One psychological test for replaceability is roughly this: what would the results be if the object of love were taken away? Would the lover mourn and lament and accept no substitutes? To be sure, as it stands this test is quite indeterminate, and there may be disagreement about whether, in a given case, the object of love was really replaceable or not. But by anyone's criteria, replacement has occurred in the preceding clone case and my wife was therefore replaceable. Further, I would argue that the fact that S is replaceable might not undermine the claim that she is really loved. My wife is loved for the particular person she is and for our history together, and so is the substitute clone, and the love for both is exactly the same. ("Same love," as I am thinking of it here, is possible even if it is love for different persons.) My wife is replaceable, but not as individuals are replaceable in Diotima's ascent to the impersonal love of Beauty. Transferability of love from my wife to another does not here, and so does not necessarily, lead us to question whether I love my wife in her particularity and for her own sake.

The more interesting case is when I know that my wife's brain and body have been destroyed and that she has been replaced by a replica, by someone who is precisely like her in all physical and mental details. How will I react?[8] The answer depends, Derek Parfit argues, on whether I believe that "replication is nearly as bad as ordinary death" or that replication is "about as good as ordinary survival."[9] If the former, then "my love cannot be simply transferred, without grief" (ibid.); if the latter (the correct view, according to Parfit), it can. Of course, if I have no knowledge of the exchange, my beliefs about replication would not come into play and there would be no mourning, warranted or not, at the substitution. Even if, knowing about the substitution, I would not love the clone and would not be persuaded by Parfit that my reaction is unjustified, my wife is in principle replaceable because there are some possible circumstances in which I would simply transfer my love for her to another without a sense of loss and love this other as I loved my wife.

I do not think Parfit speaks for most of us when he asserts "I believe that I would and that I *ought* to love" (p. 295) the replica of a person I loved and whose brain and body I know have been destroyed. Despite the fact that the substitute is an exact replica, I would care enormously about the exchange.[10] (Similarly, if I were told that *my* brain and body are to be destroyed and replaced by an exact duplicate, with all the same memories, and so on, I would not regard this prospect as calmly as Parfit does. I would be filled with fear and horror at my impending annihilation.) I would care enormously not because the object of my love is a bare particular, but because this replica, I would think, is not the person with whom I have lived my life, with whom I have shared my deepest thoughts and feelings, not the person with whom I have built up a history. Qualitative identity would not ease my grief, for it matters to me that the object of my love is one person rather than another. I may in due time come to love the replica, of course, and if I do, I would lament losing her to her replica as I lamented losing the original object of my love to her replica.

In any case, it does not disturb us much that a clone could substitute for my wife with respect to my love behavior. Complete replacement, we might say, is only a theoretical, not a realistic, possibility, and it does not lead us to retract our assertion that the loved one is irreplaceable in actual circumstances. In the usual discussions of irreplaceability, the relevant substitution class for those I love just does not include clones.

When I point to the sensitivity or intelligence of my wife as one of the things I love her for, I am not saying that sensitivity or intelligence in any person is a reason for me to love that person. It is the sensitivity or intelligence of this person, my wife, that I love her for (i.e., the very particular sensitivity or intelligence she exhibits, in the particular context in which it is). The particular way in which my wife is sensitive or intelligent is, to use Neera Badhwar's expression, the "particular stylization"[11] of her qualities: what makes these qualities uniquely hers is the very personal style of their expression. The following remarks by the critic Seymour Chatman on the apprehension of literary style are relevant here:

> Because of its complex nature, the recognition of a writer's style is not a mere act of perception, as that term is generally defined. . . . Perception entails the recognition of a thing as an instance of a CLASS of things, whereas style-recognition, as the recognition of a personality, is something more, namely the recognition of an individual as a unique complex or pattern of perceived features. That is why perception tends to be virtually instantaneous whereas the ability to recognize an author's style takes time to acquire.[12]

There is style-recognition that is not the recognition of a personality. For example, I may categorize Shelley's poetry as Romantic in style, the product of someone writing in what has come to be known as the Romantic tradition. Recognition of Shelley's style, in Chatman's sense, occurs only when I see Shelley, a Romantic poet, being a Romantic poet in his own way, Shelley's way. (I do not want to claim that all artists convey a particular, distinctive personality in their work. Some are never perceived this way—they are the voice of their age and do not speak to us in their own voice.) And this takes time, deep and prolonged familiarity with the work of Shelley.

When I am intimate with another and love another for the unique individual person he or she is, I do not just love that person for qualities that he or she possesses in common with others. Rather, the qualities for which I love the person are personalized by a particular style, a style that it takes me some time to get to know. The knowledge here is knowledge by acquaintance. Although there is no point at which it makes sense to say "I know this person completely," I know this person pretty well. I apprehend his or her own way of being an intelligent and sensitive person or of expressing these qualities, and I love him or her for being this way. (I do not love this person for the individual style alone, or for general qualities alone, but for that person's qualities-as-stylized.) Moreover, (ideally) we love a person for what the person essentially is, and what that person essentially is, as a unique individual, includes the way of expressing or manifesting the properties that make that person who he or she is.[13] Different persons can be useful to me or bring me pleasure in characteristically different ways (i.e., each might be said to have his or her own style of being useful or pleasant to me). But these might only be incidental features of a person, and as Aristotle tells us, perfect philia is based not on the incidental but on the beloved's identity properties. Loving a person for incidental qualities, even if these qualities are made uniquely someone's own by the individual's style, is loving a person for merely external properties or for his or her relations to others.

A clone of my wife would have the same fundamental qualities as my wife and would express them in exactly the same ways. (Likewise, a clone of Shelley would write in the very same style as Shelley.) So, loving my wife for her relativized qualities does not entail that I could not love a numerically different individual in exactly the same way. But the transferability of love from original to replica need not undermine the claim that my wife is loved for the unique character or personality that makes her who she is. In other words, love for my wife is not to be construed as love for the universals she exemplifies, for qualities that are abstracted from their concrete manifestation in her life, merely because some counterfactual about substitutes, about whether someone *could* take her place without grief, is true. We can, if we like, think of my wife's style and the clone's style as different tokens or instances of the same type, just as we can regard the original *Mona Lisa* and all its indistinguishable replicas as instances of the universal type, *Mona Lisa*. But this introduction of universals is no threat to the love we value. Even if loving someone for the "unique" person he or she is does not preclude the possibility of replacement of this person by an indistinguishable other, when the qualities for which I love another are highly personal and stylized, transference of love is not to be expected.[14] After all, there is still a vast difference between the transferability that personal love does admit and the often more or less easy interchangeability of things, acquaintances, sex objects, and the like.

I have argued that we love particular persons for their qualities, and further that repeatability of mere properties is no bar to uniqueness: styles are sufficiently different to make us (nontrivially) unique.[15] A particular stylization includes the distinctive way in which the various instantiated qualities of the beloved combine and intermingle with one another. Although I might have occasion to focus on some particular attractive or valuable quality of a loved one, or to distinguish between a loved one's various particular attractive qualities, my love is not just a response to particular qualities, considered individually. Rather, I cherish a particular configuration or gestalt of instantiated qualities as these are manifested in the loved one's life over an extended period of time. Moreover, this is compatible with discriminating appraisal. There may be some qualities that I find unattractive or lacking in value. But I love the other despite his or her defects because, in my view, they are outweighed by his or her attractive qualities.

Two additional points will amplify this account. First, love aids style recognition. Apprehension of another's style is not antecedently fixed, with love just tacked on to it as a kind of response to an already strongly differentiated or richly specified individual.

Rather, my love for another can provide me with a window on someone's life that is not readily available to those who interact with that person in more formal and routinized ways, and in the activity of loving another I can both elicit and discover the particular style that makes that person the unique person that individual is. And as love for another grows and deepens, so too does the apprehension of what makes that person's qualities uniquely that individual's.

Second, love often has an open-ended quality in that it is not fixed on the particular stylization of the beloved's qualities at any given time. It is not, as McTaggart's thesis suggests, the bare particular that is the object of love, for characteristics are relevant to the existence and continuation of personal love. But neither is it just the particular present person. Robert Brown observes that "the object of love cannot, at a particular time, be identical with a specifiable complex of qualities. The complex is essentially incomplete, and hence so is the object of love . . . [I]n loving someone . . . we . . . cherish . . . the incompletely specifiable beloved."[16] Brown's point might be that the object of personal love cannot be described even now and hence that love is not dependent on any reasons. But on another reading (the one I prefer), the object of love is not the unspecified beloved, but only the individual whose possibilities of personal expression are not exhausted by any particular personal style. In such love, we realize that we cannot know what personal qualities we shall discover in the beloved, qualities for which we will love that person, or how we ourselves will change as a result of our relationship. And we are prepared to love this individual, not no matter what (for surely love may quite reasonably cease to exist in some circumstances), but also not only so long as the person remains in all respects just the particular person he or she is at present.

To cherish the incompletely specifiable beloved is precisely not to cherish an individual only so long as the person conforms to expectations and regularities. Those who love resist the tendency to think of the beloved on the model of themselves and they do not typecast: the beloved is not just neatly fit into a category of personalities, identified as type-x personality and treated accordingly. Related to this, those who are fully responsive to the beloved are prepared to recognize changes in the beloved and to accommodate their love to these changes.

I have been speaking all along mainly about the irreplaceability of the loved one, but it should be added that irreplaceability covers both the person loved and the love itself. Each of our loves is a unique, irreplaceable value because it is focused on a particular person with a particular style, and each person we love is irreplaceable because our love for that person is not displaced by our love for another. (I put aside here imaginary cases involving clones.) Now I do not want to deny that we can and do compare our loves in various ways. For example, if the wife I love should die I might find somebody else I love as much. Parents also commonly claim to love all their children with an equally great love. And reflecting on the love I now have for another woman as compared with the love I once had for my wife, I may discover that I feel more fulfilled loving this other woman than I did loving my wife, that my personality meshes more harmoniously with this other woman's than it did with my wife's, and so forth. But that I can love another as much or with a love that is in some sense better does not entail that these different loves are intersubstitutable or that the later love has more than replaced the earlier. The love for this other is still a different love, a love that, in virtue of the particular personality or character of the loved one, is a distinct value and displays a distinct pattern of responsiveness and mutual engagement. The way in which each love reverberates through the substance of my life, the way in which the well-being of the other implicates my own, is specific to that love.

When someone who is loved dies or ceases to be loved, the loss cannot be completely made up by acquiring a new love. This view of personal love, it might be suggested, has a destructive side in that it could undermine the establishment of new love relationships after the loss of old ones. For it is natural for a new love to feel inadequate if he or she thinks that the loss of a loved one leaves a void in one's life that no new love can completely fill.[17] My response is this. Consider the new spouse, for example, who complains to her husband, "I can never mean to you what your previous wife meant." Her feelings of inadequacy may be due to the belief that the other has not completely "gotten over" the loss of his former wife, that he is still grieving, and that he carries with him an image of her that prevents him from seeing his new wife as an individual in her own right. I do not claim, however, that one never stops *feeling* the loss of a loved one. If, on the other hand, she feels inadequate simply because she realizes that the value of the former love is unique and irreplaceable, it might help to remind her that no other love could take her place in this sense either.[18]

As Robert Nozick observes, "the actual situation [of love] is valued above another possible one, even while realizing that had that other possibility been realized, *it* would have been valued then over this actuality—merely another possibility from its perspective then."[19] For example, it sometimes happens that I am convinced I could have loved a certain acquaintance of mine as much as I love my wife if I had not met my wife first. But I would not trade the particular love that exists for the love that might be, even if there was nothing standing in the way of its realization. Similarly, parents might admit that had they had another child than the one they actually have, they would have been as devoted to it as to the one they have. But the possible love pales in significance beside the actual one.

18

The Value of Individuals

In personal love, we value another person for being him or herself, for being the unique person he or she is. I do not just value someone under some general description, as, say, "a friend of mine," but as the very particular friend that he or she is. The discussion in the last chapter attempted to clarify this. What I now want to consider is what support there might be for the intuition that persons *have* value in virtue of being the particular persons they are, that the value of a person is partly the value of a unique self. On this view, what we value in personal love, this person's particularity, is an important part of this person's value. The person is valued for being that person alone and not as an exemplification of a type, and value resides in that person being a particular instance as distinct from others.

One philosopher who offers an account of the value of the individual, of the particular individual, is Nicolai Hartmann, and his discussion in *Ethics* can serve as our point of departure.[1] "Every one," according to Hartmann, "has personality distinctive of himself." By contrast, individuality is not distinctive of oneself but "is common to all. That in contents it is different in everyone, does not affect its universal character. The very singularity is itself universal." Personality presupposes individuality, but the former is "what distinguishes the individuality of one from that of another." Hartmann admits that the notion of "personality in general" can

be conceived "without inner contradiction," but what he is interested in, he tells us, is the value of this particular personality, of
this personality as distinguished from other personalities. We
should speak of personality in the plural, he says, and it is "in this
sense [that] we are to consider it as a value" (pp. 341–42).

It might be thought that particular individuals have value as the
particular people they are because "actual personality" (p. 341) is
a value, but Hartmann dismisses this. Personality as a value "cannot be decisively fixed for all persons" (p. 341) and neither does it
coincide with the "single actual person" (p. 348). The value that is
personality has, like all values, "an ideal self-existence" (p. 341)
independent of actuality, and so the particular individual is only to
be regarded as the "carrier of a value" (p. 348) that is not empirically given. This value is the value of someone's "ideal self," a
value that is *one* person's because, in Hartmann's curious phrase,
"he is bound to it" (p. 348), and strictly speaking, singularity pertains only to the actual empirical person, not to that person's own
ideal self. Further, personal love plays a critical role here, according to Hartmann.[2] It is "only the lover [who] knows personality as
a value." Only the lover discovers and cherishes "the ideal in the
empirical" (p. 380) and can appreciate the extent to which the
beloved realizes or falls short of his or her ideal personality.

In Hartmann's account of the value of the individual as an individual, the distinctive personality of an individual is, as a value,
ideal, and the nature of the ideal is such that it "would not be at all
contradicted, if a second real entity or several corresponded to it."
Yet Hartmann also claims that each individual has an ideal personality proper to that individual alone that the person is bound to
realize: "it is his own individual virtue, else it is no one's virtue,
because in any other person it would not be virtue" (p. 348). The
problem here is how the ideal, which is universal, can prescribe for
a single individual alone. In addition, though Hartmann (unlike
Plato) believes in the distinctive value of the individual self, his
account still devalues what is truly unique and personal in the
individual. For he claims that the value of personality is ideal, and
that from this point of view the actual personality of an empirical
individual is only "accidental, merely a fact, an affair of actual
existence" (p. 348).

I begin this chapter with Hartmann because, while his account of the value of personality is deeply flawed, he at least takes this notion seriously and sees it as a problem requiring explanation. He is interested, as I am too, in the individual as an object of personal love, of that "intimate love directed exclusively to one individual person." Only through personal love, he claims, "does the individual entity receive the recognition that is its due," the "appraisement by a special sympathetic sensing of its specific value" (p.368). Hartmann calls this sensing of the specific value of the individual entity a kind of "ethical divination" (p. 370), but as I hope now to show, it is an insight that certain leading moral theories do not express. If we look at the status of the individual in these theories, we do not find the individual mattering in the way that he or she matters in personal love.

This is pretty clear with utilitarianism. For the utilitarian, the right is that which, directly or indirectly, brings about the best state of affairs available to the agent, and states of affairs are ranked in terms of the quantity of happiness or desire satisfaction (welfare), aggregated across persons, that they involve. The unit of value is welfare as such, not the individuals who have the welfare. As agents, individuals matter only as producers of utility; as patients, they are merely "locations of their respective utilities [who] . . . do not count as individuals . . . any more than individual petrol tanks do in the analysis of the national consumption of petroleum."[3] It is, of course, persons who produce utility and experience pleasure: welfare is not free-floating and utilitarians acknowledge that intrinsic value exists only in the experiences of separate living persons. But the fact remains that for a utilitarian what is of primary importance is the quantity of welfare summed across persons, and the value of an individual or an individual's life derives from and consists in the quantity of some contribution to the general welfare. Utilitarianism's value theory effectively separates both the agent from the welfare he or she produces and the patient from the welfare he or she enjoys: the agent is to do what will bring about the best state of affairs, and the value of a state of affairs is fundamentally independent of any relation to the agent and of the identities of the persons whose welfare is affected by his or her action.

A consequentialist theory might try to accommodate the value of personality by rejecting aggregation across persons and adding considerations of love and friendship to its description of the best state of affairs. States of affairs might be ordered from best to worst in terms of a plurality of intrinsically, nonmorally valuable goods, including love and relations of friendship in which the individual is valued as an individual.[4] These goods might be ranked lexically or only attributed weights, in which case the rightness of an act would depend on how much it contributed to the weighted sum of these values. On such a view, while love and friendship may promote happiness, they are also either constitutive of the ultimate value of happiness or ultimate values alongside happiness. They are themselves valued things: as between two worlds, alike in all respects except that one contains love and friendship and the other does not, rational, well-informed and experienced people would have a settled preference for the former over the latter. But consequentialists who include love and friendship in their list of intrinsic goods, who maintain that the state of affairs consisting of people valuing other people as individuals is intrinsically valuable, do not really come closer to conveying the distinctive value of the individual self than the utilitarians I have been discussing. What is ultimately important now is the balance of intrinsic good (including the intrinsic good of love and friendship) over intrinsic evil in people's lives, not the individual in his or her particularity, and the loss of a friend or loved one finally matters only because and insofar as it affects the amount of net good in the world. Other things being equal, there is no moral reason for me to give greater weight to my love than to another's. Though it is *persons* who love and particular persons who are loved, what is valued is simply love, that is, love-in-general. The particular identity of the loved one might not be a matter of only incidental interest for the one who loves, but from the moral point of view, no particular loved one or particular love relationship is as such irreplaceably valuable.[5]

Some utilitarians regard particularistic ties of love and friendship as derivatively justifiable, because in their view more happiness overall is produced if each person makes the welfare of a few others a special concern. The person-differentiating impact of an individual's affective relationships is thus validated on the basis of a person-neutral principle. Nozick claims that this sort of validation "misconstrues the moral weight of particularistic ties," and that we need "to investigate the nature of a more consistently particularistic theory—particularistic all the way down the line."[6]

One suggestion might be this: a more consistently particularistic theory would be one that sees personal love as directed toward the distinctive value of the individual self and that validates particularistic ties in part on this basis. In any case, on a person-neutral theory of value, what we value in those we love (viz., their particular uniqueness) is one thing, and what the value of persons actually consists in is quite another.

In utilitarianism, the worth of persons is derivative from their status as loci of such activities as desiring and having pleasure and pain. They are treated as bits of utility and then the utility bits are merged together as one total lump. Who is desiring, who has pleasure or pain, is ultimately of no consequence, and so persons are replaceable, not in the sense that we never form strong emotional attachments to persons and never grieve at their loss or absence, but in the sense that the replacement of one person by another, whose life is roughly commensurate in terms of pleasure or whatever, constitutes no loss of ultimate value. Obviously with such a view of the value of persons, it comes as no surprise that utilitarianism also lacks a concept of the value of a distinctive personality. We get somewhat closer to this, however, if we turn to Kantian ethics.

In the *Foundations of the Metaphysics of Morals*, Kant maintains that human beings have dignity and that their status as ends-in-themselves is due to their possession of "an unconditional and incomparable worth."[7] This dignity is something all people have regardless of their moral character or the moral quality of their actions. Their worth is "unconditional" in that they have it "in themselves," independent of the purposes and preferences of others. That which has a "price," by contrast, has only a relative value, a value external to the valuable object itself.

One sort of price is what Kant calls "market price" (p.53), which depends upon usefulness. It is often observed, for example, that in contemporary employment practices employees are simply bought and sold as are other goods in the marketplace, treated merely as pieces of property at the disposal of the employer. Their value is wholly dependent on being valuable for the productive enterprise or valued by the employer, and when a particularly valuable member of the workforce receives a bonus or promotion, that person is not being honored for dignity, but is being rewarded for productivity. Moreover, because the worth of employees is conditional in this way, it is also not incomparable. Productivity provides the standard of comparison, and if another person B were available who could do as well or better at the same job as employee A, then other things being equal, A would be replaceable by B. Another type of price is "affective price," which something has if it "accords with a certain taste, i.e., with pleasure in the mere purposeless play of our faculties" (p. 53). Unlike market price, affective price does not presuppose any particular need or goal, but has to do with qualities that we find immediately agreeable. A person might be valued, for example, simply because he or she has a good sense of humor and is enjoyable to be with. Nevertheless, affective price is also a relative value, and whatever has this sort of value can, according to Kant, "be replaced by something else as its equivalent" (ibid).

That which has dignity, however, cannot: it "admits of no equivalent" (ibid). An employee can perhaps be replaced by someone of equivalent usefulness, but dignity is an absolute bar to replaceability. Further, a group of workers that is n-times more productive than employee A can be said to have n-times the value (i.e., market price) of employee A, and employee B who is n-times more productive than employee A can be said to have the same value (market price) as the group. But the group does not have n-times the dignity of one, nor can the dignity of one person be n-times the dignity of another. Unlike market price, the dignity of individuals is not aggregable. We can increase the number of people in the world possessing dignity, but dignity necessarily belongs to each of these individuals and to each alone; consequently, there is nothing whose dignity is thereby increased. The dignity of each of a large number of individuals does not add up to a great deal more dignity than the dignity possessed by any one of them.

The individual, however, does not have a distinctive value all of his or her own by virtue of his or her dignity. Dignity is possessed by persons generally, not by this person as distinct from others. So dignity still does not give us what we are looking for: the irreplaceability of persons, which is central to the experience of personal love, is just the irreplaceability of this particular person in virtue of his or her particularity. Of course, the persons to whom we are deeply attached are not easily substituted by others. But if persons have value only because of their dignity, then since dignity is not person-discriminating, personal love could not provide access to any fundamental value that the particular individual as such possesses. Max Scheler's remarks on Kant's conception of the person indicate how Kant fails to express this more radical sort of irreplaceability:

> Formal ethics [especially Kant's ethics] designates the person first as *"rational* person." [This] definition of the person as rational leads first to the consequence that every concretization of the idea of the person in a concrete person coincides at once with depersonalization. For that which is here called "person," namely, that "something" which is the subject of rational activity, must be attributed to concrete persons— indeed, to *all men*—in the same way and as something *identical* in all men. Hence men are not distinguishable by virtue of their personal being alone. Indeed, the concept of an "individual person" becomes, strictly speaking, a *contradictio in adjecto.* For rational acts . . . are *eo ipso* extraindividual or . . . supraindividual.[8]

On Kant's view, human beings are mixed beings, having both an animal nature and a rational nature; they are at once sensible members of the natural world with passions and inclinations and rational agents. Dignity belongs to individuals in virtue of their rational will or lawmaking capacity, their capacity of acting in accordance with the moral law and of doing so because of duty. This will is the same for all rational agents (though not all persons follow the dictates of their rational will to the same degree), and so it is quite understandable why Kant should sometimes speak of the individual as having dignity and sometimes of "lawmaking" itself as having dignity. What is irreplaceable, what admits of no equivalent, is not (as Scheler puts it) "the individual person," but the individual in virtue of something held in common with all human beings or, we might say, the rational will itself. As for humanity's animal nature, it is important for at least two reasons. First, general empirical facts about human beings define their species of rational being and impose constraints on what they can and cannot rationally will. All rational beings, in virtue of their rationality, are subject to the same fundamental practical principle—the Categorical Imperative. But not all rational creatures have the same duties, because the duties they have vary as their natures vary. Second, a full understanding of treating others as having dignity must take account of specific contingent facts about persons. What our duties demand of us in particular situations partly depends, for example, on the particular, empirically conditioned capacities for rational and autonomous action of those with whom we are dealing. But our animal nature is here taken seriously in order to specify and apply our duties, and it is our rational, not our empirical, nature that is the ground of moral duty for Kant. Moreover, on Kant's view the animal nature of human beings or of this particular human being is replaceable by a different animal nature, and indeed our animal nature is expendable altogether without diminishing the moral value of action. In the *Foundations,* he writes:

> All objects of inclinations have only a conditional worth, for if the inclinations and the needs founded on them did not exist, their object would be without worth. The inclinations themselves as sources of needs, however, are so lacking in absolute worth that the universal wish of every rational being must be indeed to free himself completely from them. (p. 46)

Things have only price, for Kant, and are replaceable; persons, on the other hand, have dignity, because of their capacity for impartially principled conduct, and their irreplaceability is grounded in the dignity of humanity. If the Kantian categories of price and dignity were exhaustive of the realm of value, actual individual human beings would not have value as the particular individual human beings they are, and the "individual person" would be irreplaceable only by virtue of being a concrete embodiment of supraindividual rationality, hence not irreplaceable at all, strictly speaking. (Hartmann, it will be recalled, viewed the individual person as a carrier of an ideal value to which that individual is linked in a unique way. In Kant, by contrast, individuals have absolute value as possessors of dignity, and they do not have the same sort of connection to *this* that individuals in Hartmann's account are supposed to have to their ideal personalities.) Now Kant is interested in laying the foundation of morality, in specifying, as Nozick calls it, "the moral basis, the characteristic [in others] in virtue of which ethical behavior is owed,"[9] and it is a matter of contention whether we need the notion of the distinctive value of the individual self for this purpose. But even if we decide that we do not, our interest in the value of the individual should extend beyond the question, what is there about the individual that gives rise to specifically moral claims?

It is sometimes alleged that in Kantian ethics it makes no difference to how we treat another that one is who one is and not some other individual. Treating another individual as an individual is treating one as the particular person one is rather impersonally, and this involves trying to see someone as that person sees him or herself. Though I do not have to take what another says about him or herself as the final word, never to be challenged, this person has a kind of practical authority about the person he or she is in that his or her self-conception has great weight for me and I take it as my point of departure. I do not just respond to this person in accordance with some rule that dictates how persons with a certain characteristic should be responded to, but I try to respond to those features that, in the individual's view, are necessary to who that person is. Indeed, in certain special kinds of relationships (viz., love and friendship), we are expected to treat the other as the particular person he or she is, and the failure to do so may be grounds for legitimate complaint. But our expectations in this regard are limited, and there are good reasons to be reluctant to take on an obligation to treat persons generally as the persons they are. For one thing, some persons might justifiably regard my attempt to respond to their self-conceptions as overly intrusive.[10]

It is, I think, a very cursory and negative interpretation of Kant's views to read them as precluding an appreciation of the particularities of other individuals.[11] A Kantian need not advocate treating our friends and loved ones impersonally, responding to them in standard and uniform ways that take little account of how they see themselves. On the contrary, in these cases, it might be said, treating others as persons requires more than rigid rule following: it requires that we be attuned to changes in their self-conceptions and that we give them special weight in our practical deliberations. The fact remains, however, that the conception of the person underlying Kant's prescriptions is not a strongly individualistic one. Unlike utilitarianism, which is a person-neutral theory, Kantian ethical theory justifies the person-relative character of our moral intuitions about the treatment of persons at a deep level. Individual human beings have an intrinsic value beyond all price and are irreplaceably valuable. But this irreplaceability is a feature of persons *simpliciter,* not of one person as distinct from others. It is of no particular interest to Kant whether or not individuals have value as individuals as well, because duty is for Kant the fundamental fact of moral life and this value plays no role in an account of duty as he understands it.

What is lacking in both utilitarianism and deontologies, Michael Stocker claims in an often cited paper,

> is simply—or not so simply—the person. For, love, friendship, affection, fellow feeling, and community all require that the other person be an essential part of what is valued. The person—not merely the person's general values nor even the person-qua-producer-or-possessor-of-general-values—must be valued. The defect of these theories in regard to love, to take one case, is not that they do not value love (which, often, they do not) but that they do not value the beloved.[12]

I have been arguing that Kantian theory does not value the beloved. Now I want to digress briefly and consider whether it values love.

It has frequently been noted, most often by critics of this moral philosophy, that acts of deep personal commitment and regard characteristic of love and friendship do not have intrinsic moral value for the Kantian. I agree that this is the view, though I hesitate to say that it indicates a defect in the theory. For a Kantian, the characteristic virtue of moral persons is conscientiousness, an effective concern to do what is right because it is right and to avoid what is wrong because it is wrong. An act's moral worth is a function of its expressing the agent's governing resolve to do what is right. But acts of personal concern characteristic of love and friendship, or what Kant calls acts of "emotional love,"[13] express aspects of our psychological nature other than our capacity for impartially principled conduct. Emotional love is here direct and spontaneous concern for another particular person, and such concern can motivate behavior that runs counter to general considerations of right and wrong. The conscientious Kantian agent does not have to be thought of as someone whose main motive for helping a friend or loved one is always a sense of duty. The agent must, however, believe that it is permissible to do so, and this belief, along with the general commitment not to do what is wrong, gives the act moral worth.[14]

Acts of emotional love might of course have some other very important kind of intrinsic value even though they do not have intrinsic *moral* value in Kant's sense, and there may yet be a plausible sense of "moral" according to which such acts do have intrinsic moral worth. But for Kant, it is only acts of "practical love" that have such worth, because they express conscientiousness. "Every man," he claims, "has a duty to others of adopting the maxim of benevolence (practical love of man), whether or not he finds them lovable" (p. 118). It is consistent with the universality of this maxim, however, to give special consideration to friends and loved ones. Kant makes it clear in the following passage that he is not advocating indiscriminate love of all people, doing good for others without regard to whether or not we have a special emotional tie to some of them:

> [O]ne man is closer to me than another, and in benevolence I am the closest to myself. Now how does this fit in with the precept "love your *neighbor* (your fellowman) as yourself"? . . . [I]n wishing I can be *equally* benevolent to everyone, whereas in acting I can, without violating the universality of my maxim, vary the degree greatly according to the different objects of my love. (p. 119)

At the same time, we should not suppose that the requirements of practical benevolence are satisfied by devoting ourselves to our friends and loved ones and that concern for the rest of humanity is optional: the impartiality of the maxim rules this out. We are to adopt a maxim of practical love, to adopt the end of helping other human beings as such (from the motive of duty), and though it may be permissible for me to favor my friend or loved one on some occasions, I must also be ready to help those for whom I do not feel particular affection (from the motive of duty) on other occasions in which I have an opportunity to help them.

Let us return to the main line of argument. According to Edward Johnson (echoing Stocker):

> The problem with utilitarianism is that, in pursuit of universal impartiality, it ends up losing individuals and replacing them with more or

less interchangeable bundles of desires. But Kantian theories seem to lose the individual too. In pursuit of the universal and "transcendental," they flense the individual down to the bare bones of abstract personhood.[15]

Rather than say Kant's theory "lose[s] the individual," I would prefer to put it this way: Kant focuses on what makes persons matter morally and what makes persons matter morally for Kant is one, but only one, of the things that makes persons matter. With Kant, I believe that human beings are rational moral agents, capable of determining their actions by reasons, and that it is in virtue of their capacity for rational agency, rather than their animality, that they possess moral dignity, that they are beings toward whom others have certain duties and who owe duties to others. But this is only part of the truth about persons. The capacity for moral agency is part of the essence of persons, but there are other things that matter about each of us as well. It also matters that each is a specific concrete individual with his or her own way of looking at him or herself and the world, that each is the particular person he or she is and not just a concrete embodiment of rationality. Each person is a unique particular in virtue of instantiating the possibilities of being human in a particular way, and that person's living constitutes an objective and unique value in the world because humanity subsists within that individual as a unique constellation of actualized possibilities.

The concept of a person is a normative and not merely descriptive one. To say of someone that one is a person is to say, in part, that one is not merely a thing to be manipulated for our personal ends. It is to say as well that we should leave the person the "space" in which to pursue his or her ends for him or herself and that we should make those ends, whose achievement would constitute the individual's happiness, to some extent our own. "Person" is a moral concept in this sense. In addition, the concern and attentiveness of personal love are of value in themselves and independent of their relation to right conduct. For example, we incur duties to our friends as a result of making friends, and parents incur duties to their children as a result of having them, but the value of our special concern for our friends and children only partly consists in its helping us to carry out our duties to them. It also has value, I suggest, as an acknowledgment and appreciation of the distinctive value of the individual friend or loved one. While we do not, I think, have a duty to make or try to make friends, or a duty to love or try to love someone in a deeply personal way, our personal loves give others a unique place in our lives that corresponds to a unique value they have, and the loves are therefore intrinsically valuable. To call them "merely personal" is to trivialize them. (It is helpful to recall in this connection Hartmann's contention that personal love, which involves the "sympathetic sensing of [another's] specific value," is an act of "ethical divination.")

A fundamental idea underlying morality is the comparative one that persons are equally important. Some persons do not count more than or less than others, but each counts the same amount as every other. Indeed, it has often been thought that this is *the* fundamental idea, in other words, that all morality tells us is to treat each individual with exactly the same moral consideration as every other. But the moral significance of persons is only partly conveyed by this basic requirement. Each person is not only of equal value with every other, but a unique individual and therefore uniquely valuable in him or herself. This is a noncomparative notion of value, and it is this unique value to which personal love provides access.

In drawing our attention to a more strongly individualistic conception of the person than we find in Kant, I am not denying that there are contexts in which a concept of equality is especially important. Nor am I suggesting that in our moral relations with friends and loved ones, we need only attend to whether we are responding appropriately to their unique qualities and values. Plainly, there are duties that we have to friends and loved ones generally and ways of treating them that deny or disregard their entitlement to equal moral consideration. And if we are trying to decide what weight our duties to our friends and loved ones have when they come into conflict with other obligations, it is not sufficient guidance to insist on the unique importance of each person. My claim is only this: it is a morally significant fact about persons that they are the particular persons they are and have intrinsic and unique value in virtue of being such.

Further, nothing I have said should be construed as an endorsement of what Lawrence Blum calls "the uniqueness view":

According to this view, each individual is unique, and what constitutes his good will be unique; morally adequate action will have to involve an appreciation of this. This will mean at least that morally appropriate action cannot be grounded in universal principles, which abstract from the uniqueness of the individual.[16]

(As I have already argued, abstracting from the uniqueness of the individual for certain purposes does not preclude the necessity of trying to appreciate another person's unique point of view. But the demands of morality would be even more exacting than they already are—excessively exacting, I think—if morally adequate action always had to involve an appreciation of the uniqueness of others.) However, I share with the uniqueness view the conviction that, in a deep sense, each person *is* uniquely precious just because each is the particular person he or she is. I have suggested as well that the distinctive value of the individual person is recognized and affirmed in and through personal love.[17] Personal love puts us in touch with a value that persons have as individuals, a value that we might overlook without it and that neither utilitarian nor Kantian morality can capture.[18]

19

Morality and Personal Relations

In commonsense morality, certain special duties loom large, duties that bind particular people to particular other people. Most of us intuitively feel, for example, that we are required by special duties to do things for our friends and loved ones. Consider William Godwin's "famous fire case."[1] We are asked to suppose first that an archbishop, a great benefactor of humanity, is trapped along with his chambermaid (presumably a person of lesser worth) in a burning building, and that I am able to save the life of only one of them. "Few of us," Godwin claims, "would hesitate to pronounce . . . which of the two ought to be preferred." The morally correct course would be to save the archbishop.

Suppose next, Godwin goes on, that the chambermaid is my wife or mother: then "that would not alter the truth of the proposition." For "of what great consequence is it that they are mine? . . . What magic is there in the pronoun 'my' that should justify us in overturning the decisions of impartial truth?" Few of us, however, are able to accept Godwin's conclusion in the second case with quite the same equanimity as Godwin. If this is what impartiality demands of us, most of us think, then so much the worse for impartiality: such impartiality cannot reasonably be expected of us. Those who want to present a convincing case for an impartialist position need to find a way of construing impartiality such that a decision to save our wife or mother does not stand condemned by it. They need to show why someone who saves his wife from the flames at the expense of the archbishop's life is not just a victim of the magic in the pronoun "my."

This brings us to one question about the moral implications of special relationships: how can we have a duty to be partial toward our friends and loved ones if, as seems to be the case, impartiality is a defining feature of morality itself? (This is not the same as asking how treating our friends and loved ones as the particular persons they are can be justified.) Distinct from this worry about partiality, another matter is sometimes discussed in this connection: how special relationships, in particular, relationships of love and friendship, compare to nonspecial relationships with respect to the degree of rigidity that moral prohibitions and requirements have in their application to others. Impartiality in this connection is contrasted not with preferential consideration but with responsiveness to individual differences in the application of general standards. It is this second issue that concerns Stephen Toulmin, for example, in his attack on the "tyranny of principles."[2] I will touch on this first before looking more closely at partiality and special duties.

Toulmin argues for what he calls an "ethics of intimacy" as a counterpart to a particular view of what morality demands in terms of impartiality. "Absolute impartiality," he claims, requires "the imposition of uniformity or equality on all relevant cases" (p.34), but impartiality in this sense is not a prime ethical demand in all of our relations with others. Moral wisdom consists partly in knowing when it is appropriate to stick more or less strictly to rules and when it is appropriate to rely more on our own judgment in applying them to individual cases; in other words, when it is appropriate to model our behavior on law and when on equity. The former has a central place in our relations with strangers, the latter in our relations with intimates: "in the ethics of strangers, respect for rules is all, and the opportunities for discretion are few," whereas "in the ethics of intimacy, discretion is all, and the relevance of strict rules is minimal" (p.35).[3]

The need for some degree of discretion in our dealings with intimates and nonintimates alike is a consequence of what might be called, borrowing an expression from H.L.A. Hart's discussion of the concept of law,[4] "the open texture" of moral rules. The general language in which moral rules are expressed marks out recurring features of action and presupposes similarity of context, and it communicates general standards of conduct in abstraction from the vagaries of particular concrete cases. At the same time, there is a limit to the guidance that general language can provide, for we cannot anticipate every possible combination of circumstances that the future will bring, and there may be situations in which it is not clear just what it is that I am required to do or prohibited from doing. This is why we cannot do without discretion altogether. A moral rule cannot unambiguously settle in advance what we should do in every particular case for there may be issues that can only be properly appreciated and settled when they arise in particular fact-situations. The importance of the open texture of moral rules is not unvarying across all spheres of human interaction, however, Toulmin would argue. Among nonintimates, this open texture is of relatively minor importance, because nonintimates do not know each other well enough (or trust each other sufficiently) to have extensive liberties with respect to deciding what the rule requires in a particular case. On the whole it is best if we standardize our responses to strangers and discretion should be allowed only a limited role. By contrast, the indeterminacy of moral rules figures prominently in relations among intimates, for lack of uniformity across different relationships and informality are part of what makes relationships personal ones. In dealing with our intimates, Toulmin maintains, "we both expect to—and are expected to—make allowances for their individual personalities and tastes, and we do our best to time our actions according to our perception of their current moods and plans" (p. 35). Intimate relations raise moral issues that can only reasonably be settled on an ongoing basis and with a sensitivity to context and individuality that precludes routinization of response.

We can illustrate this with the example of honesty. Dishonesty, when it sets up a relation that is essentially exploitative and violative of trust, is of course wrong, whether we deceive an intimate, a casual acquaintance, or a stranger. But in a sense we also hold intimates to a different standard of honesty than we hold nonintimates (I do not mean here that honesty is not as important a requirement among intimates as among nonintimates). The honest person is not just committed to telling the truth, but to *communi-*

cating it, and so cannot generally be indifferent to the background, personality, capabilities, desires, and current receptivities of the listener. In relations characterized by casual or relatively impersonal contacts, where deep and detailed knowledge of the other's life and particular identity is lacking, not much in the way of communicative sensitivity is ordinarily expected. In intimate relations, on the other hand, we have knowledge of the listener's history, sensitivities, interests and desires, and so on, and we are expected to tailor our revelations to them. Further, because intimates have more to assess in the context of sharing in order to determine what would honestly communicate, honesty among intimates is ordinarily a more difficult achievement than honesty among nonintimates.

Toulmin's moral perspective on intimate relations is not one that conceives of them as spontaneous and duty-free: intimates have a conscience about how they treat each other and presumably believe themselves to be entitled to certain kinds of treatment from one another. As we have seen, his point is only that in their dealings with one another, intimates (unlike strangers) are expected to apply moral rules with a great deal of discretion, and this is not the same as saying that moral rules have no role to play in intimate relations.

Suppose now there is some evidence that a person with whom you have a love relationship or who is your friend has wronged you. One thing that seems to be generally true of intimates, but often not true of strangers, is that even when it appears that a friend or love relation has mistreated you, you are inclined to disbelieve the appearances, to believe that you have nothing to forgive the individual for. You tend to give a friend or loved one, but not strangers in general, the benefit of the doubt as a token of your trust in that person's good will, and perhaps this relation is even entitled to the assumption that he or she has not wronged you. This being someone who cares deeply about you also plays a role when you know for a fact that the person has wronged you. For since this person is especially averse to doing you ill, it is reasonable to suppose that you have reasons for forgiveness. Your first thought is likely to be that the individual must have had some powerful reason for such an action or did not fully understand what he or she was doing. And in any case, it is safe to assume that the individual is genuinely sorry about the moral injury done to you and is pained by any hard feelings you might have toward him or her.[5] By contrast, our relations with strangers may be such that we cannot confidently assume these things about them when they have wronged us. We may say further that it speaks ill of us if we are not disposed to forgive those who love us for even relatively minor wrongs, or if we are no more tolerant of their mistreatment of us than we are of mistreatment at the hands of strangers and acquaintances.

The other issue with which I began this chapter concerns favoritism or partiality in our treatment of intimates. We are said to be obliged to do more for those people who are related to us by bonds of love and friendship than for unrelated others, to owe the former special kindnesses, services, or sacrifices. That is, personal relations require us to treat those specially related to us better than we need to, absent such a link. (Again, this is not what Toulmin argues for. He claims only that moral treatment of strangers differs from that of intimates in that the former involves the application of general rules with a minimum of discretion, the latter, application of rules with an eye to particular features of the case.) A weaker claim (viz., that it is permissible to give special treatment to our friends and loved ones) is defended by David Heyd. The objection to favoritism, he argues, should focus on those cases in which the one who gives special treatment stands to its beneficiary in an institutional relationship. For an "institutional relationship defines a group" and "part of the responsibility of the person in charge of such a group is the impartial implementation of the rules—even when he is inclined to prefer one member to another."[6] For example, the holder of a public office should refrain in an official capacity from setting the interests of some above those of others and should not allow any deviation from indifferently even-handed treatment of all those in his or her group because of some special relationship he or she might have with some of them. But outside the institutional context, one is not absolutely bound by the principles of fair distribution. "When surpassing the requirements of justice in our personal relations . . . we have the full right to favour one person rather than another even if there are no morally relevant grounds for that preference."[7]

On this analysis, the mistake of those who condemn any sort of partiality would consist in their transposing the standard of justice to be followed in institutional contexts into a universal principle of morality governing human interactions in general. But what is wrong with this? Why should the impersonal standard of justice not be of unrestricted applicability? At one point Heyd says the following about the value of supererogatory acts:

> Not being universally required [being purely optional] . . . supererogatory action breaks out of the impersonal and egalitarian framework of the morality of duty—both by displaying individual preferences and virtues, and by allowing for some forms of favouritism, partial and unilateral treatment of someone to whom the agent wishes to show special concern. . . . Supererogation is necessary as providing an opportunity to exercise certain virtues. (p. 175)

Here Heyd seems to be saying more than that "there is nothing morally wrong in the partiality involved in favours, as long as they do not violate the principles of comparative justice" (p. 150). The optionality of supererogation allows for favoritism and partiality, and these, Heyd suggests, are virtues. If the principles of comparative justice governed our dealings with our intimates, then whatever kindness or service I performed for one intimate would not be optional in relation to the others: the latter could legitimately complain of discrimination if I did not do for them what I did for the former. But what is the special value of acts of supererogatory service or kindness that favor a friend or loved one? Heyd appears to think that only by doing things for friends or loved ones that go beyond what is required do we show that we really care about *them,* that we love them and not just respect them as persons (see p. 179, e.g.). Yet surely we can act out of direct concern for our friend or loved one even if what we do is also required.[8] Moreover, we can recognize that we have a duty to give special treatment to persons who stand in some special relation to us, to our friends, for example, without losing sight of the particular friend and treating that friend merely as one member of a group all of whom have an equal claim to the same services from us.

John Cottingham also believes that there may be a duty not to show favoritism or partiality. This is, however, only a "specific duty" that arises in certain circumstances and it would be a mistake to generalize from these special cases to every ethical situation.[9]

An official in charge of distributing the corn dole, for example, must make his or her son wait in line with the rest, difficult though it might be for that individual to do this. But if it is one's own food to dispose of, then it is not only morally permissible to favor one's own child, but obligatory as well (being morally required to do this, again, is perfectly compatible with being motivated by direct concern for the child who is in need). In some cases, there may be a conflict between two specific duties—one requiring impartiality and one requiring partiality—and it is not obvious that the first should be met. Cottingham's justification for his position is this:

> I have suggested that the substantial and continuous favorable treat-
> ment which we all in fact bestow on ourselves and our loved ones is not
> only permissible but essential, since without it the very object of ethics,
> human fulfillment, would be defeated. (p.94)

The claim that it is wrong to show favoritism to our friends and loved ones amounts to "a repudiation of love" (p. 97), and any ethical system that repudiates love "sever[s] the crucial link between ethics and *eudaimonia,* the good for man or human fulfillment" (p. 90). It is not clear from Cottingham's remarks exactly how he would explain this "crucial link," but at least this much seems intended. A morality that does not give us a dispensation for a significant degree of partiality sets up a conflict between morality and personal love, for personal love cannot exist without preferential concern. But personal love is a basic good for humans, a condition of human fulfillment, and any morality that repudiates it (Godwin's, which forbids favoritism, is an extreme example) is unacceptable as a morality. No tenable ethical system can show such insensitivity toward a basic constituent of human well-being by failing to limit the scope of principles of comparative justice.[10] And if morality demands impartial justice only in specific contexts so as to allow for the love that cannot exist without favoritism, then favoritism toward our friends and loved ones does not in itself violate any moral requirement of even-handed treatment. If it did, the most that could be said for favoritism is that loyalty toward those we love sometimes excuses us from living up to the harsh standards that the moral law sets for us. But in fact what we should say is that the moral law does not set such harsh standards for the personal interactions of private individuals.

I find this convincing: an acceptable morality must not forbid us from giving our friends and loved ones preference over others. Human intimacy is a primary source of value and self-realization for most of us, and the special nature of intimacy is partly expressed in the favoritism we show our intimates. There is also a strong argument for favoritism from the point of view of a theory of right in that the capacity to act morally toward those in whom we take no special interest develops out of and is sustained by the special unselfish concern we have for our intimates. But it might be objected that Cottingham is wrong to connect love and favoritism the way he does. There is nothing morally suspect about (much of) our treatment of our intimates because it is not properly speaking preferential treatment at all. Spending most of my monthly salary on my family and giving only a bit of spare cash to charity might be called favoritism, but unlike money, much of what we give our friends and loved ones is not a scarce resource that intimates and nonintimates are in competition for. Lawrence Blum argues for this last point as follows:

> What we do for our friends is very particular to our relationship to them. . . . What is involved in comforting one's friend, for example, is particular to the friendship and grows with the friendship. . . . I cannot just pop over to someone's house who is in need of comfort and comfort him, in the way I can to my friend. . . . Thus in comforting my friend I am not doing something which I could typically be doing for another. . . . The lack of comparability between what I do for a friend and for a non-friend holds for many activities in which we please our friend or make him happy. [11]

But if there is this lack of comparability, it might be claimed, then it is misleading to say that I am favoring my friend over a stranger when, for example, I comfort my friend rather than a stranger. For I can only favor someone if I give that person something that I could give another, and I cannot give to strangers what I give to friends.

Blum's observations about the particular nature of doing good for our friends are certainly correct, but they do not weaken the link between love and favoritism. There is genuine favoritism being practiced in our dealings with our intimates because intimates and nonintimates compete for limited psychological and nonmaterial resources. The specific benefiting that I do for a friend may be such that it does not make sense to speak of doing it for a stranger: what I am doing for my friends I could not just as well be doing for strangers. But nonfriends are in competition with friends for my time, energy, and sympathy, and looked at this way, I choose against strangers when I choose to do good for my friends.

It is a mistake to think, however, that such genuine partiality toward friends and loved ones runs afoul of a constitutive norm of moral thinking (viz., impartiality) and that partiality cannot be justified from the standpoint of one among others.[12] There are reasons we can appreciate from an impartial standpoint for accepting principles that permit, and in some cases even require, a privileged status for our friends and loved ones. From this standpoint, we can appreciate the centrality of love relationships to human well-being, the importance of particularistic, preferential concern for our loved ones' interests in the formation and maintenance of deeply intimate union and the expression of personal love, and the role of such concern in developing and supporting our moral capacities.[13] Similarly, the case of promise-keeping shows that impartialist justification does not necessarily prohibit giving special consideration to some rather than to others (in other words, that impartiality in the justification of principles does not have to be mirrored in impartiality in the content of those principles). Since we can confidently pursue our ends only in a framework of relatively secure expectations about how others will relate to us, and promises help to secure expectations, some principle of promise-keeping is presumably acceptable from a point of view that gives impartial positive consideration to the interests of all. Yet the principle of promise-keeping is person-differentiating because it requires that we not treat the person to whom we have made a promise as just one among others, but rather as the person to whom we have made a promise. To ignore this is to render promising otiose.

Again, it is one thing to say that a moral justification for some principle of conduct must be specifiable in general terms that can be appreciated from a point of view that precludes favoritism, and quite another to say that impartiality is what the principle actually requires of us in our dealings with others. Impartiality does not

entail that moral norms require us to give equal weight to the interests of all, and principles allowing or requiring differential treatment of others can be authorized from an impartial standpoint that
transcends our personal standpoints, considered egocentrically.[14]

There is, Nicholas Rescher argues,[15] a quick (too quick) way to
dispose of the claim that giving special consideration to persons who
stand in some special relation to us is unjustified because it goes
against the dictum to treat everyone the same. We could say that the
dictum survives in these cases in the following form: for any person
x, if x belongs to category C, then he or she must or may be treated in
special manner M. For example, for any person x, if x belongs to the
category of person-to-whom-I-have-promised, or child, or friend,
then I am obliged to or permitted to do such-and-such things for that
person that I would not be called upon to do for someone who does
not belong to this category. But Rescher maintains that support for
differential treatment by way of hypothetical conditionalization is
suspect, for in this conditional way we can always introduce a spurious "universality into a situation that is fundamentally nonuniver-
sal, differential, and selectively preferential" (p. 75). What makes it
spurious, it seems, is that the justification is tacked on after the fact,
and that I am only universalizing when I have this child, friend, or
the like. In other words, the thesis that special treatment of my
friend or loved one is justified because "anyone at all"—provided
the person is my friend or loved one—may or must be treated in
manner M, rings hollow because it is not anyone at all but only my
friend or loved one that I am actually concerned about. Rescher also
complains that this universalization of preferential treatment is
fraudulent in that nothing is said about why certain categories of
persons qualify as the beneficiaries of my special treatment. I agree
with Rescher that we need some explanation for why we should or
may treat members of a certain group G differentially. But if
Rescher is suggesting that particularistic, selectively preferential
attachment necessarily precludes genuine impartialist justification,
I disagree. *Appeal* to impartialist considerations might interfere
with the spontaneity and directness of my concern for a friend or
loved one, but there can *be* an impartialist justification even if it
does not as such intrude upon my deliberations. I can appreciate at
any time, even in the absence of friends or loved ones at that time,
that these personal relations do ground special obligations.

It would be a caricature of impartialist moral theory to character-ize it as necessarily denying that we can be linked to particular others by special relations that make it morally proper to treat these persons in special ways. But it is just such a caricature that we find in some contemporary criticisms of traditional approaches to ethics. Christina Hoff Sommers' analysis of filial duty is a case in point.[16] Sommers distinguishes between two theses about the "ethi-cal pull" that beings exert on moral agents. The first, which she rejects, is the thesis of equal pull, attributed without argument to Kant and Mill, according to which "ethical pull is constant regard-less of circumstance, familiarity, kinship and other special rela-tions" (p. 444). Her own view is that ethical pull varies with these factors, a thesis that she calls differential pull. Yet this is hardly a novel position, nor is it rejected by Kant or Mill. In fact, Sommers' differential pull morality is just equal pull morality qualified: we are similarly obligated to others when we are in relevantly similar special relations with them.

Let us now look a bit more closely at the special duties them-selves that we have to our friends and loved ones. What effect do such relations have on our moral duties? As Robert Goodin notes,[17] commonsense morality tends to explain this in either or both of the following two ways. According to one standard view, personal relations "magnify" or strengthen previously existing moral duties. The duty not to harm another or to inflict unneces-sary suffering upon another is owed to anyone and everyone in the world at large. It is especially wrong, however, to harm our friends, family members, and the like. We also have a duty to help others who are in need or jeopardy, provided we can do so without excessive cost or risk to ourselves. This duty is imperfect because it is not owed to all others or to specified others; we are obligated or duty-bound to help people in general, but not everyone. In this case, our personal relations transform an imperfect duty into a perfect duty whose object is completely specified. (Note that what counts as excessive loss or risk in connection with helping strangers may not be excessive if it is our intimates who are in trouble. We are normally expected to take greater risks in order to help our intimates than to help strangers.) The idea here is not that we acquire new duties to our friends and loved ones that we do not have to our fellowmen as such, but rather that the general duties carry over to our personal relations, only in a stronger or perfect form. In general, personal relationships make our ordinary general duties especially stringent in relation to those to whom we are bound by mutual love and friendship, and this is why our duties to them are special.

On the second view, which is not incompatible with the first, we have duties to certain persons over and above the ordinary general ones, duties that are not just stronger versions of these. Goodin says that here special duties are to be construed as "multipliers." Consider parental duties, for example. We all have a general imperfect duty to be kind and considerate in dealing with children. But in addition, in any society where natural parents are the normal caretakers, parents who decide to bring a child into the world have special duties to that child because, in deciding to procreate, they take upon themselves responsibility for this child's well-being and development. The decision to procreate creates new duties from scratch, duties that are owed by a specific agent to a specific individual and that did not exist in a general form prior to the decision. (Of course, we are all obliged to refrain from abuse and molestation of all children, whether or not they are specifically in our charge. When it is children in our charge who are abused or molested, the wrong is regarded as particularly heinous.)

Similarly, friendship does not only transform preexisting imperfect duties into perfect ones or magnify duties that we owe, less strongly, to everyone at large. The voluntary actions of friends create new special duties de novo. There is an illuminating parallel here with relationships created by promise. "By promising to do or not to do something," H.L.A. Hart observes,

> we voluntarily incur obligations and create or confer rights on those to whom we promise; we alter the existing moral independence of the parties' freedom of choice in relation to some action and create a new moral relationship between them, so that it becomes morally legitimate for the person to whom the promise is given to determine how the promisor shall act.[18]

The profession of friendship sets up a new moral relationship in much the same way as promising. Friends, like those who make and accept promises, give one another to understand that they can be counted on to act in certain ways, do rely on each other, know that they rely each other, and so forth. Of course, friendships differ in important ways from relationships created by promise. Though friends not infrequently make definite promises of service to each other, the obligations of friendship are typically not as deliberately incurred or as definite as those that arise through promising. In both cases, however, individuals (implicitly or explicitly) make certain commitments to specific others and have special duties to them to fulfill these commitments.

The special duties that we have to our intimates may also correspond to special rights possessed by them. Duty and right are then just different names for the same ethical relationship, according to the perspective from which it is regarded. To speak of duties is to take the point of view of the agent and to indicate what must be done to avoid moral failure; to speak of rights is to take the point of view of the recipient and to indicate what must be received or accorded if there is to be no moral failure. Especially important is the fact that the mutual recognition of duties and their corresponding rights in close personal relationships is not necessarily destructive of, but can actually strengthen, mutual love and intimacy.[19] It is dangerous sentimentalism to assert that concern for rights is divisive and only impedes the spontaneous flow of goodwill.

What is antithetical to the goods associated with intimacy is a particular way of thinking about and using rights that is at home in political and impersonal contexts. Here rights are demanded by the powerless as a way of wringing recognition and respect from the powerful. Those who have been subservient press for the recognition and enforcement of rights against adversaries whose interests are threatened by a change in the status quo, and in the struggle for rights the formerly submissive gain confidence and autonomy. Once the rights are established, if they are, they are typically used self-defensively to protect the right-holder's moral space from being entered by others or interests from being thwarted by others. Clearly, however, when this way of thinking about and using rights is imported into personal relationships, those features of personal relationships that make them personal and worth having are absent. We do not want such relationships to be adversarial: the parties to them should only rarely conceive of themselves as separate beings with conflicting and antagonistic interests. Thus, while thinking in terms of rights is not out of place in healthy personal relationships,[20] in this case we have not thought about them in the appropriate way.

As long as rights are regarded as weapons of the oppressed or endangered, asserted in order to set limits to others' power over us and to protect ourselves from them, they are ill-suited to personal relations. To be sure, personal relationships can be oppressive, and insistence on rights in these relationships may help to restore or foster self-respect in those who have been oppressed by their intimates. But in the best (or healthy) personal relationships, rights will normally not have to be insisted on, and consideration of rights will augment mutual love and affection as a basis for trust.

20

Conclusion: Intimacy and Integrity

Persons of integrity are faithful to their core commitments, to those commitments, in other words, that have a privileged status in their lives because they reflect what is most important to them and give them reasons for living. The immediate object of the commitment is a principle, cause, ideal, person, country, or the like, with which they identify themselves and which they cannot betray without betraying themselves, and their commitment to the maintenance of their own integrity is parasitic on these other commitments.[1] They would betray themselves if they betrayed them because these attachments are not merely externally related to their self-conceptions. They are constituents of their identities and as such function, so to speak, as premises of their agency. (I do not mean to suggest here that a person cannot or should never re-examine his or her constitutive attachments. The question of the good in my life is not just one of how best to interpret the meaning of these attachments, but also extends to a consideration of their value.)

The constitutive loyalties of persons of integrity can be relatively narrow or quite wide. Their loyalty may be to their friends, loved ones, or family; to their profession or country; or wider still, to the whole of humanity. What all loyalties have in common is that one views their objects as somehow one's own, as belonging to oneself, not in a proprietary sense, but in the sense that one has committed oneself to them. I am not just loyal to a friend, but to *my* friend; not loyal to a country, but to *my* country; and similarly, I am only loyal to humanity if I regard it as "my species." As a rule, however, proximate objects evoke more intense loyalty than distant ones, and among proximate objects, those we love and with whom we have close affectional ties evoke the most intense loyalty of all.

Not all breaches of loyalty expose one to the charge of having violated one's integrity. One might be expected to be loyal to some extent to one's employer, for example, and perhaps one acknowledges that one should be, but it does not follow that one could not be disloyal to that employer without self-betrayal and personal disintegration. A particular instance of disloyalty is connected to the loss of integrity only when it involves the betrayal of an identity-conferring commitment. Close friendships and love relations, however, involve the kind of deep personal commitment that, as Bernard Wiliams puts it, "compels . . . allegiance to life itself."[2] Since these relationships contribute to our identity and help give our lives their point, disloyalty to our friends and loved ones is an especially serious matter considered from the point of view of the one who is disloyal.

What constitutes disloyalty to our friends and loved ones varies from case to case, since to a large degree the bases and expectations of every friendship and love relationship are different. In general, a loyal friend does not violate the trust established by the friendship, but the conditions under which such trust is violated cannot be spelled out in the abstract. Further, while close friendships and love relations involve our integrity, we normally have other core commitments as well that relate to different spheres of our lives. When our commitment to our friend or loved one comes into conflict with one of these other commitments, we do not necessarily lose our integrity if we choose against the former.

Love and friendship are loyalties to particular persons, and the interests of my friends and loved ones have a special importance and weight for me by virtue of the fact that I have committed myself to them. This is what it means to have a loyalty to them. For a consequentialist, however, these personal loyalties, and communal loyalties as well, must be subordinated to what is best from a more impartial standpoint, usually taken to be the standpoint of the species as a whole. Species loyalty, as we might call it, is more demanding than any of these less inclusive loyalties.[3] But with respect to any loyalty, even species loyalty, a consequentialist must say this: the fact that the object of a loyalty is *mine* in itself adds nothing to the moral case for my doing what is good for it. Considerations regarding *my* friends, *my* country, or *my* species are in no way directly relevant to what I should do. Their being mine is not in itself a morally weighty factor, and so loyalty itself is devalued. What matters is only that one bring about the best state of affairs, and what is best is fundamentally independent of any relation to the agent.

Consequentialists have not felt compelled to say that agents should always consciously aim at producing the best overall state of affairs. They have construed their theory as a standard of rightness rather than as a decision procedure, and offered a defense of preferential treatment of our intimates that rests on the moral importance of propinquity. Our closeness to and intimate knowledge of friends and loved ones justifies some partiality in our treatment of these persons, some special attention to satisfying *their* needs and promoting *their* well-being, the argument goes, because such closeness and knowledge are linked with the accurate identification of needs and greater effectiveness of response. If we are actually to help another, we have got to know what action would really help and be in a position to undertake it. Since we are in an especially good position to see and minister to the needs of those near and dear to us, we are obliged to do more for them than for unrelated others in an effort to spare them harm and bring them benefits. Preference for friends and loved ones is thus justified on the ground that it produces the best outcome overall. As Sidgwick puts it, "each man will obviously promote the general happiness best by rendering services to a limited number, and to some more than others."[4] But again how overall states of affairs are ranked depends in no way on its being *my* friend or loved one to whom I show favoritism. Personal bonds and loyalties are morally significant solely because of their contribution to the general good and not because of their role in the lives of particular individuals.[5]

Now it might be argued that with suitable changes in its theory of the good, consequentialism can successfully rebut the charges I have made. A pluralistic consequentialism ascribes intrinsic value to a variety of different sorts of states of affairs, among which might be particularistic loyalties and the acts that express them. For such a consequentialism, it can be of intrinsic value, for example, that people have friends and loved ones and care specially about them, and more generally, that people have and express particular loyalties. But for pluralistic consequentialism, as an agent-neutral theory of right, the value of S's expressing personal loyalty is not intrinsically affected by its being *the agent's* expressing of *his* or *her* loyalty. At best agent-neutral consequentialism can only enjoin us to bring about the intrinsically good state of affairs of people having and expressing their loyalties. Of course, from an impersonal standpoint, my friends are not more valuable than other people's friends, and my integrity is not more valuabe than is theirs. But this is not the only standpoint from which to regard our friends and integrity, nor, I believe, is it the perspective from which we principally live our lives.

For many of us, friendship is an identity-conferring commitment. I take it as intrisically relevant to what I should do that I have committed myself to this particular person, that fidelity to this commitment provides a measure against which I judge (in part) the worth of my life, and that as a result betrayal of my friend would constitute a diminishing of my integrity. That it is my own integrity that is at stake in how I conduct myself toward my friend has fundamental importance for me. Now the consequentialist attack on loyalties entails a repudiation of the notion that we have any basic, nonderivative responsibility to maintain or repair our own integrity[6]: there is ultimately no moral reason for me to care more about the loss of my own integrity than to care about such a loss on the part of another person. The consequentialist does not just recommend the adoption of an impartial viewpoint in moral assessment, for I can be impartial without denying that I have a unique relationship to my own integrity. I need only accept that others have the same special relation to their own principles and commitments as I have to my own. Rather, I am to detach myself altogether from the personal point of view—the point of view from which we care about our own integrity in a specially intimate way and give special weight to our own commitments just because they are ours—and take a wholly impersonal attitude to myself.[7] From this impersonal point of view, I am just one person among others: not because I recognize that each of us has a special relation to his or her own commitments that cannot be transferred to others, but because I see my personal concerns as merely means to or as subordinate to the end of achieving some overall good.[8]

Consequentialists not only condemn egoism, they also deny the legitimacy of another kind of self-concern, a self-concern that is reflected in attaching special value to fidelity to one's own commitments. Those who care about themselves in this way do not treat their own integrity and the integrity of others as interchangeable goods: their first allegiance is to their own. Such partiality toward one's own integrity is not to be confused with mere prudence or self-interest. Someone who refuses to do something because it would violate *his* or *her* integrity is not necessarily maximizing his or her personal utility (in fact, people often sacrifice their happiness, and sometimes even their lives, in the name of loyalty). What one thinks about when one's commitments are put to the test is better expressed as self-worth rather than self-interest. Moreover, those who regard their own integrity as their fundamental responsibility are not necessarily preoccupied with images of themselves as persons of integrity, and do not necessarily go through life shielding their principles and commitments from new experiences and the reactions of other people. They are able to experience a sense of connectedness with other people, to form deep attachments to them, to love and befriend them.

This special concern for one's own integrity is particularistic and hence similar to personal love. An individual who takes his or her own integrity seriously, more seriously than the integrity of someone else, is concerned about someone in particular, him or herself. That person values him or herself not just as an instance of a type ("person with integrity"), but as a unique[9] individual with his or her own distinctive worth ("this particular person who is me and who possesses integrity"). No one else can substitute here because the individual's own commitments have a special status in the person's scale of values precisely because they are personal. Similarly, in personal love we value the particular uniqueness of another person; it is the deepest experience of the irreplaceability of persons. Our love attaches to another in his or her own individuality, not simply as a bearer of a common general property, and so, like the special concern we have for our own integrity, it is nontransferable. When I love someone in a personal sense, that person has a distinctive value for me that is not reducible to conformity to certain general norms or a contribution to the social good. Likewise, the self for whose integrity I hold myself especially accountable stands out from others by virtue of its having a normative significance all of its own.[10]

Finally, it is not my integrity alone that I am concerned about in personal relationships. In addition to the fact that my image of myself and sense of personal worth are intimately connected with my commitments to friends and loved ones, love and close friendship involve a direct concern for the integrity of those I care about. In one sense, to love someone is to desire whatever that person desires for the reason that the person desires it (which is different from desiring something for another because it will be for the other's good as I see it). But we might say that personal love is more than this: it is directed toward the good of the whole particular person I love, and among those who have attained a personality of their own, their good is determined relative to their hierarchy of values and concerns. So if I see that the actions or choices of those I love place those things that they care most deeply about in jeopardy, I will inform them of this and, if need be, exert pressure on them to maintain integrity and support and encourage their efforts to do so. (Needless to say, I will not entice or pressure those I love into conduct that does not agree with the values with which they most closely identify.) I want my beloved to be true to his or her core commitments for my beloved's sake, and my helping him or her to maintain or restore integrity is an indication of the depth of my commitment.[11]

Notes

Introduction

1. See Alasdair MacIntyre, *After Virtue* (Notre Dame: University of Notre Dame Press, 1984); Michael Sandel, *Liberalism and the Limits of Justice* (Cambridge: Cambridge University Press, 1982).

2. Williams' characterization comes from "Persons, Character, and Morality," in *Moral Luck* (Cambridge: Cambridge University Press, 1981), pp. 2–5.

3. Ibid., p. 18.

4. "Remapping the Moral Domain: New Images of the Self in Relationship," in T. C. Heller, M. Sosna, and D. Wellbery, eds. *Reconstructing Individualism: Autonomy, Individuality and the Self in Western Thought* (Stanford, CA: Stanford University Press, 1986).

5. See Owen Flanagan, Jr., and Jonathan Adler, "Impartiality and Particularity," *Social Research* 50 (Autumn 1983): 576–96. See also Gertrud Nunner-Winkler, "Two Moralities? A Critical Discussion of an Ethic of Care and Responsibility versus an Ethic of Rights and Justice," in W. Kurtines and J. Gewirtz, eds. *Morality, Moral Behavior, and Moral Development* (New York: John Wiley and Sons, 1984), pp. 348–61.

Chapter 1

1. *The Autobiography of John Stuart Mill* (Garden City, NY: Doubleday), p. 104.

2. *Meno,* 100b.

3. "Can Virtue Be Taught?" in R. F. Dearden, P. H. Hirst and R. S. Peters, eds. *Education and Reason* (London: Routledge & Kegan Paul, 1972), pp. 44–57.

4. John Rawls, *A Theory of Justice* (Cambridge, MA: Belknap Press, 1971), p. 176.

5. "Can Ethics Provide Answers?" in M. Velasquez and C. Rostan-kowski, eds. *Ethics: Theory and Practice* (Englewood Cliffs, NJ: Prentice-Hall, 1985), p. 29.

6. "Internal and External Reasons," in *Moral Luck* (Cambridge: Cambridge University Press, 1981), p. 102.

7. Ibid, pp. 104–5.

8. Though I do no more here than scratch the surface of this debate, it should be noted that it has been thought to have special significance for the concerns of this book. Internalist accounts of reasons for action have played an important role in recent challenges to traditional moral theory—Kantian or utilitarian—for their failure to respect the personal point of view. One example is Jeffrey Olen's recent book *Moral Freedom* (Philadelphia: Temple University Press, 1988), where what he calls internalism is a crucial element of his argument that the demands of impersonal morality do not always override the demands of personal morality. Unfortunately, we cannot extract a single definition of "internalism" from the various discussions in the philosophical literature.

9. On what makes something an important and fundamental human good, see James D. Wallace, "The Importance of Importance," in *Moral Relevance and Moral Conflict* (Ithaca, NY: Cornell University Press, 1989).

10. Susan Wolf tries to make a case for this in "Moral Saints," *Journal of Philosophy* 79 (1982): 419–39.

11. "The Importance of What We Care About," *Synthese* 53 (1982), p. 257.

Chapter 2

1. "The Importance of What We Care About," *Synthese* 53 (1982), p. 260.

2. See Chapter 14, "Caring About Others"

3. *Harm To Others* (New York: Oxford University Press, 1984), pp. 33–34.

4. As Frankfurt observes, op. cit., p. 260.

5. "Caring About Caring: A Reply to Frankfurt," *Synthese* 53 (1982), p. 274.

6. "The Rights of Animals and Unborn Generations," in William Blackstone, ed. *Philosophy and Environmental Crisis* (Athens: University of Georgia Press, 1974), pp. 49–50.

7. *Harm to Others,* op. cit., p. 32.

8. *On Caring* (New York: Harper & Row, 1971), p. 10.

9. See Robert Gordon, "The Aboutness of Emotion," *American Philo-*

sophical Quarterly 11 (1974):27–36; Robert Solomon, "Emotions and Choice," in A. Rorty, ed. *Explaining Emotions* (Berkeley: University of California Press, 1980), pp. 251–81.

10. By, for example, Robert Kraut in "Love *De Re*," in P. French, T. Uehling, Jr., and H. Wettstein, eds. *Midwest Studies in Philosophy, Vol. X* (Minneapolis: University of Minnesota Press, 1986), pp. 413–30.

11. *A Theory of Justice* (Cambridge, MA: Belknap Press, 1971), p. 478.

12. *Ethics and the Limits of Philosophy* (Cambridge, MA: Harvard University Press, 1985), p. 183.

13. For more on infatuation, see Chapter 16.

14. "Caring About Caring: A Reply to Frankfurt," op. cit., p. 284.

15. *Caring: A Feminine Approach to Ethics and Moral Education* (Berkeley: University of California Press, 1984), p. 94.

Chapter 3

1. *The Rejection of Consequentialism* (Oxford: Clarendon Press, 1982).

2. See the discussion of agent-neutral and agent-relative value in Eric Mack, "Moral Individualism: Agent-Relativity and Deontic Restrictions," forthcoming in *Social Philosophy and Policy.*

3. *Persons, Rights, and the Moral Community* (New York: Oxford University Press, 1987), p. 241.

4. It might be objected that in this case, the person does not really *care* about the hobby, but only takes an interest in it. As I shall explain in a moment, I think this objection is insensitive to important differences in caring. It expresses a too-elevated view of caring.

5. In order to regard something as of *value,* rather than merely as fun to do and the like, one must reflect on it from a point of view independent of one's desires. From this standpoint, what one values may be judged to be innocent or positively valuable.

6. *Impartial Reason* (Ithaca: Cornell University Press, 1983), p. 165.

7. Jeffrey Olen thinks that the value of a project that gives worth and meaning to my life

> does not rest solely on my own dispositions. . . . If I am to reflect on my various projects, if I am to discover that some are . . . a source of value, worth, and meaning, then, however personal my reasoning may be, it seems that I must also be regarding myself as a member of a community with shared values.

See *Moral Freedom* (Philadelphia: Temple University Press, 1988), pp. 31–33.

8. Gabriele Taylor, *Pride, Shame and Guilt* (Oxford: Clarendon Press, 1985); Lynne McFall, "Integrity," *Ethics* 98(1987): 5–20.

9. It is not required that on every occasion in which a person acts with integrity, the agent be thinking that what he or she is committed to has impersonal value. The belief in impersonal value functions as a background assumption that need only enter consciousness from time to time.

10. For more on this notion of integrity, see Chapter 12.

Chapter 4

1. *Metamorphosis* (New York: Basic Books, 1959), pp. 83, 167.

2. See the section entitled "Mountain Climbing and Self-Knowledge" in Douglas Walton, *Courage: A Philosophical Investigation* (Berkeley: University of California Press, 1986), pp. 207–13.

3. This explanation of how friendship is a means to self-knowledge is more dynamic than the one John Cooper attributes to Aristotle. Cooper has Aristotle argue this way: "For knowing intuitively that he and his friend are alike in character, such a person could, by studying his friend's character, come to know his own." ("Aristotle on Friendship," in A. Rorty, ed. *Essays on Aristotle's Ethics* [Berkeley: University of California Press, 1980], p. 322.) Instead of "studying," I stress corrective or confirmatory feedback.

4. *Subjecting and Objecting* (Oxford: Basil Blackwell, 1983), p. 187.

5. *Caring: A Feminine Approach to Ethics and Moral Education* (Berkeley: University of California Press, 1984), p. 165.

6. "Persons, Character and Morality," in A. Rorty, ed. *The Identities of Persons* (Berkeley: University of California Press, 1976), p. 215.

7. *On Caring* (New York: Harper & Row, 1971), pp. 67–72.

8. See Mayeroff, ibid, p. 54.

Chapter 5

1. See Epictetus' advice in *The Enchiridion,* Sec. 26:

Is the child or wife of another dead? There is no one who would not say, "This is an accident of mortality." But if anyone's own child happens to die, it is immediately, "Alas! how wretched am I." It should be always remembered how we are affected on hearing the same thing concerning others.

Here Epictetus relies on what he takes to be the universal fact of indifference to the fate of others outside our narrow circle.

2. Annette Baier explores "three tests of our loves," all of which are "versions of a demand for a certain sort of independence or autonomy in our loves and carings," in "Caring About Caring: A Reply to Frankfurt," *Synthese* 53 (1982), pp. 280–87.

Chapter 6

1. "A Critique of Utilitarianism," in J.J.C. Smart and Bernard Williams, eds. *Utilitarianism: For and Against* (Cambridge: Cambridge University Press, 1973), pp. 116–17.

2. Bernard Williams, "Persons, Character, and Morality," in A. Rorty, ed. *The Identities of Persons* (Berkeley: University of California Press, 1976), p. 209; and "A Critique of Utilitarianism," p. 116.

3. See Loren Lomasky, "A Refutation of Utilitarianism," *Journal of Value Inquiry* 17 (1983): 269–73.

4. "The Objectivity of Morals and the Subjectivity of Agents," *American Philosophical Quarterly* 22 (1985), p. 284.

5. "Persons, Character, and Morality," op. cit., p. 210.

6. Ibid.

7. "Egoists, Consequentialists, and Their Friends," *Philosophy and Public Affairs* 16 (1987), p. 79.

8. Op. cit., p. 110.

9. *The Rejection of Consequentialism: A Philosophical Investigation of the Considerations Underlying Rival Moral Conceptions* (Oxford: Clarendon Press, 1982), p. 56.

10. "Moral Integrity and Moral Psychology: A Refutation of Two Accounts of the Conflict Between Utilitarianism and Integrity," *Journal of Value Inquiry* 20 (1986), p. 286.

11. This claim is also defended by Spencer Carr, "The Integrity of a Utilitarian," *Ethics* 86 (1976): 241–46; Sarah Conly, "Utilitarianism and Integrity," *Monist* 66 (1983): 298–311; John Harris, "Williams on Negative Responsibility and Integrity," *Philosophical Quarterly* 24 (1974): 265–73; Kenneth Rogerson, "Williams and Kant on Integrity," *Dialogue* 22 (1983): 461–78; and Gregory Trianosky, op. cit.: 279–88.

12. See, for example, Robert Merrihew Adams, "Should Ethics Be More Impersonal? A Critical Notice of Derek Parfit, *Reasons and Persons*," *Philosophical Review* 98 (1989), esp. pp. 452–53; Neera Badhwar, "Utilitarianism and the Justification of Friendship," (unpublished manuscript); and Bernard Williams, *Utilitarianism: For and Against,* op. cit., pp. 128–35. Scheffler also admits that he is "sympathetic toward this outlook," but he prefers not to take a stand on whether the separation of

justification and motivation renders consequentialism unacceptable as a moral theory. See *The Rejection of Consequentialism,* op. cit., pp. 43–53.

13. *Common-sense Morality and Consequentialism* (London: Routledge and Kegan Paul, 1985), p. 32.

Chapter 7

1. "Agent-Centered Restrictions from the Inside Out," *Philosophical Studies* 50 (1986), p. 306.

2. According to Paul Gomberg, a person has "consequentialist integrity" if one makes a consequentialist imperative one's dominant purpose and integrates all other purposes into a life that serves this overriding goal. Consequentialism, Gomberg admits, can ask a lot of us, but consequentialist integrity is neither impossible nor too demanding. See "Consequentialism and History," *Canadian Journal of Philosophy* 19 (1989): 383–403.

3. *Nobel Prize Lecture: One Word of Truth* (London, 1972).

4. "It Makes No Difference Whether or Not I Do It," *Proceedings of the Aristotelian Society,* Supplementary Vol. 49 (1975), p. 184.

5. Bernard Williams, "Utilitarianism and Moral Self-Indulgence," in H. D. Lewis, ed. *Contemporary British Philosophy 4* (London: Allen and Unwin, 1976), pp. 311–12.

6. "Sentiment and Sentimentality in Practical Ethics," *Proceedings and Addresses of The American Philosophical Association* 56 (1982), pp. 26–27.

7. Williams, op. cit., p. 315.

8. "Whatever the Consequences," in J. Thomson and G. Dworkin, eds. *Ethics* (New York: Harper and Row, 1968), p. 224.

9. Cf. Thomas Nagel's claim in "War and Massacre," *Philosophy and Public Affairs* 1 (1972), p. 132:

> If by committing murder one sacrifices one's moral purity or integrity, that can only be because there is *already* something wrong with murder. The general reason against committing murder cannot therefore be merely that it makes one an immoral person.

10. It will be remembered that in Chapter 3 I argued that serious commitment involves the belief that what is cared about just matters, and not merely in relation to me.

11. Charles E. Larmore makes the same point in *Patterns of Moral Complexity* (Cambridge: Cambridge University Press, 1987), p. 148.

12. Cf. remarks by Richard Norman, *Reasons for Action* (New York: Barnes and Noble, 1971), p. 98.

13. *A Critique of Utilitarianism* (Cambridge: Cambridge University Press, 1973), p. 98.

14. "It Makes No Difference Whether or Not I Do It," op. cit., p. 186.

15. As R. F. Holland points out in "Absolute Ethics, Mathematics and the Impossibility of Politics," in G. Vesey, ed. *Human Values* (Atlantic Highlands, NJ: Humanities Press, Inc., 1978), p. 187.

Chapter 8

1. James Gutmann also discusses these in "Integrity as a Standard of Valuation," *Journal of Philosophy* 42 (1945): 210–17.

2. I follow Robert Nozick, *Philosophical Explanations* (Cambridge, MA: Harvard University Press, 1981), pp. 100–4.

3. See ibid., p. 416.

Chapter 9

1. "Constancy and Purity," *Mind* 92 (1983), p. 499.

2. A person of integrity is faithful to commitments or principles that are authentically his or her own and not the product of mindless conformity or blind obedience to authority. Integrity is also tied to another component of our conception of autonomy: distinct self-identity or individuality. Harriet Goldhor Lerner, in her insightful book *The Dance of Anger* (New York: Harper and Row, 1985), discusses how difficult it is for women to define and maintain a separate self within their closest personal relationships. They tend to "de-self" themselves for those they care about. "De-selfing" works like this:

> We sacrifice our clear and separate identity [hence, our integrity] and our sense of responsibility for, and control over, our own life . . . a lot of energy goes into trying to "be for" the other person, and trying to make the other person think or behave differently. Instead of taking responsibility for our own selves, we tend to feel responsible for the emotional well-being of the other person and hold the other person responsible for ours. (p. 30)

Women are socialized to be excessively focused on, and fused with, the problems of others, and this prevents women from defining and maintaining a distinct self-identity.

3. "Persons, Character and Morality," in A. Rorty, ed *The Identities of Persons* (Berkeley: University of California Press, 1976), p. 209.

4. Kekes, op. cit.

5. For the distinction between active and passive senses of commitment, see S. I. Benn and G. F. Gaus, "Practical Rationality and Commitment," *American Philosophical Quarterly* 23 (1986), p. 256.

6. According to Roger Trigg, "any commitment . . . depends on two distinct elements. It presupposes certain beliefs and also involves a personal dedication to the actions implied by them." See *Reason and Commitment* (Cambridge: Cambridge University Press, 1973), p. 44.

7. "Freedom of the Will and the Concept of a Person," reprinted in Joel Feinberg, ed. *Reason and Responsibility,* 4th ed. (Belmont, CA: Dickenson, 1978), pp. 395–403.

8. For example, see Marilyn A. Friedman, "Autonomy and the Split-Level Self," *The Southern Journal of Philosophy* 24 (1986): 19–35. Friedman does not here characterize Frankfurt's account as male-biased, but I believe she would make this criticism.

9. *Critique of Pure Reason,* Norman Kemp Smith, trans. (New York: St. Martin's Press, 1965), p. 130.

10. Frankfurt, op. cit., p. 403 n.6.

11. In contrast to this, Frankfurt explores the notion of a "decisive" second-order volition in "Identification and Wholeheartedness," in F. Schoeman, ed. *Responsibility, Character and The Emotions* (Cambridge: Cambridge University Press, 1987), pp. 27–45.

12. *Pride, Shame, and Guilt* (Oxford: Clarendon Press, 1985), p. 114.

13. *Being and Nothingness,* Hazel Barnes, trans. (New York: Philosophical Library, 1956), p. 439.

14. See the discussions of existentialism in Mike W. Martin, *Self-Deception and Morality* (Lawrence, Kansas: University Press of Kansas, 1986), pp. 60–68; David Norton, *Personal Destinies* (Princeton: Princeton University Press, 1976), pp. 95–121; and G.J. Warnock, "On Choosing Values," In P. French, T. Uehling, and N. Wettstein, eds., *Midwest Studies in Philosophy III: Studies in Ethical Theory* (Minneapolis: University of Minnesota Press, 1978), pp. 28–34. This discussion of Sartre focuses on his official position, and I do not claim that he is always consistent with it. In fact, when Sartre engages in practical moral commentary, he seems to depart from it.

15. Sartre devotes much of the section entitled "The Origin of Nothingness" (Part one, Chapter one, Section V of *Being and Nothingness*) to its analysis.

16. For example, see the classic argument in Plato's *Protagoras,* and contemporary discussions by R. M. Hare in *Freedom and Reason* (Oxford: Oxford University Press, 1963), Chapter 5, and Gary Watson, "Skepticism about Weakness of Will," *Philosophical Review* 86 (1977): 316–39.

17. See discussion in Alfred Mele, *Irrationality* (New York: Oxford University Press, 1987).

18. David Kepesh, the hero of Philip Roth's *Professor of Desire* (New York: Farrar, Straus and Giroux, 1977), describes himself as a young man in the following way:

> I refuse—out of an incapacity that I elevate to a principle—to resist whatever I find irresistable, regardless of how unsubstantial and quirky, or childish and perverse, the source of the appeal might strike anyone else. (p. 14)

19. *Virtues and Vices* (Ithaca: Cornell University Press, 1978), p. 82. Cf. Philippa Foot: "It is only because fear and the desire for pleasure often operate as temptations that courage and temperance exist as virtues at all." ("Virtues and Vices," in *Virtues and Vices and Other Essays in Moral Philosophy* [Berkeley: University of California Press, 1978], p. 9)

20. *Immorality* (Princeton: Princeton University Press, 1984), p. 119.

21. Kekes, op. cit., p. 499.

22. *Eudemian Ethics* in J. Solomon and W. D. Ross, eds. *The Works of Aristotle*, Vol. IX (Oxford: Oxford University Press, 1915), 1228b24–30.

23. *Scoundrel Time* (Boston: Little, Brown, 1976).

24. *Elia Kazan: A Life* (New York: Alfred A. Knopf, 1988).

25. "Character, Virtue and Freedom," *Philosophy* 57 (1982), pp. 501–2.

26. "Integrity," *Proceedings of the Aristotelian Society* 55 (1981), p. 146.

27. *Pride, Shame, and Guilt,* op. cit., p. 121.

28. See, for example, Raphael Demos' influential article, "Lying to Oneself," *Journal of Philosophy* 57 (1960): 588–95.

29. Alfred Mele, *Irrationality,* op. cit., Chapter 9.

30. For more on the so-called paradox of self-deception, see Mike Martin's anthology, *Self-Deception and Self-Understanding* (Lawrence, Kansas: University Press of Kansas, 1985); Martin, *Self-Deception and Morality,* op. cit., pp. 18–30; and Ronald Milo, *Immorality,* op. cit., pp. 106–13.

31. Relevant here is Herbert Fingarette's remark:

> It is because the movement into self-deception is rooted in a concern for integrity of spirit that we temper our condemnation of the self-deceiver. We feel he is not a *mere* cheat. We are moved to a certain compassion in which there is awareness of the self-deceiver's authentic inner dignity as the motive of his self-betrayal. [*Self-Deception* (London: Routledge and Kegan Paul, 1969), p. 140.]

32. On the relationship between self-deception and weakness of will, see Bela Szabados, "The Self, Its Passions and Self-Deception," in Mike Martin, ed. *Self-Deception and Self-Understanding,* op. cit., pp. 149–51.

33. Two useful discussions of hypocrisy are Eva Feder Kittay, "On Hypocrisy," *Metaphilosophy* 13 (1982): 277–89; Bela Szabados, "Hypocrisy," *Canadian Journal of Philosophy* 9 (1979): 195–210. Kittay and Szabados agree that hypocrites do not always act to promote their self-interest at the expense of others. For Szabados, it is required only that we be able to "discern some personal stake which he [the hypocrite] has in his project of pretense" (p. 205).

34. *The Presentation of Self in Everyday Life* (Garden City, NY: Doubleday Anchor, 1959), p. 208; also pp. 58–66.

35. It may be asked here why persons of integrity have this attitude to hypocrisy. Hypocrisy is a form of incoherence, between belief and behavior or motive and action, and coherence is a fundamental requirement of personal integrity.

36. *Pride, Shame, and Guilt,* op. cit., p. 123.

37. Similarly, Pascal claims in his discussion of the wager that the practice of ritual, initially undertaken without much conviction, can eventually alter one's genuine inner beliefs:

> You would like to attain faith, and do not know the way; you would like to cure yourself of unbelief, and ask the remedy for it. Learn of those who have been bound like you, and who now stake all their possessions. These are people who know the way which you would follow, and who are cured of an ill of which you would be cured. Follow the way by which they began; by acting as if they believe, taking the holy water, having masses said, etc. Even this will naturally make you believe, and deaden your acuteness. [*Thoughts,* W.F. Trotter, trans. (New York: P.F. Collier and Son, 1910), p. 233ff.]

Chapter 10

1. "Freedom of the Will and the Concept of a Person," in Joel Feinberg, ed *Reason and Responsibility,* 4th ed. (Belmont, CA: Dickenson, 1978), p. 398.

2. See Harry Frankfurt, "The Importance of What We Care About," *Synthese* 53 (1982), pp. 263–65; Daniel Dennett, "I Could Not Have Done Otherwise—So What?" *Journal of Philosophy* 81 (1984), pp. 555–56.

3. See Michael Slote's example of a father who feels "he musn't let the police find his son, but must, instead, do everything in his power to help him get to a place of safety. . . . Parental love can lead someone to act this way and allow him to feel justified in doing so." [*Goods and Virtues* (Oxford: Clarendon Press, 1983), p. 86]

4. Peter van Inwagen, "The Incompatibility of Free Will and Determinism," *Philosophical Studies* 27 (1975), p. 188.

5. As Dennett argues, op. cit., pp. 556–57.

6. Ibid., p. 556.

7. "The Importance of What We Care About," op. cit., p. 263. See also Frankfurt's more extensive discussion in "Rationality and the unthinkable," in his *The Importance of What We Care About* (Cambridge: Cambridge University Press, 1988), pp. 177–90.

8. Bernard Williams distinguishes between these "two ways in which necessity may enter the structure of my thought" in "Practical Necessity," in his *Moral Luck* (Cambridge: Cambridge University Press, 1981), p. 127.

9. Character is also stressed in an interpretation Robert Gay gives of Williams' remarks on practical necessity:

> [T]he experience of practical necessity is presenting to me what is necessary if the self of my present desires and present character is to continue: anything else would not fit in with this character.

But Gay suspects that this explanation of the experience of practical necessity in terms of continuity of character cannot plausibly be thought of as a reductive one:

> [W]hen we had thrashed out the issues, it might prove that our idea of what is essential to a person's character is not independent of the experience in which a specific consideration is picked out as the one on which we *must* act.

See Gay's excellent article, "Bernard Williams on Practical Necessity," *Mind* 98 (1989), pp. 559–60.

10. Though one might fail to do what one judges one must, Gay claims that

> the space [that the] "must" and "have to" [of practical necessity] leave for simply failing to act does seem very narrow: we seem driven to suppose something like what we picture when we imagine a creature charmed by a snake, with the creature thinking "I *must* do so and so," but finding that it is fixed to the spot and *cannot* escape.

See ibid., p. 552n.

11. "The Importance of What We Care About," op. cit., p. 263. Luther's use of constraint descriptions is also not just a matter of ceremonial politeness, as in "Excuse me but I *have* to disagree with you."

12. Gay (op. cit., p. 553) makes the same point:

> [When we imagine Luther], we surely do not envisage someone who simply does
> not care about anything other than loyalty to the truth as he sees it, nor someone
> who has carefully weighed up considerations on both sides, and has decided that
> on balance loyalty to the truth matters most to him. Rather, although there are
> in the situation before him a number of considerations which might engage his
> attention and affect a deliberation of the "balance of considerations" sort, here
> and now truthfulness and what it requires of him is presented in a special
> way. . . . He may say that this is what matters most to him; but this "mattering
> most" will not be the result of any weighing up of considerations, but of the way
> this consideration has been singled out in his thinking.

13. As Williams notes in "Practical Necessity," op. cit., p. 128.

14. *Ethics and the Limits of Philosophy* (Cambridge, MA: Harvard University Press, 1985), p. 188.

15. *Goods and Virtues,* op. cit., pp. 77–93.

16. See Williams, *Ethics and the Limits of Philosophy,* op. cit., pp. 188–89:

> The agent who does such a thing may feel that he must do it, that there is no
> alternative for him, while at the same time recognizing that it would not be a
> demand on others. The thought may come in the form that it is a demand on
> him, but not on others, because he is different from others; but the difference
> will then typically turn out to consist in the fact that he is someone who has this
> very conviction.

Chapter 11

1. *The Rejection of Consequentialism* (Oxford: Clarendon Press, 1982), p. 18.

2. As Peter Winch observes in "Moral Integrity," in P. Winch, *Ethics and Action* (London: Routledge and Kegan Paul, 1972).

3. *A Theory of Justice* (Cambridge, MA: Belknap Press, 1971), p. 519.

4. "Integrity," *Ethics* 98 (1987), p. 10.

5. Several of these points about the virtuous epistemic agent are taken from James A. Montmarquet, "Epistemic Virtue," *Mind* 96 (1987): 482–97.

6. Quoted in Lee Randolph Bean, "Entrepreneurial Science and the University," *The Hastings Center Report* 12 (1982), p. 6.

7. *After Virtue* (Notre Dame: University of Notre Dame Press, 1981), p. 175.

8. Bernard Mayo attempts to show that "personal integrity . . . is very

much the same thing as moral integrity," but the argument is unconvincing. See his "Moral Integrity," in Godfrey Vesey, ed. *Human Values* (Atlantic Highlands, NJ: Humanities Press, 1978), pp. 27–43.

9. "Morality and Importance," in G. Wallace and A.D.M. Walker, eds. *The Definition of Morality* (London: Methuen, Inc., 1970), p. 95.

10. Some who were opposed to punishment for Oliver North made this argument: he may have been wrong to do as he did, but he is nonetheless a man of moral (political) integrity. I take no position on this. My point is only that the latter claim presupposes that North is seen as a member of the same moral (political) community as those who so argue.

11. The connection between recognition of integrity and the possibility of a certain kind of political community is remarked on in Ronald Dworkin, *Law's Empire* (Cambridge, MA: Belknap Press, 1986), p. 166.

12. *Virtues and Vices,* op. cit., Chapter 4.

13. *Webster's New International Dictionary of the English Language,* 2nd ed. (Springfield, MA: G. and C. Merriam Co., 1949), p. 2727.

14. For a discussion of the Thomas More affair, see Peter French, *Ethics in Government* (Englewood Cliffs, NJ: Prentice-Hall, 1983), pp. 37–44.

15. "The Problem Solvers and the Public," in Peter French, ed. *Conscientious Actions* (Cambridge, MA: Schenkman, 1974), p. 88.

16. I follow Larry May here in "On Conscience," *American Philosophical Quarterly* 20 (1982): 57–67. According to May, there is an "egoistic motivation" at the core of the phenomenon of conscience. See also Bernard Gert, *The Moral Rules* (New York: Harper, 1973), p. 208:

> If one has pride and integrity, in addition to compassion, then he has additional reasons for being moral. Being moral is required to avoid not only remorse, but also shame and guilt . . . all of these reasons have an air of self-interest about them.

17. "Doubts About the Man of Conscience," in Peter French, ed. *Conscientious Actions,* op. cit., p. 29.

Chapter 12

1. "Constancy and Purity," op. cit., p. 499.

2. *Father and Son: A Study of Two Temperaments* (New York: W. W. Norton and Co., 1963), p. 84.

3. *The Nazi Doctors* (New York: Basic Books, 1986), pp. 422, 460.

4. A person may act in a principled manner without its being the case that his or her life is conducted in accordance with a coherent set of principles. And a person's conduct still reflects a pattern even when one

does not take up a view of one's life as a whole and guide oneself by an overall judgment of how to structure one's different principles within a system of principles. For as Kekes (op. cit., p. 499) notes, "patterns may be deliberate or fortuitous. The latter is a property every life has . . . for that pattern is simply the aggregate of [a person's] actions."

5. The first notion of living an integrated life might be labeled Aristotelian, the second, Nietzschean. I thank John Kleinig for pointing out these different interpretations to me.

6. Kekes, op. cit., p. 515.

7. "Integrity," *Ethics* 98 (1987), p. 13.

8. There are other ways to render one's commitments coherent as well. There may be a deeper kind of integration: commitments might not just be externally adjusted to one another, but one might be transformed in light of another. For example, what is possible for me in relationships of friendships might be altered by my moral convictions.

9. "Of Husbanding Your Will," in D.M. Frame, trans. *The Complete Essays of Montaigne* (Stanford, CA: University Press, 1958), pp. 770, 774.

10. Gerald Postema characterizes Montaigne's attitude here as a "strategy of detachment." See "Self-Image, Integrity, and Professional Responsibility," in D. Luban, ed. *The Good Lawyer: Lawyers' Roles and Lawyers' Ethics* (Totowa, NJ: Rowman and Allanheld, 1984), pp. 286–314.

11. See Ruth Barcan Marcus' remarks about the avoidance of moral dilemmas in "Moral Dilemmas and Consistency," *Journal of Philosophy* 72 (1980): 121–36.

12. I do not mean to deny, however, that conflict between our commitments may in fact deepen our understanding of them and provide opportunities for personal development.

13. "Doesn't Life Require Compromise?" in *The Virtue of Selfishness* (New York: New American Library, 1964), pp. 85–86.

14. *Law's Empire* (Cambridge, MA: Belknap Press, 1986), pp. 181–82.

15. Martin Benjamin, in his book-length treatment of integrity and compromise in ethics and politics, argues that the decision to seek or accept a compromise in cases of ethical disagreement is "at bottom a matter of judgment," and that "the principal values framing or guiding the exercise of judgment in the circumstances of compromise are individual integrity, overall utility (including social integrity), and equal respect." But he emphasizes that these values will conflict in certain circumstances and that they underdetermine choice about compromise. Different people will interpret and weigh these values differently, and so there is no single answer for everyone to the question whether a certain compromise is integrity-preserving. See his *Splitting the Difference: Compromise and Integrity in*

Ethics and Politics (Lawrence, Kansas: University Press of Kansas, 1990), esp. pp. 121–28.

Chapter 13

1. I say "somewhat ambiguous" because it is not completely clear from the text why Jones risks his life by joining the rebels.

2. "Moral Sensitivity," *Philosophy* 59 (1984), p. 15.

Chapter 14

1. Robespierre is an extreme example of this. Taking his cue from Rousseau's *Social Contract,* Robespierre set out to create a new world in which good men could find utopian happiness, a "republic of virtue." In single-minded devotion to this cause, Robespierre committed unspeakable atrocities.

2. As Lawrence Blum points out in "Compassion," in R. Kruschwitz and R. C. Roberts, eds., *The Virtues* (Belmont, CA: Wadsworth, 1987), pp. 232–33.

3. Philip Pettit's article, "The Paradox of Loyalty" [*American Philosophical Quarterly* 25 (1988): 163–71] has helped me to articulate the sense in which this is so.

4. Disinterested care means that x does not desire y's good as a means to x's own, and that x does not desire y's good only insofar as it is compatible with x's own independent good. Disinterested care most definitely does not entail that x derives no benefit "of his own" from caring about y. Kierkegaard argues that the best way to determine if x's attitude to y is not instrumental is to see whether x's love for y continues after y's death. [*Works of Love* (New York: Harper and Row, 1962), pp. 281–82.] Whether or not this is so, we can certainly maintain love for someone who is dead or permanently absent. What love for such persons involves requires a separate discussion, but I leave these cases aside.

5. "Friends and Future Selves," *The Philosophical Review* 95 (1986), p. 562.

6. Ibid., pp. 561–62.

7. The special concern for one's own integrity is taken up again in the conclusion.

8. But if x loves y, then, as David Annis argues, x *normally* wants this; if not, we need an explanation of mitigating circumstances before categorizing the attachment as love. See "Emotion, Love and Friendship," *International Journal of Applied Philosophy* 4 (1988): 1–7.

9. "Privacy: A Rational Context," in R. Wasserstrom, ed., *Today's Moral Problems* (New York: Macmillan, 1980), p. 369.

10. "Privacy, Intimacy, and Personhood," in R. Wasserstrom, ed., ibid, pp. 371–91.

11. Alan Soble argues that Reiman's conception is actually no less proprietary than Fried's:

> Whether an account of love smells of the market turns (as Reiman said) on whether the shared item is parceled out selectively to create scarcity. On this score, Reiman's account, if I am right, does no better than Fried's.

The Structure of Love (New Haven: Yale University Press, 1990), p. 185.

12. For example, see Joseph Kupfer, "Privacy, Autonomy, and Self-Concept," *American Philosophical Quarterly* 24 (1987): 81–89; and Robert Gerstein, "Intimacy and Privacy," *Ethics* 89 (1978): 76–81. Though I do not explicitly take up the issue of privacy again in what follows, some of what I say about intimacy seems to presuppose a background of privacy.

Chapter 15

1. Cf. R.S. Peters' characterization of a personal relationship as one involving "some reciprocal response of individual to individual . . . receptivity and outgoingness towards another at an affective level . . . as an individual human being." This is necessary for a personal relation, but as Peters notes, "usually when we talk of personal relationships we mean a development of [this] minimal type of relationship." See his "Personal Understanding and Personal Relationships," in T. Mischel, ed., *Understanding Other Persons* (Totowa, NJ: Rowman and Littlefield, 1974), pp. 54–56.

2. See Magda Denes, "Existential Approaches to Intimacy," in M. Fischer and G. Stricker, eds., *Intimacy* (New York: Plenum Press, 1983), pp. 136–39.

3. Lyn H. Lofland, *A World of Strangers: Order and Action in Urban Public Space* (New York: Basic Books, 1973), pp. 16–17.

4. *Behavior in Public Places* (New York: Free Press, 1963), p. 24. The following references to Goffman are from this book.

5. Focused interaction among strangers is not always constrained by prevailing social norms. Consider the case of Christian families who hid Jews (strangers to them) from the Nazis during the war years.

6. Virginia Held distinguishes between the domain of "particular flesh and blood others for whom we have actual feelings in our insides and in

our skin" and the domain of " "all others" of standard moral theory." The domain of particular others, she claims, is not limited to family members, neighbors, friends, and the like, but can include "actual starving children in Africa with whom one feels empathy or even the anticipated children of future generations." I find this confused. Held's point seems to be that I can care deeply about starving children in Africa and about children of future generations. Persons who are remote from us, whether spatially or temporally, can still engage our "actual feelings" and elicit our concern. But the notion of particularity should not be used here. How can children in Africa or future children be flesh and blood others for me, the way my friends are, for example, if I have never met them and their particular identities are unknown to me? See her "Feminism and Moral Theory," in E. Kittay and D. Meyers, eds. *Women and Moral Theory* (Totowa, NJ: Rowman and Littlefield, 1987), pp. 117–19.

7. I borrow here from John Rawls's characterization of an institution in *A Theory of Justice* (Cambridge, MA: Belknap Press, 1971), p. 55.

8. See Ralph H. Turner, "Role: Sociological Aspects," in D. Sills, ed., *International Encyclopedia of the Social Sciences,* Vol. 13 (New York: Macmillan, 1968), pp. 553–55.

9. On acquaintanceship as a cognitive relationship, see Murray S. Davis, *Intimate Relations* (New York: Free Press, 1973), pp. 94–104.

10. These relational features of acquaintanceship are culled from ibid., pp. 30–55.

11. Not all cases in which one is oriented toward and cares about another individual as a particular person presuppose acquaintance. Julius Moravcsik makes this point in "Communal Ties," *Proceedings and Addresses of the American Philosophical Association* 62 (1988): 211–25.

12. *Who's Afraid of Virginia Woolf?* (New York: Atheneum, 1982), pp. 158–59, 240–41.

13. See "Marriage, Love, and Procreation," in R. Baker and F. Elliston, eds., *Philosophy and Sex* (Buffalo, NY: Prometheus, 1975), pp. 195–198.

14. Alan Soble [*The Structure of Love* (New Haven: Yale University Press, 1990), p. 211] claims that "two lovers x and y might show concern for each other, share intense experiences with each other, and so forth, and yet never breathe a word or think a thought about their future. They live in the now." It might also be claimed that x and y who have a love-hate relationship can live in the now. X and y can still be committed to each other, however, even if they live in the now.

15. For a discussion of the difference between collective and private interests, see Gerald Postema, "Collective Evils, Harms, and the Law," *Ethics* 97 (1987): 414–40.

16. This is perhaps an appropriate place to mention that love and friend-

ship are messier phenomena than my rather selective discussion might suggest. Even in the best relationships, there are bound to be conflicts, disagreements, and misunderstandings; prudential reasoning, and not just feelings of love, accounts for the way we treat the other person; relationships wax and wane over long stretches of time; they can lose their spontaneity and impede rather than foster growth; and so forth. I believe these are important matters, but I have little or nothing to say about them because I think they introduce complications that do not affect the main claims and lines of argument in this part of the book.

Chapter 16

1. We must be careful here not to make this seem too deliberate. As Laurence Thomas notes, "it is all too obvious that as a rule we do not self-consciously choose our friends in the way we choose, say, the clothes we wear." See his "Friendship," *Synthese* 72 (1987), p. 218. Further, I do not claim that friendship is a voluntary relationship in all cultures. In our culture, no particular individuals are assigned by custom or tradition to be one's friends, but there are variations across cultures in the way in which the practice of friendship is carried on.

2. This interpretation of Plato has been disputed. Terence Irwin, for example, argues that

> Plato does not commit himself to this view [that the pupil ceases to love the objects at lower stages when he reaches higher stages]. . . . The lower stages are means to the higher, but Plato does not suggest they are only means. The lower beautifuls partake in the Form, and embody it imperfectly; Plato does not claim they are imperfect because they are purely instrumental, but only because they are incomplete expressions of beauty. [*Plato's Moral Theory* (Oxford: Clarendon Press, 1977), p. 169]

Another philosopher who rejects the traditional interpretation is A. W. Price, *Love and Friendship in Plato and Aristotle* (Oxford: Clarendon Press, 1989). He concludes his discussion of the *Symposium* in Chapter 2 as follows:

> An individual is retained as an object of love throughout the later stages of the ascent, though the kind of life that the lover, under guidance, achieves for him and for himself changes very considerably. (p. 53)

3. *The Nature of Love,* Vol. 1 (Chicago: University of Chicago Press, 1984), p. 82.

4. *Symposium,* in B. Jowett, trans., *Plato: The Republic and Other Works* (Garden City, NY: Anchor, 1973), p. 354.

5. "In each stage of the lover's ascent," according to Martha Nussbaum, "the aspiring lover, aided by his teacher, sees relationships between one beauty and another, acknowledges that these beauties are comparable and interchangeable, differing only in quantity." [*Fragility of Goodness: Luck and Ethics in Greek Tragedy and Philosophy* (Cambridge: Cambridge University Press, 1986), p. 180] Particular loved persons are seen to be interchangeable with one another early in the ascent. Ultimately, the lover transcends attachment to persons (and laws, institutions, etc.), and not just to a particular person. The teaching of Nussbaum's Diotima is not so much that particular persons are interchangeable as that all concrete manifestations of beauty—differing from one another only quantitatively—are expendable.

6. Nussbaum argues that the *Phaedrus* represents a conscious retraction by Plato of the *Symposium*'s strictures on emotional attachment to an individual. See ibid., pp. 200–33. My remarks on Platonic love focus on a position that, if Nussbaum is correct, Plato himself came to abandon.

7. I follow here Nussbaum's discussion of the *Symposium* in *Fragility of Goodness,* op. cit., pp. 180–83.

8. *Two Cheers for Democracy* (London: E. Arnold, 1939).

9. "The Individual as Object of Love in Plato," in *Platonic Studies* (Princeton: Princeton University Press, 1973), p. 31.

10. *The Natural History of Love* (New York: Minerva Press, 1959), pp. 363–71. For other conceptions of romantic love, see Willard Gaylin, *Rediscovering Love* (New York: Penguin, 1987); and Robert Solomon, *About Love: Reinventing Romance for Our Times* (New York: Simon and Schuster, 1988).

11. *Analyzing Love* (Cambridge: Cambridge University Press, 1987), pp. 77–78.

12. See Robert C. Solomon, *Love: Emotion, Myth and Metaphor* (Garden City, NY: Anchor, 1981), p. 181.

13. "The Phenomena of Love and Hate," *Philosophy* 53 (1978), p. 10.

14. "Love," *Proceedings of the Aristotelian Society* 76 (1976), pp. 154–56.

15. See Alan Soble, *The Structure of Love* (New Haven: Yale University Press, 1990), pp. 206–14.

16. So argues Nussbaum in "Plato on Commensurability and Desire," *Proceedings of the Aristotelian Society,* Supp. Vol. 58 (1984).

17. This is a point made by Robert Brown, op. cit., pp. 62–65.

18. "Between Consenting Adults," *Philosophy and Public Affairs* 14 (1985), p. 272.

19. *Nicomachean Ethics,* T. Irwin, trans. (Indianapolis: Hackett, 1985),

1168a8–9. All subsequent references in this chapter to the *Nicomachean Ethics* are from the Irwin translation.

20. In an ingenious article, Elijah Milgram attributes to Aristotle an account of friendship that is modeled after his explanation of parental love. See "Aristotle on Making Other Selves," *Canadian Journal of Philosophy* 17 (1987): 361–76.

21. *Philosophy of Right,* T. M. Knox, trans. (London: Oxford University Press, 1967), p. 117.

22. Joseph Kupfer discusses various obstacles to friendship between parents and their adult children in his perceptive paper, "Can Parents and Children Be Friends?" *American Philosophical Quarterly* 27 (1990): 15–26.

23. "Unreasonable Care: The Establishment of Selfhood," in G. Vesey, ed. *Human Values* (Atlantic Highlands, NJ: Humanities Press, 1978), pp. 1–26. With keen insight into the dynamics of parent–child interactions, Newson discusses several ways in which parental upbringing gives the child a belief in "his own intrinsic worth, his own fundamental *considerability.*"

24. *Nicomachean Ethics,* 1156a11–14.

25. The argument that pleasure and utility friendships have a substantial noninstrumental component—and are for this reason classified by Aristotle as forms of friendship—but are still essentially instrumental, comes from John Cooper, "Aristotle on Friendship," in A. Rorty, ed., *Essays in Aristotle's Ethics* (Berkeley: University of California Press, 1980), pp. 308–15.

26. Vlastos, op. cit.

27. "Plato and Aristotle on Friendship and Altruism," *Mind* 86 (1977): 532–54. According to Annas, Aristotle "could be said not to have fully attained the notion of loving someone truly as an individual, rather than as a bearer of desired qualities."

28. "Aristotle on the Good of Friendship," *Australasian Journal of Philosophy* 63 (1985): 269–82. Schoeman argues that there is a deep problem with Aristotle's account of friendship:

> Whereas we wanted the relationship to express concern for the friend for the friend's sake, it [on Aristotle's view] comes out as having concern for the friend for the sake of the friend's virtues. . . . But when we love the goodness of the person, we perhaps can best characterize that relationship as one of respect, not love or friendship.

29. Vlastos' criticism of Plato (and hence Aristotle), as I have interpreted it, focuses on the issue of replaceability. But he also seems to be making a different point, viz. that Platonic love is not love for the individual because its object is only the good qualities of the other, whereas

people have bad as well as good qualities. If this is why the individual is not loved, then were the other to have only good qualities, loving them would be loving the individual.

30. This is how Nancy Sherman interprets the second psychological principle expressed in the quote from Aristotle. See her "Aristotle on Friendship and the Shared Life," *Philosophy and Phenomenological Research* 47 (1987), p. 604.

31. Two different questions can be asked about history and replaceability:
1. Could my relationship with another person have had the same history as the relationship I have with this person?
2. Could my future relationship with another person have the same history as my present relationship with this person?

The difference here is that in (1) we are asked to compare loves abstractly, whereas in (2) we are asked to compare loves that are temporally ordered. This difference is significant if, as Amelie Rorty maintains, one feature of the historicity of love is that we are "permanently transformed" by our loves. If each love changes me and my self-conception, I will come to a new love as one who has been transformed by my former love, and the history of my new love will reflect this changed self. See her "The Historicity of Psychological Attitudes: Love is Not Love Which Alters Not When It Alteration Finds," in P. French, T. Uehling, Jr., and H. Wettstein, eds. *Midwest Studies in Philosophy,* Vol. X (Minneapolis: University of Minnesota Press, 1986), esp. p. 404.

32. Nussbaum discusses the value of friendship for Aristotle in *Fragility of Goodness,* op. cit., pp. 362–68.

33. As noted by Laurence Thomas, op. cit., pp. 221–23.

34. Cf. this remark by Max Deutscher:

> A pure capitulation to the point of view of the other as he or she sees it for himself or herself, disguised no doubt as "a total respect for his/her autonomy" is a lack of love and serious or objective interest. More in cowardice or indifference than in love, it is a refusal to offer the difference and outsidedness of observation and remark which only a different and loving observer and involver can give. [*Subjecting and Objecting* (Oxford: Basil Blackwell, 1983), p. 196]

35. To say they value the friendship is not to tell how they will decide when, in a particular case, maintaining the relationship conflicts with other things they value in other areas of their lives.

36. Friendships have a better chance of developing and surviving in some social settings than others. For example, in mobile societies individuals tend to become detached from enduring and significant relationships, and friendships tend to be more short-lived than in stable communities.

Some cultures might also inculcate values that are antithetical to the values of friendship.

37. *Nicholas Nickelby* (New York: Bantam, 1983), Chap. 20, pp. 242–43.

38. *The Maxims of La Rouchefoucauld*, L. Kronenberg, trans. (New York: Vintage, 1959), #83.

Chapter 17

1. John McT. E. McTaggart, *The Nature of Existence*, Vol. 2 (Cambridge: Cambridge University Press, 1927), Bk. V, Chap. xli, Sections 465–68.

2. "The Phenomena of Love and Hate," *Philosophy* 53 (1978), pp. 12–14.

3. On my reading of McTaggart, he holds that personal love can be caused by the belief that the beloved has certain qualities, but that the beloved's qualities can never be the lover's reason for loving. Love understood in this way is personal in a sense—because there is something about the beloved that explains why the lover's love gets attached to her—but I require more (or something else). On my conception of personal love, the lover *x* must be able to supply reasons for loving *y* in terms of *y*'s qualities.

4. Martin Warner suggests that we cannot coherently combine (1) and (2). If we accept (2), we are committed to the denial of (1). See his fascinating paper, "Love, Self, and Plato's *Symposium*," *Philosophical Quarterly* 29 (1979): 329–39.

5. In *Mozart's Librettos,* R. Pack and M. Lelash, trans. (Cleveland: World Publishing Co., 1965), p. 235.

6. *Philosophical Explanations* (Cambridge, MA: Belknap Press, 1981), p. 455.

7. Robert Kraut proposes this test for replaceability in "Love *De Re,*" in P. French, T. Uehling, Jr., and H. Wettstein, eds., *Midwest Studies in Philosophy,* Vol. X (Minneapolis: University of Minnesota Press, 1986), p. 428. We need, he notes, explicit criteria for replaceability: "How long must Walter lament for his lost Sandra to qualify as not willing to substitute another for her. . . . Must Walter turn suicidal to qualify as having really loved her"?

8. Mark Bernstein considers the following scenario:

> I have a wife, Nancy, whom I love very much. Let us suppose that I were informed that tomorrow my wife Nancy would no longer be part of my life. . . . In her stead, a Nancy* would appear, a qualitatively indistinguishable individual from Nancy.

Though qualitatively identical, Bernstein maintains, I would not automatically transfer my love from Nancy to Nancy*. See his "Love, Particularity, and Selfhood," *Southern Journal of Philosophy* 23 (1985): 287–93. Ronald de Sousa tells a similar story, inspired by Stanislaw Lem's novel *Solaris:*

> Kris, the narrator, is one of a crew of researchers vainly attempting to establish communication with Solaris, a sentient but uncommunicative planet. . . . Doppelgängers of persons from their past materialize in the research station. It is assumed that each doppelgänger is manufactured by the sentient planet according to the information stored in the victim's own brain. Kris is confronted with a doppelgänger of Rheya, a lover from his past who is long since dead. Embroidering slightly on Lem, let us assume that the information used to manufacture the pseudo-Rheya is as complete as possible, matching not only explicit beliefs but also inferences, both logical and informal, that Kris might conceivably be in a position to make. . . . In short, we can ensure that in qualitative terms Kris cannot possibly discover that the doppelgänger is not the original. And yet— here is the important point—he knows that this cannot possibly be the real Rheya, because the real Rheya is long dead. And that is why the doppelgänger arouses horror rather than joy. The distinction presupposed by Kris's distress is a purely numerical one. . . . Yet he is so horrified by the appearance of the doppelgänger that . . . he tries to get rid of her by any means possible.

Why is Kris horrified?

> The reason must be that Kris cares about the particular identity of that singular person, Rheya, more than he cares about her properties. The reason, in short, stems from Kris's capacity for singular reference, or nonfungible identification. [*The Rationality of Emotion* (Cambridge, MA: MIT Press, 1987), pp. 99–103]

Ought Kris to mind, de Sousa asks, that the doppelgänger is not the original? If he does mind, does this not only show that his love is completely irrational? De Sousa's answer (see p. 132), drawing on an elaborate typology of objects of emotions and a further distinction between cause and explanation, is no.

9. *Reasons and Persons* (Oxford: Clarendon Press, 1984), pp. 294–95.

10. Parfit would respond that if we do care enormously, it is for a bad reason. Once we are convinced of the truth of reductionism with respect to persons, we will see that this reaction is unjustified. I would follow Susan Wolf and argue that accepting the truth of reductionism does not by itself lead to this result. See her "Self-Interest and Interest in Selves," *Ethics* 96: (1986): 704–20. The following remark of hers is particularly pertinent:

> Love would have to be understood as love for what the loved one is like [in a Parfitian world]. To some extent, this is as it should be. But in our world, other facts typically enter in. (p. 711)

Also useful here are Robert Merrihew Adams' observations on the rationality of caring about personal identity, in "Should Ethics Be More Impersonal? A Critical Notice of Derek Parfit, *Reasons and Persons,*" *Philosophical Review* 98 (1989), esp. pp. 455–61. The rationality of the ways we ordinarily care about personal identity, he claims,

> is established, *within* a form of life to which they belong, by our finding that they *make sense.* . . . We are able to interpret our lives in terms of them. (p. 458)

This argument, as Adams stresses, does not rely on nonreductionist beliefs about personal identity.

11. "Friends as Ends in Themselves," *Philosophy and Phenomenological Research* 48 (1987), pp. 19–21.

12. "Semantics of Style," in J. Kristeva et al., eds., *Essays in Semiotics* (The Hague: Mouton, 1971), pp. 417–18.

13. I do not want to claim that personal love is only based on the beloved's essential properties. Our loves are often unobjectionably based on both essential and incidental properties.

14. Cf. the discussion of irreplaceability in Robert Solomon, *Love: Emotion, Myth and Metaphor* (Garden City, NY: Anchor, 1981), pp. 201–11. Solomon focuses on the historical dimension of love and the irreplaceability of shared histories. "History," he asserts, "is perhaps the best possible insurance against dispensability" (p. 209). The best insurance against dispensability of the beloved, Solomon conjectures, is not the beloved's first-order properties by themselves, but her second-order relational properties of having contributed to and continuing to contribute to a shared history with her lover. *X* may have a meaningful shared history with *y* and a meaningful shared history with *z*, but *y* is significantly unique for *x* in that the shared histories are not interchangeable.

15. Cf. these remarks by Robert Nozick in *The Examined Life* (New York: Simon and Schuster, 1989):

> Plato got the matter reversed . . . as love grows you love not general aspects or traits but more and more particular ones, not intelligence in general but that particular mind, not kindness in general but those particular ways of being kind . . . . [L]eaving aside various "science fiction" possibilities—no other person *could* have precisely those traits. . . . [A person] comes to be loved, not for

any general dimensions or "score" on such dimensions—that, if anything, gets taken for granted—but for his or her own particular and nonduplicable way of embodying such general traits. (pp. 81–82)

16. *Analyzing Love* (Cambridge: University Press, 1987), pp. 106–8.

17. I thank Christopher Gowans for urging me to think more about this.

18. Alan Soble argues that if we eventually cease to feel the loss of a loved one because we find someone else to love, as often happens, this shows that the loss of a loved one *can* be completely made up by acquiring a new beloved, and hence that personal love does not as a rule involve unique, irreplaceable values in any interesting sense. [See *Structure of Love* (New Haven: Yale University, Press, 1990), pp. 292–93.] I disagree. Loves are individuated by the character of their respective objects, and even if x is just as happy loving z as he or she was loving a different y, the love for z has not completely replaced the love for y. Further, in love, one's identity is wrapped up in a particular relationship with a particular person. How then could x replace y with a different z? For when the loved one changes, the one who loves changes, and so the person who now loves z would have a different identity from the person who once loved y.

19. *Philosophical Explanations,* op. cit., p. 456.

Chapter 18

1. *Ethics*, Vol. 2, S. Coit, trans. (London: Allen and Unwin, 1951), Chap. 32. All page references to Hartmann are from this edition.

2. Ibid., Chap. 33.

3. Introduction to A. Sen and B. Williams, eds. *Utilitarianism and Beyond* (Cambridge: Cambridge University Press, 1982), p. 4.

4. For example, see G. E. Moore's discussion of ideal-utilitarianism in *Principia Ethica* (Cambridge: Cambridge University Press, 1903), pp. 188–89.

5. It can also plausibly be argued, with respect to friendship and other important aspects of life, that consequentialism is a *self-effacing* theory. On a certain construal of friendship, consequentialist motivations are incompatible with the attitudes and dispositions characteristic of friendship. But friendship is among the intrinsic goods the consequentialist prizes. So he should, in a manner of speaking, forget the consequentialist justification of friendship. Being self-effacing, however, is a serious problem for a moral theory if morality is necessarily social.

6. *Philosophical Explanations* (Cambridge, MA: Belknap Press, 1981), p. 457.

7. L. W. Beck, trans. (Indianapolis: Bobbs-Merrill, 1959), p. 54. All parenthetical page references to Kant in the next several paragraphs are to this translation.

8. *Formalism in Ethics and Non-Formal Ethics of Values,* M. Frings and R. Funk, trans. (Evanston, IL: Northwestern University Press, 1973), pp. 371–72.

9. *Philosophical Explanations,* op. cit., p. 452.

10. See Elizabeth Spelman, "On Treating Persons as Persons," *Ethics* 88 (1977): 150–61.

11. For an example of such an interpretation, see Robin Dillon, "Care and Respect," presented at Explorations in Feminist Ethics Conference, Duluth, Minnesota, October 1988. My interpretation of Kant is more in line with the one Onora O'Neill gives in "Between Consenting Adults," *Philosophy and Public Affairs* 14 (1985). According to O'Neill, "to treat human beings as persons . . . we . . . must take their particular capacities for rationality and autonomy into account" (p. 264), and this requires, I believe, that we pay attention to the kinds of things with which they identify in their lives.

12. "The Schizophrenia of Modern Ethical Theories," *Journal of Philosophy* 63 (1976), p. 459.

13. *The Doctrine of Virtue,* M. Gregor, trans. (New York: Harper and Row, 1964), p. 117. Parenthetical page references to Kant in the next paragraph are from this translation.

14. Barbara Herman, and following her, Marcia Baron, distinguish between two ways in which the sense of duty can operate: as a primary and as a secondary motive. In the latter case, the motive of duty operates as a limiting condition and does not provide the agent with the motivation to act as he or she does. See Herman, "Integrity and Impartiality," *Monist* 66 (1983), pp. 236–37; and Baron, "The Alleged Moral Repugnance of Acting from Duty," *Journal of Philosophy* 81 (1984), pp. 206–9. Henning Jensen also defends Kant against the objection that he would always have us act from duty rather than from such motives as love and compassion, in "Kant and Moral Integrity," *Philosophical Studies* 57 (1989): 193–205.

15. "Ignoring Persons," in O. H. Green, ed., *Respect for Persons* (New Orleans: Tulane University Press, 1982), p. 93.

16. *Friendship, Altruism and Morality* (London: Routledge and Kegan Paul, 1980), pp. 94–95.

17. For a similar view, see Robert R. Ehman, "Personal Love and Individual Value," *Journal of Value Inquiry* 10 (1976): 91–105.

18. The value of the individual as an individual is not reducible to the value of repeatable characteristics, but neither is it the transcendent individual manifesting itself as the rationality of the agent.

Chapter 19

1. *Enquiry Concerning Political Justice* (Oxford: Clarendon Press, 1971), Bk. 2, Chap. 2.

2. "The Tyranny of Principles," *The Hastings Center Report* 11 (1981): 31–39.

3. In another essay, Toulmin draws a distinction between "dealing with people in accordance with specifiable, generalized roles" and "human interactions in which all the parties concerned display the highest degree of conscious sensitivity to the detailed and specific actualities of one another's positions and feelings." The latter, he claims, "most fully and characteristically represent interactions between *persons.*" See his "Rules and Their Relevance for Understanding Human Behavior," in T. Mischel, ed., *Understanding Other Persons* (Totowa, NJ: Rowman and Littlefield, 1974), pp. 211–14. Toulmin does not here discuss the moral implications of this distinction.

4. *The Concept of Law* (Oxford: Clarendon Press, 1961), pp. 121–32.

5. For a sensitive discussion of the bearing of friendship on forgiveness, see Norvin Richards, "Forgiveness," *Ethics* 99 (1988), pp. 92–93.

6. "Ethical Universalism, Justice and Favouritism," *Australasian Journal of Philosophy* 56 (1978), p. 28.

7. *Supererogation* (Cambridge: Cambridge University Press, 1982), p. 99. Parenthetical page references to Heyd in the next paragraph are to this work.

8. That Heyd fails to adequately explain the special value of supererogatory acts is argued by Shelly Kagan in, "Does Consequentialism Demand Too Much? Recent Work on the Limits of Obligation," *Philosophy and Public Affairs* 13 (1984), pp. 240–45.

9. "Ethics and Impartiality," *Philosophical Studies* 43 (1983): 83–99.

10. Somewhat more tentatively, George Sher argues that

> the assumption that such conflict [between a morality that is sensitive to the demands of relationship and a morality of duty and principle] is inevitable should itself not go unquestioned. Even if we concede that relationships impose demands which *differ* from the demands of moral principles—and I think we ought to concede this—it remains possible that each set of demands might be adjusted to, and might be bounded by, the other. ["Other Voices, Other Rooms?" in E. Kittay and D. Meyers, eds., *Women and Moral Theory* (Totowa, NJ: Rowman and Littlefield, 1987), p. 184]

On this, see also Thomas Nagel, *The View From Nowhere* (New York: Oxford University Press, 1986), pp. 200–4.

11. *Friendship, Altruism, and Morality* (London: Routledge and Kegan Paul, 1980), p. 56.

12. Several philosophers have argued that we need to distinguish between two types of morality: personal and social. The former consists of principles that need not be characterized by impartiality, the latter of principles that are so characterized, and the two moralities may conflict. For example, see Lynne McFall, "Integrity," *Ethics* 98 (1987), pp. 17–20; and John Kekes, "Morality and Impartiality," *American Philosophical Quarterly* 18 (1981): 295–303. I have not adopted this way of speaking because it misleadingly suggests that partiality cannot itself be defended from an impartial standpoint.

13. Following R. M. Hare, Jonathan Adler distinguishes between an intuitive and a critical level of moral thinking. At the critical level, he claims, we can give an impartialist justification for inculcating particularistic loyalties to friends and loved ones. See his "Particularity, Gilligan, and The Two-Levels View: A Reply," *Ethics* 100 (1989): 149–56. Alan Gewirth argues that the right to form families and friendships with their preferential relations derives from "the universalist principle of the equal human right to freedom." See his "Ethical Universalism and Particularism," *Journal of Philosophy* 85 (1988): 283–302. I am more comfortable with this neo-Kantian impartialist justification of favoritism than with the one offered by utilitarians. Gewirth's principle can play a role in moral decision making that is compatible with the dispositions and attitudes of love and friendship, but the principle of utility may not be able to.

14. Lawrence Blum argues that an impartialist justification cannot be given for "principles (or reasons) which take the form that agents who stand in certain specific relations with other persons have a reason to do certain things toward that person which other agents do not." A genuinely impartialist derivation "would have to see the special relationships as generating agent-neutral value," but "we feel that particular relationships are not simply generators of agent-neutral good, but are rather expressive of a good which is internal to those special relationships." ["Iris Murdoch and the Domain of the Moral," *Philosophical Studies* 50 (1986), pp. 352–54.] I am not persuaded by this argument. The availability of an impartialist justification for special treatment of friends and loved ones does not force us to radically alter the way in which we conceive of the value of personal relationships.

15. *Unselfishness* (Pittsburgh: University of Pittsburgh Press, 1975), pp. 74–76.

16. "Filial Morality," *Journal of Philosophy* 83 (1986): 439–56.

17. In "What is So Special About Our Fellow Countrymen?" *Ethics* 98 (1988), pp. 671–73.

18. "Are There Any Natural Rights?" in A. I. Melden, ed., *Human Rights* (Belmont, CA: Wadsworth, 1970), pp. 68–69.

19. For more on this, see John Deigh, "Morality and Personal Relations," in G. Graham and H. LaFollette, eds., *Person to Person* (Philadelphia: Temple University Press, 1989), pp. 106–23.

20. I here take issue with the view of John Hardwig in "Should Women Think in Terms of Rights?" *Ethics* 94 (1984): 441–55. Hardwig's analysis of the role of rights in intimate relations suggests that we should leave our self-respect at the door when we enter a personal relationship. Consider this remarkable claim:

> You can invade my privacy, interrupt what I am doing, fail to respect my privacy, verbally abuse or perhaps even physically assault me, and it is all right so long as I know you are my friend. (p. 444)

Conclusion

1. See Chapter 7.

2. "Persons, Character, and Morality," in A. Rorty, ed., *The Identities of Persons* (Berkeley: University of California Press, 1976), p. 215.

3. According to Andrew Oldenquist, the utilitarian view is that "the wider the loyalty, the greater the moral claim it has on us." See "Loyalties," *Journal of Philosophy* 79 (1982), p. 180. Oldenquist challenges this position.

4. *Methods of Ethics*, 7th ed. (London, 1907), p. 242.

5. The point I am making about consequentialism is not that a committed consequentialist must be a cold fish, without special and strong attachments to other individuals. It is rather that one cannot consistently regard these attachments as having any nonderivative importance because they are one's *own* attachments. One must regard them as *someone's* attachments.

6. For more, see Chapter 7.

7. From the personal point of view, my own commitments and projects have a special importance and weight for me because they are mine, including those that do not directly involve other people.

8. Christine Korsgaard has argued that utilitarians look at our actions from the theoretical standpoint, the standpoint from which "we see ourselves as wholly determined by natural forces, the mere undergoers of our experiences." By contrast, Kantian moral philosophy takes the standpoint of practical reason, the standpoint from which we "regard ourselves as agents, as the thinkers of our thoughts and the originators of our actions," as the livers of a particular life. She maintains further that the perspective of practical reason (or what I call the personal point of view) is the appro-

priate one for morality: it is from this standpoint that "moral thought and moral concepts . . . are generated." Now utilitarianism cannot accord any special importance to *my* commitments in moral deliberation because it does not take the standpoint of the agent, but if Korsgaard is right, utilitarians are asking moral questions from the wrong standpoint. Korsgaard's views are presented in the context of her critical discussion of Parfit, "Personal Identity and the Unity of Agency: A Kantian Response to Parfit," *Philosophy and Public Affairs* 18 (1989): 101–32.

9. This is not true in all possible worlds. Suppose there are many coexisting replicas of me. Would this matter to me? Would I then be as concerned about the integrity of each of my replicas as I am about my own? In such a case, I might regard my own integrity as my special responsibility, even though I know I am not unique. What matters, I might say, is that I am I, not that I am unique.

10. Intimacy is also of especial importance with respect to the possession of integrity. As noted in Chapter 4, friendship is arguably the best means available to us for arriving at a secure knowledge of our own lives and characters, and self-knowledge is a precondition of integrity.

11. In addition to x's wanting for y what y wants because y wants it (is this really love at all?) and x's wanting for y what is good for y in y's sense of what is good for y, Alan Soble notes that "the concern of personal love is an uneasy mixture of x's seeking the good for y in y's sense and x's seeking it in x's sense." See *The Structure of Love* (New Haven: Yale University Press, 1990), p. 269.

Index